I0016863

Odoo Development Cookbook

Build effective applications by applying Odoo development
best practices

Holger Brunn

Alexandre Fayolle

Daniel Reis

BIRMINGHAM - MUMBAI

Odoo Development Cookbook

Copyright © 2016 Packt Publishing

All rights reserved. No part of this book may be reproduced, stored in a retrieval system, or transmitted in any form or by any means, without the prior written permission of the publisher, except in the case of brief quotations embedded in critical articles or reviews.

Every effort has been made in the preparation of this book to ensure the accuracy of the information presented. However, the information contained in this book is sold without warranty, either express or implied. Neither the authors, nor Packt Publishing, and its dealers and distributors will be held liable for any damages caused or alleged to be caused directly or indirectly by this book.

Packt Publishing has endeavored to provide trademark information about all of the companies and products mentioned in this book by the appropriate use of capitals. However, Packt Publishing cannot guarantee the accuracy of this information.

First published: April 2016

Production reference: 1260416

Published by Packt Publishing Ltd.
Livery Place
35 Livery Street
Birmingham B3 2PB, UK.

ISBN 978-1-78588-364-4

www.packtpub.com

Credits

Authors

Holger Brunn

Alexandre Fayolle

Daniel Reis

Reviewers

Guewen Baconnier

Stefan Rijnhart

Acquisition Editor

Manish Nainani

Content Development Editor

Mehvash Fatima

Technical Editors

Menza Mathew

Deepti Tuscano

Copy Editors

Merilyn Pereira

Alpha Singh

Project Coordinator

Kinjal Bari

Proofreader

Safis Editing

Indexer

Monica Ajmera Mehta

Production Coordinator

Arvindkumar Gupta

Cover Work

Arvindkumar Gupta

About the Authors

Holger Brunn has been a fervent open source advocate since he came in to contact with the open source market sometime in the nineties. With an academic background in philosophy and sociology, he turned his interest to generalized logic, which proves helpful in many aspects of his IT work. Turning into a professional programmer was a side effect of his hobbyist interest, combined with a part-time job with a very open-minded mentor to whom he owes a lot of gratitude.

He has programmed for ERP and similar systems in different positions since 2001. For the last eight years, he has dedicated his time to TinyERP, which became OpenERP and evolved into Odoo. Currently, he works at Therp BV in the Netherlands as a developer and is an active member of the Odoo Community Association (OCA). He's most interested in fundamental work on technical modules, but also enjoys contributing to other projects, with a focus on UI and website widgets, CRM, and knowledge management.

Alexandre Fayolle started working with Linux and free software in the mid 1990s and quickly became interested in the Python programming language. Between 1999 and 2012, he helped manage Logilab, a company he cofounded, he specialized in Python development, and had the opportunity to work on projects for large companies such as EDF, Arcelor-Mittal, and GdF Suez (now Engie) using the Cubicweb framework.

He also tackled fun projects involving machine learning, natural language processing, and multi-agent systems. In 2012, he joined Camptocamp to share his expertise on Python, PostgreSQL, and Linux with the team implementing Odoo (OpenERP at the time). He currently manages projects for Camptocamp and is strongly involved in the Odoo Community Association. In his spare time, he likes to play the vibraphone in a jazz quartet, but has recently been known for writing a book about Odoo, which he hopes you'll enjoy.

Daniel Reis has been working in the IT industry for over 15 years in developer, consultant, and management roles. Most of this work was at the Capgemini multinational consultancy firm, implementing proprietary business solutions for reference companies in a variety of sectors, such as industry, telecommunications, and banking. Daniel has a BSc in applied mathematics and a master's in business administration from the ISCTE Business School.

He's worked with Odoo solutions (formerly OpenERP) since 2010, and he is an active contributor in the Odoo community association projects. He has been a speaker at the Open Days annual conference and other open source events. He is the author of the first Odoo development book: *Odoo Development Essentials*, also by Packt Publishing.

He currently works at Securitas, the global security services company, where he has introduced Python, Odoo, and other open source solutions into the company's IT applications portfolio.

I thank my wife, Maria José, for all the support and patience that made this book possible.

About the Reviewers

Guewen Baconnier is a discrete guy who does not enjoy being put forward. He works at Camptocamp where he's been a TinyERP programmer before moving to OpenERP and now Odoo. He is a free software enthusiast and an active member of the Odoo Community Association (OCA), where his responsibilities involve, among others, being the lead developer of the OCA Connector Framework. Guewen also loves books so should you come across him, there is a good chance he may have his nose in one, either reading a technical book to keep up with his boundless curiosity and hunger to learn, or reading a novel to journey in some fictional universe, or whatever good read fell into his hands. He likes to hike in the countryside with his beloved wife. He is also the happy father of two nice kids, with whom he enjoys spending time, strolling, going to the library, reading books, and playing Kerbal Space Program.

> I would like to thank my wife and kids for supporting my tiredness on the morrows of long evenings of reviewing. And I would like to thank Alexandre Fayolle who helped me shape this short biography. Finally, thanks to my colleagues and to all contributors of the OCA from whom I learn every day.

Stefan Rijnhart is a life-long open source advocate and has been a full time Odoo consultant and developer since 2010. He enjoys collaborating in the Odoo Community Association (OCA), which he finds to be mutually beneficial to his customers' projects. In the OCA, Stefan played a key role in the creation of the OpenUpgrade migration project for Odoo and in the Odoo Community Backports project (OCB). Offline, you can find him riding a carrier bicycle through the streets of Amsterdam with his son on the front seat, or playing music with his band. Get in touch with Stefan at `http://opener.amsterdam`.

www.PacktPub.com

eBooks, discount offers, and more

Did you know that Packt offers eBook versions of every book published, with PDF and ePub files available? You can upgrade to the eBook version at www.PacktPub.com and as a print book customer, you are entitled to a discount on the eBook copy. Get in touch with us at customercare@packtpub.com for more details.

At www.PacktPub.com, you can also read a collection of free technical articles, sign up for a range of free newsletters and receive exclusive discounts and offers on Packt books and eBooks.

https://www2.packtpub.com/books/subscription/packtlib

Do you need instant solutions to your IT questions? PacktLib is Packt's online digital book library. Here, you can search, access, and read Packt's entire library of books.

Why subscribe?

- ▶ Fully searchable across every book published by Packt
- ▶ Copy and paste, print, and bookmark content
- ▶ On demand and accessible via a web browser

Table of Contents

Preface

Odoo, formerly known as OpenERP, is a great platform for developers. The framework at its core is very rich and allows building client–server applications from scratch as well as adapting existing applications to your needs through a clever extension mechanism and a very modular design. The latest versions have brought a wealth of new possibilities with the addition of a full-featured website development stack. The scope is huge and it is easy for newcomers to feel lost.

For years, Odoo developers have been learning their craft by reading the code of the addon modules, which are built on top of the framework to provide enterprise management features. While effective, the process is long and error prone, since it is difficult to know whether the source code you are learning from is using the latest possibilities offered by the framework, or if you are looking at an older module that has not been updated to use these features. To make things worse, some code flows are intrinsically hard to follow because they're partly in the business logic layer, partly in the database layer, partly in the request handling layer, and partly in the client side code. The introduction of a new API in version 8 has made things even more confusing, since most of the code base was not immediately ported to this new API.

This book is meant to save you time by tapping in to the years of experience accumulated by long-time Odoo contributors to learn the current best practices in Odoo development by focusing on the new features of version 9, and also giving a solid base in the existing mature functionality of the framework. Since Odoo has a long tradition of guaranteeing backward compatibility, most of the presented material should still work with the upcoming versions.

What this book covers

This book contains 16 chapters. We tried hard to make each chapter as independent as possible, and to make the various recipes in each chapter self-contained.

Chapter 1, Installing the Odoo Development Environment, explains how to create a development environment for Odoo, start Odoo, create a configuration file, and activate the developer tools of Odoo.

Chapter 2, Managing Odoo Server Instances, is about addon installation and upgrading. It provides useful tips for working with addons installed from GitHub, and organizing the source code of your instance.

Chapter 3, Creating Odoo Modules, explains the structure of an Odoo addon module and gives a step-by-step guide for creating a simple module from scratch.

Chapter 4, Application Models, focuses on Odoo model descriptions, and explains the various field types and the different inheritance models available in Odoo.

Chapter 5, Basic Server Side Development, introduces the v8 API of Odoo, presents the commonly used methods of the Model class, and explains how to write business logic methods.

Chapter 6, Advanced Server Side Development Techniques, deals with more advanced topics useful when writing business methods such as writing wizards to walk the user through a process or writing onchange methods. It also covers porting code from the old API to the v8 API.

Chapter 7, Debugging and Automated Testing, proposes some strategies for server-side debugging and an introduction to the Python debugger. It also explains how to write and run automated tests using YAML or Python for your addon modules.

Chapter 8, Backend Views, explains how to write business views for your data models and how to call server-side methods from these views. It covers the usual views (list view, form view, and search view) as well as the views introduced in recent versions of Odoo (Kanban, graph, calendar, pivot, and so on)

Chapter 9, Module Data, shows how to ship data along with the code of your module. It also explains how to write a migration script when a data model provided by an addon is modified in a new release.

Chapter 10, Access Security, explains how to control who has access to what in your Odoo instance, by creating security groups, writing access control lists to define what operations are available to each group on a given model, and, if necessary, by writing record level rules.

Chapter 11, Internationalization, deals with the translation of the user interfaces of your addons.

Chapter 12, Automation and Workflows, illustrates the different tools available in Odoo to implement business process for your records. It also shows how server actions and automated rules can be used to support business rules.

Chapter 13, Web Server Development, deals with the core of the web server in Odoo. It explains how to map URLs to methods and how to control who can access these URLs.

Chapter 14, CMS Website Development, shows how to customize websites built with Odoo, by writing your own templates and providing new snippets for use in the website builder.

Chapter 15, Web Client Development, dives into the JavaScript part of Odoo and explains how you can provide new widgets and make RPC calls to the server. It also gives tips about debugging and testing this part of your code.

Chapter 16, Server Deployment, provides advice on how to install and configure Odoo for production, including setting up a reverse proxy to encrypt network communications over HTTPS and ensuring that Odoo starts when the server boots.

Who this book is for

This book is targeted at Python developers who want to learn Odoo development or consolidate their Odoo skills. Some experience with the JavaScript programming language and web development in general is required to fully benefit from the frontend chapters.

This book focuses on core application development. It does not cover how to use the business applications provided by Odoo. You may want to refer to *Working with Odoo*, by Greg Moss, for this.

This book does not provide explanations about how the internals of the enterprise management applications work. To understand this, you will have to read the source code and experiment for yourself. Being familiar with the contents of the *Odoo Development Cookbook* should make your life easier, as it contains pointers to parts of the code you can read to learn about a specific topic.

What you need for this book

The set up recipes in *Chapter 1, Installing the Odoo Development Environment*, and *Chapter 15, Web Client Development*, expect that you are working on a server running Debian GNU/Linux, or a derivative distribution such as Ubuntu, in a reasonably up-to-date release. If you are running another distribution, things should be fairly straightforward; the main differences should be in the names of the packages to install, and possibly the location of the configuration files of PostgreSQL and Nginx.

If your workstation is running Windows or MacOS, we advise you to set up a Debian virtual machine to work with Odoo. While it is possible to develop natively on Windows or Mac, having a development environment as close as possible to the deployment environment is a good way to avoid nasty surprises and GNU/Linux is the recommended deployment platform for Odoo.

Is there a recommended Integrated Development Environment (IDE) for Odoo? This is a frequently asked question by newcomers. The best answer is to use whatever tool you are familiar with. Popular choices include Eclipse or PyCharm, but a very high number of experimented developers, including the core Odoo developers, use just a programming text editor such as vim, GNU emacs, or Sublime Text to have syntax highlighting and useful helpers such as automatic indentation, while using the Python debugger for debugging. It is recommended to start with the basic tools because IDEs have a tendency to hide complexity you should be familiar with in order to fix the harder problems.

Sections

In this book, you will find several headings that appear frequently (Getting ready, How to do it, How it works, There's more, and See also).

To give clear instructions on how to complete a recipe, we use these sections as follows:

Getting ready

This section tells you what to expect in the recipe, and describes how to set up any software or any preliminary settings required for the recipe.

How to do it...

This section contains the steps required to follow the recipe.

How it works...

This section usually consists of a detailed explanation of what happened in the previous section.

There's more...

This section consists of additional information about the recipe in order to make the reader more knowledgeable about the recipe.

See also

This section provides helpful links to other useful information for the recipe.

Conventions

In this book, you will find a number of text styles that distinguish between different kinds of information. Here are some examples of these styles and an explanation of their meaning.

Code words in text, database table names, folder names, filenames, file extensions, pathnames, dummy URLs, user input, and Twitter handles are shown as follows: "The parsing of the configuration file by Odoo is done using the Python `ConfigParser` module."

A block of code is set as follows:

```
[DEFAULT]
project = /home/odoo/projects/project1
env = dev
prefix = %(project)s/%(env)s

[options]
addons-path = %(prefix)s/odoo/addons,%(prefix)s/OCA/server-tools
data_dir = %(prefix)s/data_dir
```

When we wish to draw your attention to a particular part of a code block, the relevant lines or items are set in bold:

```
{    'name': 'Chapter 03 code',
     'depends': ['base', 'decimal_precision],
     'data': ['views/library_book.xml'] }
```

Any command-line input or output is written as follows:

```
$ sudo apt-get install git python2.7 postgresql nano python-virtualenv
```

New terms and **important words** are shown in bold. Words that you see on the screen, for example, in menus or dialog boxes, appear in the text like this: "Click on the **Manage Databases** link."

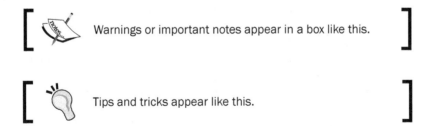

Warnings or important notes appear in a box like this.

Tips and tricks appear like this.

Reader feedback

Feedback from our readers is always welcome. Let us know what you think about this book—what you liked or disliked. Reader feedback is important for us as it helps us develop titles that you will really get the most out of.

To send us general feedback, simply e-mail `feedback@packtpub.com`, and mention the book's title in the subject of your message.

If there is a topic that you have expertise in and you are interested in either writing or contributing to a book, see our author guide at `www.packtpub.com/authors`.

Customer support

Now that you are the proud owner of a Packt book, we have a number of things to help you to get the most from your purchase.

Downloading the example code

You can download the example code files for this book from your account at `http://www.packtpub.com`. If you purchased this book elsewhere, you can visit `http://www.packtpub.com/support` and register to have the files e-mailed directly to you.

You can download the code files by following these steps:

1. Log in or register to our website using your e-mail address and password.
2. Hover the mouse pointer on the **SUPPORT** tab at the top.
3. Click on **Code Downloads & Errata**.
4. Enter the name of the book in the **Search** box.
5. Select the book for which you're looking to download the code files.
6. Choose from the drop-down menu where you purchased this book from.
7. Click on **Code Download**.

You can also download the code files by clicking on the **Code Files** button on the book's webpage at the Packt Publishing website. This page can be accessed by entering the book's name in the **Search** box. Please note that you need to be logged in to your Packt account.

Once the file is downloaded, please make sure that you unzip or extract the folder using the latest version of:

- ▸ WinRAR / 7-Zip for Windows
- ▸ Zipeg / iZip / UnRarX for Mac
- ▸ 7-Zip / PeaZip for Linux

Downloading the color images of this book

We also provide you with a PDF file that has color images of the screenshots/diagrams used in this book. The color images will help you better understand the changes in the output. You can download this file from `http://www.packtpub.com/sites/default/files/downloads/Bookname_ColorImages.pdf`.

Errata

Although we have taken every care to ensure the accuracy of our content, mistakes do happen. If you find a mistake in one of our books—maybe a mistake in the text or the code—we would be grateful if you could report this to us. By doing so, you can save other readers from frustration and help us improve subsequent versions of this book. If you find any errata, please report them by visiting `http://www.packtpub.com/submit-errata`, selecting your book, clicking on the **Errata Submission Form** link, and entering the details of your errata. Once your errata are verified, your submission will be accepted and the errata will be uploaded to our website or added to any list of existing errata under the Errata section of that title.

To view the previously submitted errata, go to `https://www.packtpub.com/books/content/support` and enter the name of the book in the search field. The required information will appear under the **Errata** section.

Piracy

Piracy of copyrighted material on the Internet is an ongoing problem across all media. At Packt, we take the protection of our copyright and licenses very seriously. If you come across any illegal copies of our works in any form on the Internet, please provide us with the location address or website name immediately so that we can pursue a remedy.

Please contact us at `copyright@packtpub.com` with a link to the suspected pirated material.

We appreciate your help in protecting our authors and our ability to bring you valuable content.

Questions

If you have a problem with any aspect of this book, you can contact us at
`questions@packtpub.com`, and we will do our best to address the problem.

1

Installing the Odoo Development Environment

In this chapter, we will cover the following topics:

- ▸ Easy installation of Odoo from source
- ▸ Managing Odoo environments using the `start` command
- ▸ Managing Odoo server databases
- ▸ Storing the instance configuration in a file
- ▸ Activating the Odoo developer tools
- ▸ Updating Odoo from source

Introduction

There are lots of ways to set up an Odoo development environment. This chapter proposes one of these, although you will certainly find a number of other tutorials on the web explaining other approaches. Keep in mind that this chapter is about a development environment, which has different requirements from a production environment, covered in *Chapter 16, Server Deployment*.

Easy installation of Odoo from source

For Odoo deployment, it is recommended to use a GNU/Linux environment. You may be more at ease using Microsoft Windows or Mac OS X, but the fact is that most of the Odoo developers are using GNU/Linux and you are much more likely to get support from the community for OS-level issues happening on GNU/Linux than on Windows.

It is also recommended to develop using the same environment (same distribution, same version) as the one which will be used in production. This will avoid nasty surprises such as discovering on the day of deployment that some library has a different version than expected, with a slightly different and incompatible behavior. If your workstation is using a different OS, a good approach is to set up a virtual machine on your workstation and to install a GNU/Linux distribution in the VM.

> To avoid copying files between your workstation where you are running your development environment and the virtual machine which runs Odoo, you can configure a SAMBA share inside the virtual machine and store the source code there. You can then mount the share on your workstation in order to edit the files easily.

This book assumes you are running Debian GNU/Linux as its stable version (Jessie at the time of writing). Ubuntu is another popular choice, and since it is built on top of Debian, most of the examples in this book should work unchanged. Whatever Linux distribution you choose, you should have some notion of how to use it from the command line, and having a few ideas about system administration will certainly not cause any harm.

Getting ready

We assume that Linux is up and running and that you have an account with root access, either because you know the root password or because `sudo` has been configured. In the following pages, we will be using `$(whoami)` whenever the login of your work user is required in a command line. This is a shell command which will substitute your login in the command you are typing.

Some operations will definitely be easier if you have a GitHub account. Go to `https://github.com` and create one if you don't have one already.

How to do it...

To install Odoo from source, you need to follow these steps:

1. Run the following commands to install the main dependencies:

```
$ sudo apt-get install git python2.7 postgresql nano \
python-virtualenv
```

2. Download and install `wkhtmltopdf`:

   ```
   $ wget http://nightly.odoo.com/extra/wkhtmltox-0.12.1.2_linux-
   jessie-amd64.deb
   ```

   ```
   $ sudo dpkg -i wkhtmltox-0.12.1.2_linux-jessie-amd64.deb
   ```

Caution!

This is a package provided by the Odoo maintainer for Debian Jessie. If you are using another distribution, browse to `http://download.gna.org/wkhtmltopdf/0.12/0.12.1/` and download the package for your operating system.

3. Now, use this to install the build dependencies:

   ```
   $ sudo apt-get install gcc python2.7-dev libxml2-dev \
   libxslt1-dev libevent-dev libsasl2-dev libldap2-dev libpq-dev \
   libpng12-dev libjpeg-dev
   ```

4. Configure PostgreSQL:

   ```
   $ sudo -u postgres createuser --createdb $(whoami)
   $ createdb $(whoami)
   ```

5. Configure `git`:

   ```
   $ git config --global user.name "Your Name"
   $ git config --global user.email youremail@example.com
   ```

6. Clone the Odoo code base:

   ```
   $ mkdir ~/odoo-dev
   $ cd ~/odoo-dev
   $ git clone -b 9.0 --single-branch https://github.com/odoo/odoo.git
   $ cd odoo
   ```

7. Create an `odoo-9.0` virtual environment and activate it:

   ```
   $ virtualenv ~/odoo-9.0
   $ source ~/odoo-9.0/bin/activate
   ```

8. Install the Python dependencies of Odoo in `virtualenv`:

   ```
   $ pip install -r requirements.txt
   ```

9. Create and start your first Odoo instances:

```
$ createdb odoo-test
$ python odoo.py -d odoo-test --addons-path=addons \
--dbfilter=odoo-test$
```

10. Point your browser to `http://localhost:8069` and authenticate using the `admin` account and `admin` as password.

You can download the example code files for this book from your account at `http://www.packtpub.com`. If you purchased this book elsewhere, you can visit `http://www.packtpub.com/support` and register to have the files e-mailed directly to you.

You can download the code files by following these steps:

> ▶ Log in or register to our website using your e-mail address and password

> ▶ Hover the mouse pointer on the **SUPPORT** tab at the top

> ▶ Click on **Code Downloads & Errata**

> ▶ Enter the name of the book in the **Search** box

> ▶ Select the book for which you're looking to download the code files

> ▶ Choose from the drop-down menu where you purchased this book from

> ▶ Click on **Code Download**

You can also download the code files by clicking on the **Code Files** button on the book's webpage at the Packt Publishing website. This page can be accessed by entering the book's name in the **Search** box. Please note that you need to be logged in to your Packt account.

Once the file is downloaded, please make sure that you unzip or extract the folder using the latest version of:

> ▶ WinRAR / 7-Zip for Windows

> ▶ Zipeg / iZip / UnRarX for Mac

> ▶ 7-Zip / PeaZip for Linux

How it works...

Dependencies come from various sources. First, you have the core dependencies of Odoo, the Python interpreter that is used to run the source code, and the PostgreSQL database server used to store the instance data. **Git** is used for source code versioning and getting the source code of Odoo itself.

Since we will need to edit some files as `root` or as `postgres` (the PostgreSQL administrative user) on our server, we need to install a console-based text editor. We suggest `nano` as it is very simple to use, but feel free to choose any editor with which you feel at ease as long as it works on the console, such as `vim`, `e3`, or `emacs-nox`.

Wkhtmltopdf is a runtime dependency of Odoo used to produce PDF reports. The version required by Odoo 9.0 is 0.12.1, which is not included in current GNU/Linux distributions. Fortunately for us, the maintainers of wkhtmltopdf provide prebuilt packages for various distributions on `http://wkhtmltopdf.org/downloads.html` (in the archive section). However, Debian Jessie is not there, so the Odoo maintainers provide their own version of the package on `http://nightly.odoo.com/extra/`.

There are lots of other runtime dependencies that are Python modules, which we can install using `pip` in a virtual environment. However, some of these Python modules can feature some dependencies on native C libraries for which the Python bindings need to be compiled. We therefore install the development packages for these C libraries as well as the Python development package and a C compiler. Once these build dependencies are installed, we can use `pip -r requirements.txt` (a file which comes from the Odoo source code distribution) to download, compile, and install the Python modules.

Virtual environments

Python virtual environments, or **virtualenv** for short, are isolated Python workspaces. They are very useful to Python developers because they allow different workspaces with different versions of various Python libraries installed, possibly on different Python interpreter versions.

You can create as many environments as you wish using the command `virtualenv path/to/newenv`. This will create a `newenv` directory in the specified location, containing a `bin/` subdirectory and a `lib/python2.7` subdirectory.

In `bin/` you will find several scripts:

- `activate`: The script is not executed, it is sourced using the built-in `source` shell. This will activate the environment by adjusting the `PATH` environment variable to include the `bin/` directory of the `virtualenv`. It also installs a shell function called `deactivate`, which you can run to exit the `virtualenv`, and changes the shell prompt to let you know which `virtualenv` is currently activated

- `pip`: This is a special version of the `pip` command which acts inside the `virtualenv` only.

- `python`: This is a wrapper around your system Python interpreter which uses the packages installed in the `virtualenv`.

> The built-in `source` shell is also available (as a single dot, followed by a space, and the path to the file to source). The shortcut form is perfectly fine, but we will stick to `source` in this book for readability.

There are two main ways of using a `virtualenv`. You may activate it as we show in the recipe (and call `deactivate` when you're done) or you may use the scripts in the `bin/` directory of the environment explicitly by calling them with their full path, in which case you don't need to activate the `virtualenv`. This is mainly a matter of taste, so you should experiment and find out which style suits you better for which case.

You may have executable Python scripts with the first line looking like the following:

```
#! /usr/bin/env python
```

These will be easier to use with an activated `virtualenv`. This is the case with the `odoo.py` script, which you can therefore call in the following way:

```
$ ./odoo.py -d odoo-test --addons-path=addons --db-filter=odoo-test$
```

PostgreSQL configuration

On a GNU/Linux system, Odoo works very well with the default values of `psycopg2`, the Python module used to access a **PostgreSQL** database:

- Passwordless authentication if the database user has the same name as the current user on local connections
- Local connection uses Unix domain sockets
- The database server listens on port 5432

In that case, there is nothing special to do: we use the `postgres` administrative user to create a database user which shares our login name and give it the right to create new databases. We then create a new database with the same name as the new user, which will be used as a default database when using the `psql` command.

When on a development server, it is OK to give the PostgreSQL user more rights and to use the `--superuser` command-line option rather than just `--createdb`. The net effect is that this user can then also create other users and globally manage the database instance. If you feel `--superuser` is too much, you may still want to use `--createrole` in addition to `--createdb` when creating your database user. Avoid doing this on production servers as it would give additional leverage to an attacker exploiting a vulnerability in some part of the deployed code (see *Chapter 16, Server Deployment*).

If you want to use a database user with a different login, you will need to provide a password for the user. This is done by passing the `--pwprompt` flag on the command line when creating the user, in which case the command will prompt you for the password.

If the user has already been created and you want to set a password (or modify a forgotten password) you can use the following command:

```
$ psql -c "alter role $(whoami) with password 'newpassword'"
```

 If this command fails with an error message saying that the database does not exist, it is because you did not create a database named after your login name in step 3. That's fine; just add the `--dbname` option with an existing database name such as `--dbname template1`.

Git configuration

At some point in the book, you will need to use `git commit`. This will fail unless some basic configuration is performed; you need to provide Git with your name and email address. Git will remind you to do this with a nice error message, but you may as well do it now.

 This is also something to keep in mind if you are using a service such as Travis for continuous integration, and your test scripts need to perform some git merges: you have to provide a dummy name and e-mail for the merging to succeed.

Downloading the Odoo source code

Downloading the Odoo code base is done by performing a `git clone` operation. Be patient as this will take some time. The options `--branch 9.0 --single-branch` avoid downloading other branches and save a little time. The `--depth` option can also be used to avoid downloading the whole repository history, but the downside of that option is that you will not be able to explore that history when looking for issues.

The Odoo developers also propose nightly builds, which are available as tarballs and distribution packages. The main advantage of using a git clone is that you will be able to update your repository when new bug fixes are committed in the source tree. You will also be able to easily test any proposed fixes and track regressions, so you can make your bug reports more precise and helpful for the developers.

Starting the instance

Now comes the moment you've been waiting for. To start our first instance, we first create a new empty database and then use the `odoo.py` script with the following command-line arguments:

- ► `-d database_name`: Use that database by default.

- ▸ `--db-filter=database_name$`: Only try to connect to databases matching the supplied regular expression. One Odoo installation can serve multiple instances living in separate databases and this argument limits the available databases. The trailing `$` is important as the regular expression is used in match mode; this avoids selecting names starting with the specified string.

- ▸ `--addons-path=directory1,directory2,...`: This is a comma separated list of directories in which Odoo will look for addons. This list is scanned at the instance creation time to populate the list of available add-on modules in the instance.

If you are using a database user with a database login different from your Linux login, you need to pass the following additional arguments:

- ▸ `--db_host=localhost`: use a TCP connection to the database server

- ▸ `--db_user=database_username`: use the specified database login

- ▸ `--db_password=database_password`: the password to use to authenticate against the PostgreSQL server

To get an overview of all the available options, use the `--help` argument. We will see much more about the `odoo.py` script in this chapter as well as in *Chapter 2, Managing Odoo Server Instances.*

When Odoo is started on an empty database, it will first create the database structure needed to support its operations. It will also scan the addons path to find the available addon modules, and insert some the initial records in the database. This includes the `admin` user with the default password `admin` which you will use to authenticate with.

Odoo includes an HTTP server. By default, it listens on all local network interfaces on TCP port `8069` so pointing your web browser to `http://localhost:8069/` leads you to your newly created instance.

There is more...

In the recipe, we downloaded the latest stable version of Odoo using the following command:

```
$ git clone -b 9.0 --single-branch https://github.com/odoo/odoo.git
```

This uses the official branch maintained by Odoo. One issue with this branch is that bug fixes contributed by the community are not always merged in a timely fashion. The **Odoo Community Association (OCA)** maintains a parallel branch in which fixes and improvements are peer-reviewed by the community and tend to be merged faster than on the official branch. It is not a fork of Odoo, and the latest version of Odoo is merged back into that branch daily. You may want to use it for your developments and deployments, in which case you need to clone Odoo like this:

```
$ git clone -b 9.0 --single-branch https://github.com/OCA/OCB.git odoo
```

Managing Odoo environments using the start command

We will often want to use custom or community modules with our Odoo instance. Keeping them in a separate directory makes it easier to install upgrades to Odoo or troubleshoot issues from our custom modules. We just have to add that directory to the addons path and they will be available in our instance, just like the core modules are.

It is possible to think about this module directory as an Odoo environment. The Odoo `start` command makes it easy to organize Odoo instances as directories, each with its own modules.

Getting ready

For this recipe we need to have already installed Odoo. We assume that it will be at `~/odoo-dev/odoo`, and that the `virtualenv` is activated.

This means that the following command should successfully start an Odoo server:

```
$ ~/odoo-dev/odoo/odoo.py
```

How to do it...

To create a work environment for your instance, you need to follow these steps:

1. Change to the directory where Odoo is:

   ```
   $ cd ~/odoo-dev
   ```

2. Choose a name for the environment and create a directory for it:

   ```
   $ mkdir my-odoo
   ```

3. Change to that directory and start an Odoo server instance for that environment:

   ```
   $ cd my-odoo/
   $ ../odoo/odoo.py start
   ```

How it works...

The Odoo `start` command is a shortcut to start a server instance using the current directory. The directory name is automatically used as the database name (for the `-d` option), and the current directory is automatically added to the addons path (the `--addons-path` option) as long as it contains an Odoo addon module. In the preceding recipe you won't see the current directory in the addons path because it doesn't contain any modules yet.

There's more

By default the current directory is used, but the `--path` option allows you to set a specific path to use instead. For example, this would work from any directory:

```
$ ~/odoo-dev/odoo/odoo.py start --path=~/odoo-dev/my-odoo
```

The database to use can also be overridden using the usual `-d` option. In fact, all the other usual `odoo.py` command-line arguments, except `--addons-path`, will work. For example, to set the server listening port, use the following command:

```
$ ../odoo/odoo.py start --xmlrpc-port=8080
```

As we can see, the Odoo `start` command can be a convenient way to quickstart Odoo instances with their own module directory.

Managing Odoo server databases

When working with Odoo, all the data of your instance is stored in a PostgreSQL database. All the standard database management tools you are used to are available, but Odoo also proposes a web interface for some common operations.

Getting ready

We assume that your work environment is set up and you have an instance running. Do not start it using the `odoo.py start` command shown in the previous recipe, as it configures the server with some options which interfere with multi-database management.

How to do it...

The Odoo database management interface provides tools to create, duplicate, remove, back up, and restore a database. There is also a way to change the master password which is used to protect access to the database management interface.

Access the Database Management interface

To access the database, the following steps need to be performed:

1. Go to the login screen of your instance (if you are authenticated, log out).
2. Click on the **Manage Databases** link. This will navigate to `http://localhost:8069/web/database/manager` (you can also point your browser directly to that URL.).

Set or change the master password

If you've set up your instance with default values, and not yet modified it as explained in the following section, the database management screen will display a warning telling you that the master password is not set, and advising you to set one, with a direct link:

1. To set the **Master Password**, you can click on that link. You will get a dialog box asking you to provide the new password:

2. Type in a non-trivial new password and click on **Continue**.

3. When the master password is already set, click the **Set Master Password** button at the bottom of the screen to change it

4. In the displayed dialog box, type the previous master password and the new one, and then click on **Continue**.

The master password is in the server configuration file under the `admin_password` key. If the server was started without specifying a configuration file, a new one will be generated in `~/.openerp_serverrc`. See the next recipe for more information about the configuration file.

Creating a new database

This dialog box can be used to create a new database instance which will be handled by the current Odoo server:

1. In the database management screen, click on the **Create Database** button at the bottom of the screen.

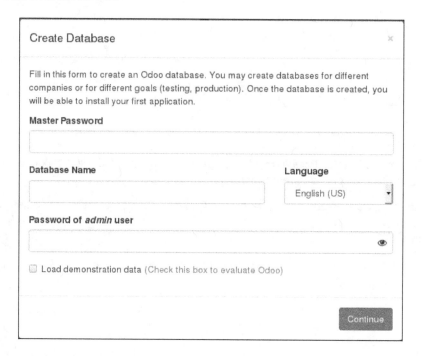

2. Fill the form in as follows:

   ❑ **Master password:** The master password for this instance.

   ❑ **Database name:** Input the name of the database you wish to create.

   ❑ **Language:** Select the language you wish to be installed by default in the new database.

   ❑ **Password of admin user:** Type the password you want to set for the admin user of the new instance.

❑   **Load demonstration data**: Check this box to have demonstration data. This is useful to run tests or set up a demonstration for a customer, but should not be checked for a database meant to contain production data.

3. Click on the **Continue** button, and wait a little until the new database is initialized. You will then be redirected to the instance, connected as the Administrator.

Troubleshooting

If you are redirected to a login screen, this is probably because the option `--db-filter` was passed to Odoo and the new database name did not match the new database name. Note that the `odoo.py start` command does this silently, making only the current database available. To work around this, simply restart Odoo without the `start` command, as shown in the first recipe of this chapter. If you have a configuration file (see the *Storing the instance configuration in a file* recipe later in this chapter), then check that the `db_filter` option is unset or set to a value matching the new database name.

Duplicating a database

Very often you will have an existing database and you want to experiment with it to try a procedure or run a test, but without modifying the existing data. The answer is simple: duplicate the database and run the tests on the copy. Repeat as many times as required:

1. In the database management screen, click on the **Duplicate** link next to the name of the database you wish to clone.

Duplicate Database   ✕

Master Password

[   ]

Database Name

[odoo   ]

New Name

[   ]

[Continue]

2. Fill in the form:
   - ❑ **Master Password**: the master password of the Odoo server
   - ❑ **New Name**: the name you want to give to the copy

3. Click on the **Continue** button.

4. You can then click on the name of the newly created database in the database management screen to access the login screen for that database.

Removing a database

When you have finished your tests, you will want to clean up the duplicated databases. To do this, perform the following steps:

1. In the database management screen, click on the **Delete** link next to the name of the database you want to remove.

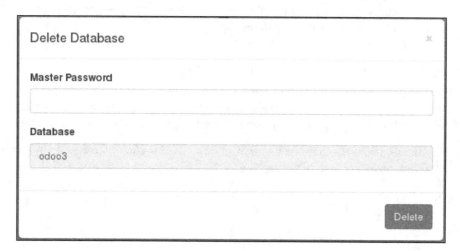

2. Fill in the form; enter the **Master Password**, which is the master password of the Odoo server.

3. Click the **Delete** button.

> **Caution! Potential data loss!**
> If you selected the wrong database, and have no backup, there is no way to recover the lost data.

Backing up a database

For creating a backup, the following steps need to be performed:

1. In the database management screen, click the **Backup** link next to the database you want to back up.

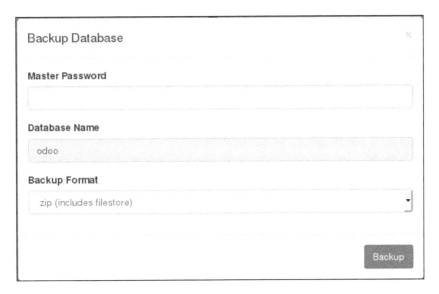

2. Fill in the form:

    ❑   **Master Password**: the master password of the Odoo server.

    ❑   **Backup Format**: always use **zip** for a production database, as it is the only real full backup format. Only use the **pg_dump** format for a development database where you don't really care about the file store (admin by default).

3. Click the **Backup** button. The backup file will be downloaded to your browser.

Restoring a database backup

If you need to restore a backup, this is what you need to do:

1. In the database management screen, click the **Restore Database** button at the bottom of the screen.

2. Fill in the form:

   ❏ **Master Password**: the master password of the Odoo server.
   ❏ **File**: a previously downloaded Odoo backup.
   ❏ **Database Name**: provide the name of the database in which the backup will be restored. The database must not exist on the server.
   ❏ **Generate a new database uuid**: leave unchecked if you are installing a database which has been deleted from the server; otherwise check the box. There is little difference between them, and if in doubt, leaving it unchecked is a safe choice.

3. Click the **Continue** button.

 Note: It is not possible to restore a database on top of itself. If you try to do this, you will get an error message (**Database restore error: Database already exists**). You need to remove the database first.

How it works...

These features, apart from the **Change master password** screen, run `postgresql` administration commands on the server and report back through the web interface.

The master password is a very important piece of information which only lives in the Odoo server configuration file and is never stored in the database. There used to be a default value of `admin`, but using this value is a security liability as it is well known. In Odoo v9, this is identified as an "unset" master password and you get urged to change it when accessing the database administration interface. Even if it is stored in the configuration file under the `admin_passwd` entry, this is *not* the same as the password of the `admin` user; these are two independent passwords: the master password is set for an Odoo server process, which itself can handle multiple database instances, each of which has an independent `admin` user with his own password.

 Security considerations: Remember that we are considering a development environment in this chapter. The Odoo database management interface is something which needs to be secured when you are working on a production server as it gives access to a lot of sensitive information, especially if the server hosts Odoo instances for several different clients. This will be covered in *Chapter 16, Server Deployment*.

To create a new database, Odoo uses the PostgreSQL `createdb` utility and calls the internal Odoo function to initialize the new database in the same way as when you start Odoo on an empty database.

To duplicate a database, Odoo uses the `--template` option of `createdb` passing the original database as an argument. This essentially duplicates the structure of the template database in the new database using internal and optimized PostgreSQL routines, which is much faster than creating a backup and restoring it (especially when using the web interface which requires downloading the backup file and uploading it again).

Backup and restore operations use the `pg_dump` and `pg_restore` utilities respectively. When using the `.zip` format, the backup will also include a copy of the file store which contains a copy of the documents when you configure Odoo to not keep these in the database, which is the default in 9.0. Unless you configure it otherwise, these files live in `~/.local/share/Odoo/filestore`.

> If the backup gets large, downloading it may fail, either because the
> Odoo server itself is not able to handle the large file in memory or if the
> server runs behind a reverse proxy (see *Chapter 16, Server Deployment*)
> because there is a limit to the size of HTTP responses set in the proxy.
> Conversely, for the same reasons, you will likely experience issues with
> the database restore operation. When you start running into these issues,
> it is time to invest in a more robust external backup solution.

There is more...

Experienced Odoo developers generally don't use the database management interface, and
perform the operations from the command line. To initialize a new database with demo data
for instance, the following one-liner can be used:

```
$ createdb testdb && odoo.py -d testdb
```

The additional bonus of this command line is that you can request installation of addons
while you are at it using for instance `-i sale,purchase,stock` (more on this in *Chapter 2,
Managing Odoo Server Instances*).

To duplicate a database, stop the server, and run the following command:

```
$ createdb -T dbname newdbname
$ cd ~/.local/share/Odoo/filestore # adapt if you have changed the data_
dir
$ cp -r dbname newdbname
$ cd -
```

Note that in the context of development, the file store is often omitted.

> The use of `createdb -T` only works if there are no active sessions
> on the database, which means you have to shut down your Odoo
> server before duplicating the database from the command line.

To remove an instance, run the following command:

```
$ dropdb dbname
$ rm -rf ~/.local/share/Odoo/filestore/dbname
```

To create a backup (assuming the PostgreSQL server is running locally), use the following
command:

```
$ pg_dump -Fc -f dbname.dump dbname
$ tar cjf dbname.tgz dbname.dump ~/.local/share/Odoo/filestore/dbname
```

To restore the backup, run the following command:

```
$ tar xf dbname.tgz
$ pg_restore -C -d dbname dbname.dump
```

Caution!

If your Odoo instance uses a different user to connect to the database you need to pass `-U username` so that the correct user is the owner of the restored database.

Storing the instance configuration in a file

The `odoo.py` script has dozens of options, and it is tedious to remember them all and to remember to set them properly when starting the server. Fortunately, it is possible to store them all in a configuration file and to only specify by hand the ones you want to alter, for example, for development.

How to do it...

To generate a configuration file for your Odoo instance, run the following command:

```
$ odoo.py --save --config myodoo.cfg --stop-after-init
```

You can add additional options, and their values will be saved in the generated file. All the unset options will be saved with their default value set. To get a list of possible options, use:

```
$ odoo.py --help | less
```

This will provide you with some help about what the various options perform. To convert from the command line form to the configuration form, use the long option name, remove the leading dashes, and convert the dashes in the middle to underscores: `--without-demo` becomes `without_demo`. This works for most options, but there are a few exceptions listed in the next section.

Edit the file `myodoo.cfg` (use the table in the following section for some parameters you may want to change). Then to start the server with the saved options, run the following command:

```
$ odoo.py -c myodoo.cfg
```

The `--config` option is commonly abbreviated as `-c`

How it works...

At start up, Odoo loads its configuration in three passes. First a set of default values for all options is initialized from the source code. Then the configuration is parsed, and any value defined in the file overrides the defaults. Finally, the command-line options are analyzed and their values override the configuration obtained from the previous pass.

As mentioned earlier, the names of the configuration variables can be found from the names of the command-line options by removing the leading dashes and converting the middle dashes to underscores. There are a few exceptions, notably:

Command line	Configuration file
`--db-filter`	`dbfilter`
`--no-xmlrpc`	`xmlrpc = True / False`
`--database`	`db_name`
`--debug`	`debug_mode = True / False`
`--i18n-import / --i18n-export`	`Unavailable`

Here is a list of options commonly set through the configuration file:

Option	Format	Usage
`without_demo`		Prevents module demo data from being loaded.
`addons_path`	Comma separated list of paths	A list of directory names in which the server will look for addons (see *Chapter 2, Managing Odoo Server instances*).
`admin_passwd`	Text	The master password (see previous recipe).
`data_dir`	Path to a directory	A directory in which the server will store session information, addons downloaded from the Internet, and documents if you enable the file store.
`db_host`	Host name	The name of the server running the PostgreSQL server. Use `False` to use local Unix Domain sockets, and `localhost` to use TCP sockets locally.
`db_user`	Database user login	
`db_password`	Database user password	This is generally empty if `db_host` is `False` and `db_user` has the same name as the user running the server. Read the man page of `pg_hba.conf` for more information on this.

Option	Format	Usage
database	Database name	Used to set the database name on which some commands operate by default). This does not limit the databases on which the server will act. See the following dbfilter option for this.
dbfilter	A regular expression	The expression should match the name of the databases considered by the server. If you run the website, it should match a single database, so it will look like ^databasename$. More information on this is in *Chapter 16, Server Deployment*.
xmlrpc_interface	IP address of a network interface	Defaults to 0.0.0.0, meaning the server listens on all interfaces
xmlrpc_port longpolling_port	Port number	The ports on which the Odoo server will listen. You will need to specify both to run multiple Odoo servers on the same host. longpolling_port is only used if workers is not 0.
logfile	Path to a file	The file in which Odoo will write its logs.
log_level	Log verbosity level	Specify the level of logging. Accepted values (in increasing verbosity order): critical, error, warn, info, debug, debug_rpc, debug_rpc_answer, debug_sql.
workers	Integer	The number of worker processes. See *Chapter 16, Server Deployment*, for more information.
no_database_list	True / False	Set to True to disable listing of databases. See *Chapter 16, Server Deployment*, for more information.

There is more...

The parsing of the configuration file by Odoo is done using the Python ConfigParser module. This module supports defining values for variables from the values of other variables using the %(section.variable)s notation. You can omit section if the value comes from the same section or if it is defined in the special [DEFAULT] section.

For instance, if you want to define the database login to be the same as the database name, you can write the following in your Odoo configuration file:

```
[options]
db_name = projectname
db_user = %(options.db_name)s
```

A very common use is to define a common prefix for the paths of the addons:

```
[DEFAULT]
project = /home/odoo/projects/project1
env = dev
prefix = %(project)s/%(env)s

[options]
addons-path = %(prefix)s/odoo/addons,%(prefix)s/OCA/server-tools
data_dir = %(prefix)s/data_dir
```

Activating the Odoo developer tools

When using Odoo as a developer, you need to know how to activate **Developer Mode** in the web interface to access the advanced settings menu and developer information.

How to do it...

To activate Developer Mode in the web interface:

1. Connect to your instance and authenticate (not necessarily as `admin`; this function is available to all users, but the Administrator has more tools available).

2. Click on the down arrow next to your user name in the top right corner of the page .

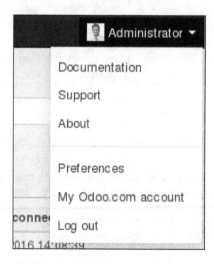

3. In the drop-down menu, click on **About**.

4. In the dialog box which is displayed, click on **Activate the developer mode** in the top right corner.

It is also possible to activate the developer mode by editing the URL: before the **#** sign, insert **?debug=**. For instance, if you are starting from: **http://localhost:8069/web#menu_id=102&action=94**, then you need to change this to: **http://localhost:8069/web?debug=#menu_id=102&action=94**.

5. To exit developer mode, you can edit the URL and remove that string, close your browser tab and open a new one, or use the **Leave Debug Mode** option at the bottom of the debug drop-down menu next to the user menu in the top right of the screen.

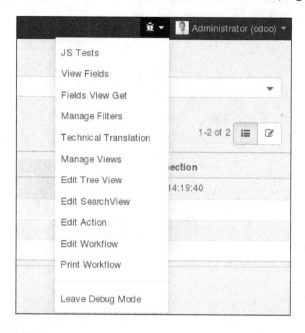

How it works...

When in developer mode, three things happen:

- The JavaScript and CSS code sent to the browser is not minified, which means that the web development tools of your browser are easy to use for debugging the JavaScript code (more on this in *Chapter 15, Web Client Development*).

- You get tooltips when hovering over a field in a form view or over a column in list view providing technical information about the field (internal name, type, and so on).

- A drop-down menu with a Bug icon is displayed next to the user's menu in the top right corner giving access to technical information about the model being displayed, the various related view definitions, the workflow, custom filter management, and so on.

Caution!

Test your addons both with and without developer mode, as the unminified versions of the JavaScript libraries can hide bugs which only bite you in the minified version.

Updating Odoo from source

We saw in the first recipe how to install Odoo from source by using the git repository. The main benefit of this setting is being able to update the source code of Odoo using git to get the latest bug fixes.

Getting ready

Stop any instance currently running with the Odoo source you are about to update.

Make a backup of all the databases you care about in case something goes bad. This is obviously something you need to do for production databases. See the *Managing Odoo server databases* recipe for instructions.

Then make a note of the current version of the source you are running. The best way is to create a lightweight tag using the following command:

```
$ cd ~/odoo-dev/odoo
$ git checkout 9.0
$ git tag 9.0-before-update-$(date --iso)
```

How to do it...

To update the source code of Odoo, use the following command:

```
$ git pull --ff-only
```

This will fetch the latest version of the source code committed to the current branch.

To update an instance running on this code, run the following command:

```
$ odoo.py -c myodoo.cfg --stop-after-init -u base
```

 -u is the shortcut notation for the --update option of odoo.py.

If you don't have a database set in the configuration file, you will have to add the -d database_name option. That command is to be repeated for all the instances running with this version of the source code.

If the update fails, don't panic, you have backups.

1. Read the error message carefully. Save it to a file, as it will be useful to make a bug report later.

2. If you cannot figure out what the problem is, restore the service; restore the Odoo source code to the previous version, which is known to work using the tag you set before updating the source version:

    ```
    $ git reset --hard 9.0-before-update-$(date --iso)
    ```

3. Drop the broken databases and restore them from the backups you made (see the *Managing Odoo server databases* recipe for instructions).

4. Restart your instances and tell your users that the upgrade has been postponed.

> Note that in real life, this should never happen on a production database, because you would have tested the upgrade beforehand on a copy of the database, fixed the issues, and only done the upgrade on the production server after making sure that it runs flawlessly. But sometimes, you still get surprises, so even if you are really sure, make a backup.

How it works...

Updating the source code is done by making sure we are on the correct branch using `git checkout`, and then fetching the new revisions using `git pull`. The `--ff-only` option will cause a failure if you have local commits not present in the remote repository. If this happens and you want to keep your changes, you can use `git pull` (without `--ff-only`) to merge the remote changes with yours; otherwise, use `git reset --hard origin/9.0` to force the update, discarding your local modifications.

The update command uses the following options:

▸ `-c`: specify the configuration file

▸ `--stop-after-init`: stop the instance when the update is over

▸ `-u base` or `--update base`: requests the update of the `base` module

When updating a module, Odoo does the following:

- ▸ It updates the database structure for the models defined in the module for which the structure changes. For updates on the stable branch of Odoo, there should be no such changes, but this can happen for your own addons or third party addons.
- ▸ It updates the database records stored in data files of the module, most notably the views. It then recursively updates the installed modules which have declared a dependency on the module.

Since the `base` module is an implicit dependency of all Odoo modules, updating it will trigger an update of all the installed modules in your instance. To update all installed modules, the alias `all` can be used instead of `base`.

2

Managing Odoo Server Instances

In this chapter, we will learn about:

- ▶ Configuring the addons path
- ▶ Updating the addon modules list
- ▶ Standardizing your instance directory layout
- ▶ Installing and upgrading local addon modules
- ▶ Installing addon modules from GitHub
- ▶ Applying changes to addons
- ▶ Applying and trying proposed pull requests

Introduction

In *Chapter 1, Installing the Odoo Development Environment*, we have seen how to set up an Odoo instance using only the standard "core" addons, which are shipped by the editor. This chapter focuses on adding noncore addons to an Odoo instance, be it your own addons, or third-party addons such as the ones maintained by the **Odoo Community Association** (**OCA**).

> **About the terminology – addon versus module**
>
> In this book, we will use the term **addon** or **addon module** to refer to a Python package that respects the expected format to be installed in Odoo. The user interface often uses the word **module** for this, but we prefer keeping this term for Python modules or packages that are not necessarily Odoo addons.

Configuring the addons path

The **addons path** is a configuration parameter that lists the directories, which will be searched for addon modules by Odoo when it initializes a new database.

Directories listed in the addons path are expected to contain subdirectories, each of which is an addon module.

Getting ready

This recipe assumes you have an instance ready, with a configuration file generated as described in *Chapter 1, Installing the Odoo Development Environment*. The source code of Odoo is available in `~/odoo-dev/odoo`, and the configuration file is in `~/odoo-dev/my-instance.cfg`.

How to do it...

To add the directory `~/odoo-dev/local-addons` to the addons path of the instance, follow these steps:

1. Edit the configuration file for your instance `~/odoo-dev/my-instance.cfg`

2. Locate the line starting with `addons_path =`. By default, it should look like the following:

    ```
    addons_path = ~/odoo-dev/odoo/openerp/addons,~/odoo-dev/odoo/
    addons
    ```

3. Modify the line by appending a comma followed by the name of the directory you want to add to the addons path:

    ```
    addons_path = ~/odoo-dev/odoo/openerp/addons,~/odoo-dev/odoo/
    addons,~/odoo-dev/local-addons
    ```

    You can tidy that line a little by adding a root variable and using it to shorten the path definition (see *Chapter 1, Installing the Odoo Development Environment*, for more on this):

    ```
    root = ~/odoo-dev
    addons_path = %(root)s/odoo/openerp/addons,%(root)s/odoo/
    addons,%(root)s/local-addons
    ```

4. Restart your instance:

    ```
    $ ~/odoo-dev/odoo/odoo.py -c my-instance.cfg
    ```

How it works...

When Odoo is restarted, the configuration file is read. The value of the `addons_path` variable is expected to be a comma-separated list of directories. Relative paths are accepted, but they are relative to the current working directory, and therefore should be avoided in the configuration file.

At this point, the new addons present in `~/odoo-dev/local-addons` are not available in the list of available addon modules of the instance. For this, you need to perform an extra operation explained in the next recipe, *Updating the addon modules list*.

There's more...

When you call the `odoo.py` script for the first time to initialize a new database, you can pass the `--addons-path` command line argument with a comma-separated list of directories. This will initialize the list of available addon modules with all the addons found in the supplied addons path. When you do this, you have to explicitly include the base addons directory (`odoo/openerp/addons`) as well as the core addons directory (`odoo/addons`). Be careful—if you put a space after the commas—you will need to quote the list of directories. You can use the `--save` option to also save the path to the configuration file:

```
$ odoo/odoo.py -d mydatabase \
--addons-path="odoo/openerp/addons,odoo/addons,local-addons" \
--save -c odoo-project.cfg -stop-after-init
```

In this case, using relative paths is OK, since they will be converted to absolute paths in the configuration file.

Updating the addon modules list

As we said in the previous recipe, when you add a directory to the addons path, just restarting the Odoo server is not enough to be able to install one of the new addon modules. A specific action is required for Odoo to scan the addons path and update the list of available addon modules.

Getting ready

Start your instance, and connect to the instance using the Administrator account and activate the developer mode (see *Chapter 1, Installing the Odoo Development Environment*).

How to do it...

To update the list of available addon modules in your instance, you need to perform the following steps:

1. Open the **Apps** menu:

2. Click on **Update Apps List**:

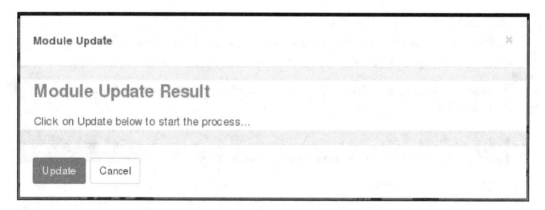

3. In the dialog, click on the **Update** button.
4. At the end of the update, you can click on the first **Apps** entry to see the updated list of available addon modules. You will need to remove the default filter on **Apps** in the search box to see all of them.

How it works...

When the **Update** button is clicked on, Odoo will read the addons path configuration variable, and for each directory in the list, it will look for immediate subdirectories containing an addon **manifest file,** which is a file named `__openerp__.py`, stored in the addon module directory. Odoo reads the manifest expecting to find a Python dictionary. Unless the manifest contains a key `installable` set to `False`, the addon module metadata is recorded in the database. If the module was already present, the information is updated; otherwise, a new record is created. If a previously available addon module is not found, the record is not deleted from the list.

Standardizing your instance directory layout

We recommend that your development and production environments all use a similar directory layout. This standardization will prove helpful when you have to perform maintenance operations, and it will also ease your day to day work.

This recipe creates a directory structure that groups files having similar life cycles or similar purpose together in standardized subdirectories. Feel free to alter this structure to suit your needs, but be sure to have this documented somewhere.

How to do it...

To create the proposed instance layout, you need to perform the following steps:

1. Create one directory per instance:

    ```
    $ mkdir ~/odoo-dev/projectname
    $ cd ~/odoo-dev/projectname
    ```

2. Create a Python `virtualenv` in a subdirectory called `env/`:

    ```
    $ virtualenv env
    ```

3. Create some subdirectories, as follows:

    ```
    $ mkdir src local bin filestore logs
    ```

    The functions of the subdirectories are as follows:

    -   `src/`: This contains the clone of Odoo itself and of the various third-party addons projects (see step 4 in this recipe)
    -   `local/`: This is used to save your instance-specific addons
    -   `bin/`: This includes various helper executable shell scripts
    -   `filestore/`: This is used as a file store
    -   `logs/` (optional): This is used to store the server log files

4. Clone Odoo and install the requirements (see *Chapter 1, Installing the Odoo Development Environment*, for details):

```
$ git clone https://github.com/odoo/odoo.git src/odoo
$ env/bin/pip -r src/odoo/requirements.txt
```

5. Save the following shell script as `bin/odoo`:

```
#!/bin/sh
ROOT=$(dirname $0)/..
PYTHON=$ROOT/env/bin/python
ODOO = $ROOT/src/odoo/odoo.py
PYTHON ODOO -c $ROOT/projectname.cfg "$*"
exit $?
```

6. Make the script executable:

```
$ chmod +x bin/odoo
```

7. Generate a configuration file for your instance:

```
bin/odoo --stop-after-init  --save \
--addons-path src/odoo/openerp/addons,src/odoo/addons,local \
--data-dir filestore
```

8. Add a `.gitignore` file, asking to exclude `data/`, `env/`, and `src/`:

```
# dotfiles, with exceptions:
.*
.gitignore
# python compiled files
*.py[co]
# emacs backup files
*~
# not tracked subdirectories
/env/
/src/
/filestore/
/logs/
```

9. Create a Git repository for this instance and add the files you've added to Git:

```
$ git init
$ git add .
$ git commit -m "initial version of projectname"
```

How it works...

We generate a clean directory structure with clearly labeled directories and dedicated roles. Especially, we separate the following:

- The code maintained by other people (in `src/`)
- The local specific code
- The data of the instance

By having one virtualenv per project, we are sure that the projects' dependencies are not going to interfere with the dependencies of other projects that can be running a different version of Odoo or use different third-party addon modules, which need different versions of Python dependencies. This comes at the cost of a little disk space.

In a similar way, using separate clones of Odoo and third-party addon modules for our different projects, we are able to let each of these evolve independently and only install updates on the instances that need them; hence, reducing the risk of introducing regressions.

The `bin/odoo` script allows to run the server without having to remember the various paths or activate the virtualenv. It also sets the configuration file for us. You can add additional scripts in there to help you in your day-to-day work, for instance, a script to check out the different third-party projects that you need to run your instance.

Regarding the configuration file, we only show the bare minimum options to set up here, but you obviously can set more, such as the database name, the database filter, or the port on which the project listens. Please refer to *Chapter 1, Installing the Odoo Development Environment*, for more information on this topic.

Finally, by managing all this in a Git repository, it becomes quite easy to replicate the setup on a different computer and share the development among a team.

Speedup tip

To ease project creation, you can create a template repository containing the empty structure, and fork that repository for each new project; this will save you from retyping the `bin/odoo` script and the `.gitignore` file, and any other template file you need (continuous integration configuration, `README.md`, `ChangeLog`, and so on).

See also

If you like this approach, we suggest trying out the buildout recipe in *Chapter 16, Server Deployment*, which goes one step further in this way by using buildout to create the instance environment.

Installing and upgrading local addon modules

The core of the functionality of Odoo comes from the addon modules. You have a wealth of addons available as part of Odoo itself as well as addon modules that you can download from the Internet or write yourself.

In this recipe, we will show how to install and upgrade addon modules through the web interface and from the command line.

The main benefits of using the command line for these operations are being able to act on more than one addon at a time and having a clear view of the server logs as the installation or update progresses, which is very useful when in the development mode or when scripting the installation of an instance.

Getting ready

You have an Odoo instance with its database initialized, the addons path is properly set, and the addons list is up to date.

How to do it...

There are two possible methods to install or update addons—you can use the web interface or the command line.

From the web interface

To install a new addon module in your database using the web interface, use the following steps:

1. Connect to the instance using the Administrator account. Open the **Apps** menu:

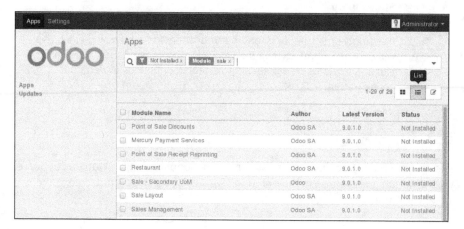

2. Click on **Apps**.

3. Use the search box to locate the addon you want to install. Here are few tips to help you in this task:

   ❑ Activate the **Not Installed** filter

   ❑ If looking for a specific functionality addon rather than a broad functionality addon, remove the **Apps** filter

   ❑ Type a part of the module name in the search box, and use this as a **Module** filter

   ❑ You may find that using the list view gives something more readable

4. Click on the **Install** button under the module name (in the icons view or in the form view).

To update an already installed module in your database, use the following steps:

1. Connect to the instance using the Administrator account.

2. Open the **Apps** menu.

3. Click on **Apps**:

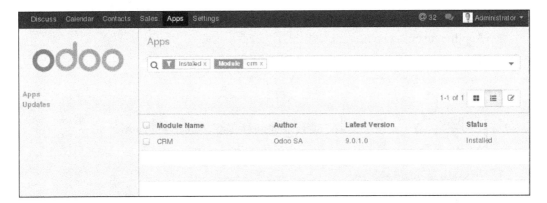

4. Use the search box to locate the addon you want to install. A few tips:

   ❑ Activate the **Installed** filter

   ❑ If looking for a specific functionality addon rather than a broad functionality addon, remove the **Apps** filter

   ❑ Type a part of the addon module name in the search box, and use this a **Module** filter

   ❑ You may find that using the list view gives something more readable

5. Display the module in the form view, and click on the **Upgrade** button under the module name.

From the command line

To install some new addons in your database, follow the following steps:

1. Find the names of the addons. This is the name of the directory containing the file `__openerp__.py` without the leading path.

2. Stop the instance. If you are working on a production database, make a backup.

3. Run the following command:

    ```
    $ odoo/odoo.py -c instance.cfg -d dbname -i addon1,addon2 --stop-
    after-init
    ```

 You may omit `-d dbname` if this is set in your configuration file.

4. Restart the instance.

To update an already installed addon module in your database, follow the steps given here:

1. Find the name of the addon module to update; this is the name of the directory containing the `__openerp__.py` file without the leading path.

2. Stop the instance. If you are working on a production database, make a backup.

3. Run the following command:

    ```
    $ odoo/odoo.py -c instance.cfg -d dbname -u addon1 \
    --stop-after-init
    ```

 You may omit `-d dbname` if this is set in your configuration file.

4. Restart the instance.

How it works...

The addon module installation and update are two closely related processes, but there are some important differences, as highlighted in the next two sections.

Addon installation

When you install an addon, Odoo checks its list of available addons for an *uninstalled* addon with the supplied name. It also checks for the dependencies of that addon and, if any, it will recursively install them before installing the addon.

The installation process of a single module consists of the following steps:

1. If any, run the addon `preinit` hook.

2. Load the model definitions from the Python source code and update the database structure if necessary (see *Chapter 4, Application Models,* for details).

3. Load the data files of the addon and update the database contents if necessary (see *Chapter 9, Module Data,* for details).

4. Install the addon demo data if demo data is enabled in the instance.

5. If any, run the addon `postinit` hook.

6. Run a validation of the view definitions of the addon.

7. If demo data is enabled and test is enabled, run the tests of the addon (see *Chapter 7, Debugging and Automated Testing,* for details).

8. Update the module state in the database.

9. Update the translations in the database from the addon's translations (see *Chapter 11, Internationalization,* for details).

> `preinit` and `postinit` hooks are defined in the `__openerp__.py` file using the `pre_init_hook` and `post_init_hook` keys, respectively. The value of the key is the name of a Python function which must be defined in the `__init__.py` file of the addon module. The **preinit** (resp. **postinit**) hook is called with a database cursor (resp. a database cursor and a registry object) and may perform modification in the database to prepare (resp. finalize) the module installation. Note that these are not run when the module is updated (you can use migration steps for this, see below).

Addon update

When you update an addon, Odoo checks in its list of available addon modules for an installed addon with the given name. It also checks for the reverse dependencies of that addon (these are the addons that depend on the updated addon), and, if any, it will recursively update them.

The update process of a single addon module consists of the following steps:

1. Run the addon module's pre migration steps, if any (see *Chapter 9, Module Data,* for details).

2. Load the model definitions from the Python source code and update the database structure if necessary (see *Chapter 4, Application Models,* for details).

3. Load the data files of the addon and update the database contents if necessary (see *Chapter 9, Module Data* for details).

4. Update the addon's demo data if demo data is enabled in the instance.

5. If any, run the addon post migration steps (see *Chapter 9, Module Data* for details).

6. Run a validation of the view definitions of the addon.

7. If demo data is enabled and test is enabled, run the tests of the addon (see *Chapter 7, Debugging and Automated Testing*, for details).

8. Update the module state in the database.

9. Update the translations in the database from the addon's translations (see *Chapter 11, Internationalization,* for details).

Note that updating an addon module which is not installed does nothing at all. However, installing an addon module that is already installed reinstalls the addon, which can have some unintended effects with some data files containing data that is supposed to be updated by the user and not updated during the normal module update process (see *Using the noupdate and forcecreate flags* in *Chapter 9, Module Data*). There is no risk of error from the user interface, but this can happen from the command line.

There's more...

Be careful about the dependency handling. Consider an instance where you want to have the addons `sale`, `sale_stock`, and `sale_specific` installed, with `sale_specific` depending on `sale_stock` and `sale_stock` depending on `sale`. To install all three, you only need to install `sale_specific`, as it will recursively install the *dependencies* `sale_stock` and `sale`. To update all three, you need to update `sale`, as this will recursively update the *reverse dependencies* `sale_stock` and `sale_specific`.

Another tricky part is when you add a dependency to an addon that already has a version installed. To continue with the previous example, imagine that you add a dependency on `stock_dropshipping` in `sale_specific`. Updating the addon `sale_specific` will not automatically install the new dependency, neither will requesting the installation of `sale_specific`. In this situation, you can get very nasty error messages because the Python code of the addon is not successfully loaded but the data of the addon and the models tables in the database are present. To solve this, you need to stop the instance and manually install the new dependency.

Installing addon modules from GitHub

GitHub is a great source of third-party addons. A lot of Odoo partners use GitHub to share the addons they maintain internally, and the Odoo Community Association (OCA) collectively maintains several hundreds of addons on GitHub. Before starting to write your own addon, be sure to check that nothing already exists that you could use as is or as a starting point.

This recipe will show you how to clone the partner-contact project of the OCA from GitHub and make the addon modules it contains available in your instance.

Getting ready

Suppose you want to change the way addresses are handled in your instance; your customer needs a third field in addition to Odoo's two (`street` and `street2`) to store addresses. You could certainly write your own addon to add a field on `res.partner`, but the issue is a bit trickier than it seems if you want the address to be properly formatted on invoices. Fortunately, someone on a mailing list tells you about the `partner_address_street3` addon that is maintained by the OCA as part of the `partner-contact` project.

The paths used in this recipe reflect the layout proposed in the *Standardizing your instance directory layout* recipe.

How to do it...

To install `partner_address_street3`, follow these steps:

1. Go to your project's directory:

   ```
   $ cd ~/odoo-dev/my-odoo
   ```

2. Clone the 9.0 branch of the `partner-contact` project in the `src/` directory:

   ```
   $ git clone --branch 9.0 \
   https://github.com/OCA/partner-contact.git src/partner-contact
   ```

3. Change the addons path to include that directory and update the addons list of your instance (see previous recipes, *Configure the addons path* and *Update the addon modules list*, of this chapter).

4. Install the `partner_address_street3` addon (see the previous previous recipe, *Install and upgrade local addon modules*).

How it works...

All the Odoo Community Association code repositories have their addons contained in separate subdirectories, which is coherent with what is expected by Odoo regarding the directories in the addons path; therefore, just cloning the repository somewhere and adding that location in the addons path is enough.

There's more...

Some maintainers follow a different approach and have one addon module per repository, living at the root of the repository. In that case, you need to create a new directory, which you will add to the addons path and clone all the addons from that maintainer you need in this directory. Remember to update the addon modules list each time you add a new repository clone.

Applying changes to addons

Most addons available on GitHub are subject to change and do not follow the rules that Odoo enforces for its stable release. They may receive bug fixes or enhancements, including issues or feature requests that you submitted, and these changes may introduce database schema changes or updates in the data files and views. This recipe explains how to install the updated versions.

Getting ready

Suppose you reported an issue with `partner_address_street3` and received a notification that the issue was solved in the lasted revision of the 9.0 branch of the `partner-contact` project, you will want to update your instance with this latest version.

How to do it...

To apply a source modification to your addon from GitHub, you need to perform the following steps:

1. Stop the instance using that addon.

2. Make a backup if it is a production instance (see the recipe *Manage Odoo server databases* in *Chapter 1, Installing the Odoo Development Environment*).

3. Go to the directory where partner-contact was cloned:

   ```
   $ cd ~/odoo-dev/my-odoo/src
   ```

4. Create a local tag for the project so that you can revert to that version in case things break:

   ```
   $ git checkout 9.0
   $ git tag 9.0-before-update-$(date --iso)
   ```

5. Get the latest version of the source code:

   ```
   $ git pull --ff-only
   ```

6. Update the `partner_address_street3` addon in your databases (see previous recipe *Install and upgrade local addon modules*).

7. Restart the instance.

How it works...

This is just a simple application of all the previous recipes we've seen; we get a new version of the addon and we update it in our instances.

If `git pull --ff-only` fails, you can revert to the previous version using this command:

```
$ git reset --hard 9.0-before-update-$(date --iso)
```

Then, you can try `git pull` (without `--ff-only`), which will cause a merge, but this means you have local changes on the addon.

 There is an entry in the **Settings** menu labeled **Upgrade modules**, but it does not work for our purpose.

See also

If the update step breaks, refer to the *Updating Odoo from Source* recipe in *Chapter 1, Installing the Odoo Development Environment*, for the recovery instructions. Remember to always test an update on a copy of a database production first.

Applying and trying proposed pull requests

In the GitHub world, a Pull Request (or PR for short) is a request made by a developer for the maintainers of a project to include some new developments. Such a PR may contain a bug fix or a new feature. These requests are reviewed and tested before being pulled in the main branch.

This recipe explains how to apply a PR to your Odoo project in order to test an improvement or a bug fix.

Getting ready

As in the previous recipe, suppose you reported an issue with `partner_address_street3` and received a notification that the issue was solved in a pull request, which is not yet merged in the 9.0 branch of the project. The developer asks you to validate the fix in PR #123. You need to update a test instance with this branch.

You should not try out such branches directly on a production database, so first create a test environment with a copy of the production database (see *Chapter 1, Installing the Odoo Development Environment*, and *Chapter 16, Server Deployment*).

How to do it...

To apply and try out a GitHub pull request for an addon, you need to perform the following steps:

1. Stop the instance.

2. Go to the directory where partner-contact was cloned:

    ```
    $ cd ~/odoo-dev/my-odoo/src
    ```

3. Create a local tag for the project so that you can revert to that version in case things break:

    ```
    $ git checkout 9.0
    ```

    ```
    $ git tag 9.0-before-update-$(date --iso)
    ```

4. Pull the branch of the pull request. The easiest way is to use the number of the PR, which should have been communicated to you by the developer. In our example, this is the pull request number 123:

    ```
    $ git pull origin pull/123/head
    ```

5. Update the `partner_address_street3` addon module in your database and restart the instance (see the previous recipe, *Installing and upgrading local addon modules*).

6. Test the update—try to reproduce your issue, or try out the feature you wanted.

If it does not work, comment on the PR page of GitHub, explaining what you did and what did not work, so that the developer can update the PR.

If it works, say so on the PR page too; this is an essential part of the PR validation process and it will speed up the merging in the main branch. You can use the text **:+1:**, which is rendered as a "thumb up" icon, meaning you approve the PR.

How it works...

We are using a GitHub feature that enables pull requests to be pulled by number using the `pull/nnnn/head` branch name, where nnnn is the number of the PR. The `git pull` command will merge the remote branch in ours, applying the changes in our code base. After this, we update the addon module, test, and report back to the author of the change about any failure or success.

There's more...

You can repeat step four for different pull requests in the same repository if you want to test them simultaneously. If you are really happy with the result, you can create a branch to keep a reference to the result of the applied changes:

```
$ git checkout -b 9.0-custom
```

Using a different branch will help you remember that you are not using the version from GitHub, but a custom one.

From then on, if you need to apply the latest revision of the 8.0 branch from GitHub, you will need to *pull* them without using `--ff-only`:

```
$ git pull origin 9.0
```

3
Creating Odoo Modules

In this chapter, we will cover the following topics:

- ▸ Creating and installing a new addon module
- ▸ Completing the addon module manifest
- ▸ Organizing the addon module file structure
- ▸ Adding Models
- ▸ Adding Menu Items and Views
- ▸ Adding Access Security
- ▸ Using scaffold to create a module

Introduction

All these components that we just mentioned will be addressed in detail in later chapters.

Now that we have a development environment and know how to manage Odoo server instances and databases, you can learn how to create Odoo addon modules.

Our main goal here is to understand how an addon module is structured and the typical incremental workflow to add components to it.

For this chapter, you are expected to have Odoo installed and to follow the recipes in *Chapter 1, Installing the Odoo Development Environment*. You are also expected to be comfortable in discovering and installing extra addon modules, as described in the *Chapter 2, Managing Odoo Server Instances*, recipes.

Creating and installing a new addon module

In this recipe, we will create a new module, make it available in our Odoo instance, and install it.

Getting ready

We will need an Odoo instance ready to use.

If the first recipe in *Chapter 1, Installing the Odoo Development Environment*, was followed, Odoo should be available at ~/odoo-dev/odoo. For explanation purposes, we will assume this location for Odoo, although any other location of your preference could be used.

We will also need a location for our Odoo modules. For the purpose of this recipe, we will use a local-addons directory alongside the odoo directory, at ~/odoo-dev/local-addons.

How to do it...

The following steps will create and install a new addon module:

1. Change the working directory in which we will work and create the addons directory where our custom module will be placed:

    ```
    $ cd ~/odoo-dev
    $ mkdir local-addons
    ```

2. Choose a technical name for the new module and create a directory with that name for the module. For our example we will use my_module:

    ```
    $ mkdir local-addons/my_module
    ```

 A module's technical name must be a valid Python identifier; it must begin with a letter, and only contain letters (preferably lowercase), numbers, and underscore characters.

3. Make the Python module importable by adding an __init__.py file:

    ```
    $ touch local-addons/my_module/__init__.py
    ```

4. Add a minimal module manifest, for Odoo to detect it. Create an __openerp__.py file with this line:

    ```
    {'name': 'My module'}
    ```

5. Start your Odoo instance including our module directory in the addons path:

    ```
    $ odoo/odoo.py --addons-path=odoo/addons/,local-addons/
    ```

If the `--save` option is added to the Odoo command, the addons path will be saved in the configuration file. Next time you start the server, if no addons path option is provided, this will be used.

6. Make the new module available in your Odoo instance; log in to Odoo using `admin`, enable the **Developer Mode** in the **About** box, and in the Apps top menu select **Update Apps List**. Now Odoo should know about our Odoo module.

7. Select the **Apps** menu at the top and, in the search bar in the top right, delete the default **Apps filter** and search for `my_module`. Click on its **Install** button and the installation will be concluded.

How it works...

An Odoo module is a directory containing code files and other assets. The directory name used is the module's technical name. The `name` key in the module manifest is its title.

The `__openerp__.py` file is the module manifest. It contains a Python dictionary with information about the module, the modules it depends on, and the data files that it will load.

In the example, a minimal manifest file was used, but in real modules, we will want to add a few other important keys. These are discussed in the next recipe, _Completing the module manifest_.

The module directory must be Python-importable, so it also needs to have an `__init__.py` file, even if it's empty. To load a module, the Odoo server will import it. This will cause the code in the `__init__.py` file to be executed, so it works as an entry point to run the module Python code. Because of this, it will usually contain import statements to load the module Python files and submodules.

Modules can be installed directly from the command line using the `--init`, or `-i`, option. In the past, we had to use the **Update Module List** to make it available to the Odoo instance. However, at this moment, this is done automatically when the **--init** or **--update** are used from the command line.

Completing the addon module manifest

The manifest is an important piece for Odoo modules. It contains important information about it and declares the data files that should be loaded.

Getting ready

We should have a module to work with, already containing an __openerp__.py manifest file. You may want to follow the previous recipe to provide such a module to work with.

How to do it...

We will add a manifest file and an icon to our addon module:

1. To create a manifest file with the most relevant keys, edit the module __openerp__. py file to look like this:

```python
# -*- coding: utf-8 -*-
{
    'name': "Title",
    'summary': "Short subtitle phrase",
    'description': """Long description""",
    'author': "Your name",
    'license': "AGPL-3",
    'website': "http://www.example.com",
    'category': 'Uncategorized',
    'version': '9.0.1.0.0',
    'depends': ['base'],
    'data': ['views.xml'],
    'demo': ['demo.xml'],
}
```

2. To add an icon for the module, choose a PNG image to use and copy it to static/description/icon.png.

How it works...

The first line, containing coding: utf-8, is necessary for Python to process the file content as Unicode UTF-8. This way, we can use non-ASCII characters in the manifest.

The remaining content is a regular Python dictionary, with keys and values. The example manifest we used contains the most relevant keys:

▸ name: This is the title for the module.

▸ summary: This is the subtitle with a one-line description.

▸ description: This is a long description, written in plain text or **ReStructuredText** (**RST**) format. It is usually surrounded by triple quotes, used in Python to delimit multiline texts. For an RST quickstart reference, visit http://docutils. sourceforge.net/docs/user/rst/quickstart.html.

- `author`: This is a string with the name of the authors. When there is more than one, it is common practice to use a comma to separate their names, but note that it still should be a string, not a Python list.

- `license`: This is the identifier for the license under which the module is made available. It is limited to a predefined list, and the most frequent option is `AGPL-3`. Other possibilities include `LGPL-3`, `Other OSI approved license`, and `Other proprietary`.

- `website`: This is a URL people should visit to know more about the module or the authors.

- `category`: This is used to organize modules in areas of interest. The list of the standard category names available can be seen at `https://github.com/odoo/odoo/blob/master/openerp/addons/base/module/module_data.xml`. But it's also possible to define other new category names here.

- `version`: This is the modules' version numbers. It can be used by the Odoo app store to detect newer versions for installed modules. If the version number does not begin with the Odoo target version (for example, `8.0`), it will be automatically added. Nevertheless, it will be more informative if you explicitly state the Odoo target version, for example, using 8.0.1.0.0 or 8.0.1.0 instead of 1.0.0 or 1.0.

- `depends`: This is a list with the technical names of the modules it directly depends on. If none, we should at least depend on the `base` module. Don't forget to include any module defining XML IDs, Views, or Models referenced by this module. That will ensure that they all load in the correct order, avoiding hard-to-debug errors.

- `data`: This is a list of relative paths to the data files to load with module installation or upgrade. The paths are relative to the module root directory. Usually, these are XML and CSV files, but it's also possible to have YAML data files. These are discussed in depth in *Chapter 9, Module Data*.

- `demo`: This is the list of relative paths to the files with demonstration data to load. These will only be loaded if the database was created with the **Demonstration Data** flag enabled.

The image that is used as the module icon is the PNG file at `static/description/icon.png`.

> Odoo is expected to have significant changes between major versions, so modules built for one major version are likely to not be compatible with the next version without conversion and migration work. Because of this, it's important to be sure about a module's Odoo target version before installing it.

There's more

Instead of having the long description in the module manifest, it's possible to have it in its own file. Since version 8.0, it can be replaced by a README file, with either a `.txt`, `.rst`, or an `.md` (Markdown) extension. Otherwise, include a `description/index.html` file in the module.

This HTML description will override a description defined in the manifest file.

There are a few more keys that are frequently used:

- `application`: If this is `True`, the module is listed as an application. Usually, this is used for the central module of a functional area.

- `auto_install`: If this is `True`, it indicates that this is a "glue" module, which is automatically installed when all its dependencies are installed.

- `installable`: If this is `True` (the default value), it indicates that the module is available for installation.

Organizing the addon module file structure

An addon module contains code files and other assets such as XML files and images. For most of these files, we are free to choose where to place them inside the module directory.

However, Odoo uses some conventions on the module structure, so it is advisable to follow them.

Getting ready

We are expected to have an addon module directory with only the `__init__.py` and `__openerp__.py` files.

How to do it...

To create the basic skeleton for the addon module:

1. Create the directories for code files:

   ```
   $ cd path/to/my-module
   $ mkdir models
   $ touch models/__init__.py
   $ mkdir controllers
   ```

```
$ touch controllers/__init__.py
$ mkdir views
$ mkdir security
$ mkdir data
$ mkdir demo
$ mkdir i18n
$ mkdir -p static/description
```

2. Edit the module's top __init__.py file so that the code in subdirectories is loaded:

```
# -*- coding: utf-8 -*-
from . import models
from . import controllers
```

This should get us started with a structure containing the most used directories, similar to this one:

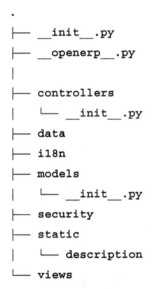

```
.
├── __init__.py
├── __openerp__.py
│
├── controllers
│   └── __init__.py
├── data
├── i18n
├── models
│   └── __init__.py
├── security
├── static
│   └── description
└── views
```

How it works...

To provide some context, an Odoo addon module can have three types of file:

- The **Python code** is loaded by the `__init__.py` files, where the `.py` files and code subdirectories are imported. Subdirectories containing code Python, in turn, need their own `__init__.py`

- **Data files** that are to be declared in the `data` and `demo` keys of the `__openerp__.py` module manifest in order to be loaded. These are usually XML and CSV files for the user interface, fixture data, and demonstration data.

- **Web assets** such as JavaScript code and libraries, CSS, and QWeb/HTML templates also play an important part. There are declared through an XML file extending the master templates to add these assets to the web client or website pages.

The addon files are to be organized in these directories:

- `models/` contains the backend code files, creating the Models and their business logic. A file per Model is recommended, with the same name as the model, for example, `library_book.py` for the `library.book` model. These are addressed in depth in *Chapter 4, Application Models*.

- `views/` contains the XML files for the user interface, with the actions, forms, lists, and so on. As with models, it is advised to have one file per model. Filenames for website templates are expected to end with the `_template` suffix. Backend Views are explained in *Chapter 8, Backend Views*, and website Views are addressed in *Chapter 14, CMS Web Site Development*.

- `data/` contains other data files with module initial data. Data files are explained in *Chapter 9, Module Data*.

- `demo/` contains data files with demonstration data, useful for tests, training or module evaluation.

- `i18n/` is where Odoo will look for the translation `.pot` and `.po` files. See *Chapter 11, Internationalization*, for more details. These files don't need to be mentioned in the manifest file.

- `security/` contains the data files defining access control lists, usually a `ir.model.access.csv` file, and possibly an XML file to define access Groups and Record Rules for row level security. See *Chapter 10, Access Security*, for more details on this.

- `controllers/` contains the code files for the website controllers, for modules providing that kind of feature. Web controllers are covered in *Chapter 13, Web Server Development*.

▶ `static/` is where all web assets are expected to be placed. Unlike other directories, this directory name is not just a convention, and only files inside it can be made available for the Odoo web pages. They don't need to be mentioned in the module manifest, but will have to be referred to in the web template. This is discussed in more detail in *Chapter 14, CMS Website Development*.

 When adding new files to a module, don't forget to declare them either in the `__openerp__.py` (for data files) or `__init__.py` (for code files); otherwise, those files will be ignored and won't be loaded.

Adding models

Models define the data structures to be used by our business applications. This recipe shows how to add a basic model to a module.

We will use a simple book library example to explain this; we want a model to represent books. Each book has a name and a list of authors.

Getting ready

We should have a module to work with. If we follow the first recipe in this chapter, we will have an empty `my_module`. We will use that for our explanation.

How to do it...

To add a new Model, we add a Python file describing it and then upgrade the addon module (or install it, if it was not already done). The paths used are relative to our addon module location (for example, `~/odoo-dev/local-addons/my_module/`):

1. Add a Python file to the module, `models/library_book.py`, with the following code:

```python
# -*- coding: utf-8 -*-
from openerp import models, fields
class LibraryBook(models.Model):
    _name = 'library.book'
    name = fields.Char('Title', required=True)
    date_release = fields.Date('Release Date')
    author_ids = fields.Many2many('res.partner',
        string='Authors')
```

2. Add a Python initialization file with code files to be loaded by the module `models/__init__.py`, with the following code:

```python
from . import library_book
```

3. Edit the module Python initialization file to have the `models/` directory loaded by the module:

```
from . import models
```

4. Upgrade the Odoo module, either from the command line or from the apps menu in the user interface. If you look closely at the server log while upgrading the module, you should see this line:

```
openerp.modules.module: module my_module: creating or updating
database tables
```

After this, the new `library.book` model should be available in our Odoo instance. If we have the technical tools activated, we can confirm that by looking it up at **Settings | Technical | Database Structure | Models**.

How it works...

Our first step was to create a Python file where our new module was created.

Odoo models are objects derived from the Odoo `Model` Python class.

When a new model is defined, it is also added to a central model registry. This makes it easier for other modules to later make modifications to it.

Models have a few generic attributes prefixed with an underscore. The most important one is `_name`, providing a unique internal identifier to be used throughout the Odoo instance.

The model fields are defined as class attributes. We began defining the `name` field of the `Char` type. It is convenient for models to have this field, because by default, it is used as the record description when referenced from other models.

We also used an example of a relational field, `author_ids`. It defines a many-to-many relation between `Library Books` and the partners — a book can have many authors and each author can have many books.

There's much more to say about models, and they will be covered in more depth in *Chapter 4, Application Models*.

Next, we must make our module aware of this new Python file. This is done by the `__init__`. py files. Since we placed the code inside the `models/` subdirectory, we need the previous `init` file to import that directory, which should in turn contain another `init` file importing each of the code files there (just one in our case).

Changes to Odoo models are activated by upgrading the module. The Odoo server will handle the translation of the model class into database structure changes.

Although no example is provided here, business logic can also be added to these Python files, either by adding new methods to the Model's class, or by extending existing methods, such as `create()` or `write()`. This is addressed in *Chapter 5, Basic Server Side Development*.

Adding Menu Items and Views

Once we have Models for our data structure needs, we want a user interface for our users to interact with them. This recipe builds on the `Library Book` Model from the previous recipe and adds a menu item to display a user interface featuring list and form Views.

Getting ready

The addon module implementing the `library.book` Model, provided in the previous recipe, is needed. The paths used are relative to our addon module location (for example, `~/odoo-dev/local-addons/my_module/`).

How to do it...

To add a view, we will add an XML file with its definition to the module. Since it is a new Model, we must also add a menu option for the user to be able to access it.

Be aware that the sequence of the following steps is relevant, since some use references to IDs defined in previous steps:

1. Create the XML file to add the data records describing the user interface `views/library_book.xml`:

```xml
<?xml version="1.0" encoding="utf-8"?>
<openerp>
  <data>
    <!-- Data records go here -->
  </data>
</openerp>
```

2. Add the new data file to the addon module manifest, `__openerp__.py` by adding it to the `views/library_book.xml`:

```python
# -*- coding: utf-8 -*-
{
    'name': "Library Books",
    'summary': "Manage your books",
    'depends': ['base'],
    'data': ['views/library_book.xml'],
}
```

3. Add the Action that opens the Views in the `library_book.xml` file:

```
<act_window
    id="library_book_action"
    name="Library Books"
    res_model="library.book" />
```

4. Add the menu item to the `library_book.xml` file, making it visible to the users:

```
<menuitem
    id="library_book_menu"
    name="Library"
    action="library_book_action"
    parent=""
    sequence="5" />
```

If you try and upgrade the module now, you should be able to see a new top menu option (you might need to refresh your web browser). Clicking on it should work and will open Views for `Library Books` that are automatically generated by the server.

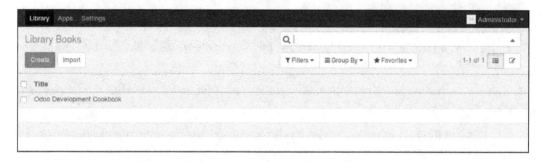

5. Add a custom form view to the `library_book.xml` file:

```
<record id="library_book_view_form" model="ir.ui.view">
    <field name="name">Library Book Form</field>
    <field name="model">library.book</field>
    <field name="arch" type="xml">

        <form>
          <group>
            <field name="name"/>
            <field name="author_ids" widget="many2many_tags"/>
          </group>
          <group>
            <field name="date_release"/>
          </group>
        </form>

    </field>
</record>
```

6. Add a custom Tree (List) view to the `library_book.xml` file:

```xml
<record id="library_book_view_tree" model="ir.ui.view">
  <field name="name">Library Book List</field>
  <field name="model">library.book</field>
  <field name="arch" type="xml">

    <tree>
      <field name="name"/>
      <field name="date_release"/>
    </tree>

  </field>
</record>
```

7. Add custom `Search` options to the `library_book.xml` file:

```xml
<record id="library_book_view_search" model="ir.ui.view">
  <field name="name">Library Book Search</field>
  <field name="model">library.book</field>
  <field name="arch" type="xml">

    <search>
      <field name="name"/>
      <field name="author_ids"/>
      <filter string="No Authors"
              domain="[('author_ids','=',False)]"/>
    </search>

  </field>
</record>
```

How it works...

At the low level, the user interface is defined by records stored in special Models. The first two steps create an empty XML file to define the records to be loaded and then add them to the module's list of data files to be installed.

Data files can be anywhere inside the module directory, but the convention is for the user interface to be defined inside a `views/` subdirectory using file names after the Model the interface is for. In our case, the `library.book` interface is in the `views/library_book.xml` file.

The next step is to define a Window Action to display the user interface in the main area of the web client. The Action has a target Model defined by `res_model` and sets the title to display to the user using `name`. These are just the basic attributes. It supports additional attributes, giving much more control of how the Views are rendered, such as what Views are to be displayed, adding filters on the records available, or setting default values. These are discussed in detail in *Chapter 8, Backend Views*.

In general, data records are defined using a `<record>` tag, but in our example, the Window Action was defined using the `<act_window>` tag. This is a shortcut to create records for the `ir.actions.act_window` Model, where Window Actions are stored.

Similarly, menu items are stored in the `ir.ui.menu` Model, but a convenience `<menuitem>` shortcut tag is available and was used.

These are the menu items' main attributes used here:

- ▸ `name`: This is the menu item text to be displayed.
- ▸ `action`: This is the identifier of the action to be executed. We use the ID of the Window Action created in the previous step.
- ▸ `sequence`: This is used to set the order at which the menu items of the same level are presented.
- ▸ `parent`: This is the identifier for the parent menu item. Our example menu item had no parent, meaning that it is to be displayed at the top of the menu.

At this point, our module can display a menu item, and clicking on it opens Views for the `Library Books` model. Since nothing specific is set on the Window Action, the default is to display a List (or Tree) view and a form view.

We haven't defined any of these Views, so Odoo will automatically create them on the fly. However, we will surely want to control how our Views look, so in the next two steps, a form and a tree view are created.

Both Views are defined with a record on the `ir.ui.view` model. The attributes we used are as follows:

- ▸ `name`: This is a title identifying this view. It is frequent to see the XML ID repeated here, but it can perfectly be a more human readable title.
- ▸ `model`: This is the internal identifier of the target model, as defined in its `_name` attribute.
- ▸ `arch`: This is the view architecture, where its structure is actually defined. This is where different types of View differ from each other.

Form Views are defined with a top `<form>` element, and its canvas is a two-column grid. Inside the form, `<group>` elements are used to vertically compose fields. Two groups result in two columns with fields, that are added using the `<field>` element. Fields use a default widget according to their data type, but a specific widget can be used with the help of the `widget` attribute.

Tree Views are simpler; they are defined with a top `<tree>` element containing `<field>` elements for the columns to be displayed.

Finally, we added a Search view to expand the search option in the box at the top right. Inside the `<search>` top-level tag, we can have `<field>` and `<filter>` elements. Field elements are additional fields that can be searched from the box. Filter elements are predefined filter conditions that can the activated with a click.

Using scaffold to create a module

When creating a new Odoo module, there is some boilerplate that needs to be set up. To help quick starting new modules, Odoo provides the `scaffold` command.

The recipe shows how to create a new module using the `scaffold` command, which will put in place a skeleton of the files directories to use.

Getting ready

We need Odoo installed and a directory for our custom modules.

We will assume that Odoo is installed at `~/odoo-dev/odoo` and our custom modules will be at `~/odoo-dev/local-addons`.

How to do it...

The `scaffold` command is used from the command line:

1. Change the working directory to where we will want our module to be. This can be whatever directory you choose, but within an addons path to be useful. Following the directory choices used in the previous recipe, it should be as follows:

   ```
   $ cd ~/odoo-dev/local-addons
   ```

2. Choose a technical name for the new module and use the `scaffold` command to create it. For our example, we will choose `my_scaffolded`:

   ```
   $ ~/odoo-dev/odoo/odoo.py scaffold my_scaffolded
   ```

3. Edit the `__openerp__.py` default module manifest provided and change the relevant values. You will surely want to at least change the module title in the `name` key.

This is how the generated addon module should look like:

```
$ tree my_scaffolded
my_scaffolded
├── controllers.py
├── demo.xml
├── __init__.py
├── models.py
├── __openerp__.py
├── security
│   └── ir.model.access.csv
└── templates.xml
```

How it works...

The `scaffold` command creates the skeleton for a new module based on a template.

By default, the new module is created in the current working directory, but we can provide a specific directory where to create the module, passing it as an additional parameter. For example:

```
$ ~/odoo-dev/odoo/odoo.py scaffold my_module ~/odoo-dev/local-addons
```

A `default` template is used but a `theme` template is also available, for website theme authoring. To choose a specific template, the `-t` option can be used. We are also allowed to use a path for a directory with a template.

This means that we can use our own templates with the `scaffold` command. The built-in themes can be used as a guide, and they can be found in the Odoo subdirectory `./openerp/cli/templates`. To use our own template, we could use something like this:

```
$ ~/odoo-dev/odoo/odoo.py scaffold -t path/to/template my_module
```

There's more...

Unfortunately, the default template does not adhere to the current Odoo guidelines. We could create our own template by copying the default one, at `odoo/openerp/cli/templates/default/`, and modifying to better suit the structure described in the *Organizing the module file structure* recipe. A command similar to this could get us started on that:

```
$ cp -r ~/odoo-dev/odoo/openerp/cli/templates/default ~/odoo-dev/template
```

Later, we can use it with the following command:

```
$ ~/odoo-dev/odoo/odoo.py scaffold -t ~/odoo-dev/template my_module
```

4

Application Models

In this chapter, we will cover the following topics:

- ▶ Defining the Model representation and order
- ▶ Adding data fields to a Model
- ▶ Using a float field with configurable precision
- ▶ Adding a monetary field to a Model
- ▶ Adding relational fields to a Model
- ▶ Adding a hierarchy to a Model
- ▶ Adding constraint validations to a Model
- ▶ Adding computed fields to a Model
- ▶ Exposing Related fields stored in other models
- ▶ Adding dynamic relations using Reference fields
- ▶ Adding features to a Model using inheritance
- ▶ Using Abstract Models for reusable Model features
- ▶ Using Delegation inheritance to copy features to another Model

Introduction

In order to concisely get the point through, the recipes in this chapter make small additions to an existing addon module. We chose to use the module created by the recipes in *Chapter 3, Creating Odoo Modules*. To better follow the examples here, you should have that module created and ready to use.

Defining the Model representation and order

Models have structural attributes defining their behavior. These are prefixed with an underscore and the most important is _name, which defines the internal global identifier for the Model.

There are two other attributes we can use. One to set the field used as a representation, or title, for the records, and another one to set the order they are presented in.

Getting ready

This recipe assumes that you have an instance ready with my_module, as described in *Chapter 3, Creating Odoo Modules.*

How to do it...

The my_module instance should already contain a Python file called models/library_book.py, which defines a basic model. We will edit it to add a new class-level attribute after _name:

1. To add a human-friendly title to the model, add the following:

   ```
   _description = 'Library Book'
   ```

2. To have records sorted first by default from newer to older and then by title, add the following:

   ```
   _order = 'date_release desc, name'
   ```

3. To use the short_name field as the record representation, add the following:

   ```
   _rec_name = 'short_name'
   short_name = fields.Char('Short Title')
   ```

When we're done, our library_book.py file should look like this:

```python
# -*- coding: utf-8 -*-
from openerp import models, fields
class LibraryBook(models.Model):
    _name = 'library.book'
    _description = 'Library Book'
    _order = 'date_release desc, name'
    _rec_name = 'short_name'
    name = fields.Char('Title', required=True)
    short_name = fields.Char('Short Title')
    date_release = fields.Date('Release Date')
    author_ids = fields.Many2many('res.partner', string='Authors')
```

We should then upgrade the module to have these changes activated in Odoo.

How it works...

The first step adds a friendlier description title to the model's definition. This is not mandatory, but can be used by some addons. For instance, it is used by the tracking feature in the `mail` addon module for the notification text when a new record is created. For more details, see *Chapter 12, Automation and Workflows*.

By default, Odoo orders the records using the internal `id` value. But this can be changed to use the fields of our choice by providing a `_order` attribute with a string containing a comma-separated list of field names. A field name can be followed with the `desc` keyword to have it sorted in reverse order.

Only fields stored in the database can be used. Non-stored computed fields can't be used to sort records.

 The syntax for the `_sort` string is similar to SQL `ORDER BY` clauses, although it's stripped down. For instance, special clauses such as `NULLS FIRST` are not allowed.

Model records have a representation used when they are referenced from other records. For example, a `user_id` field with the value 1 represents the **Administrator** user. When displayed in a form view, we will be shown the user name rather than the database ID. By default, the `name` field is used. In fact, that is the default value for the `_rec_name` attribute, and that's why it's convenient to have a `name` field in our Models.

If no `name` field exists in the model, a representation is generated with the model and record identifiers, similar to **(library.book, 1)**.

There's more...

Record representation is available in a magic `display_name` computed field added automatically to all models since version 8.0. Its values are generated using the Model method `name_get()`, which was already in existence in previous Odoo versions.

Its default implementation uses the `_rec_name` attribute. For more sophisticated representations, we can override its logic. This method must return a list of tuples with two elements: the ID of the record and the Unicode string representation for the record.

For example, to have the title and its release date in the representation, such as **Moby Dick (1851-10-18)**, we could define the following:

```
def name_get(self):
    result = []
    for record in self:
        result.append(
            (record.id,
             u"%s (%s)" % (record.name, record.date_released)
            ))
    return result
```

Do notice that we used a Unicode string while building the record representation, `u"%s (%s)"`. This is important to avoid errors, in case we find non-ASCII characters.

Adding data fields to a model

Models are meant to store data, and this data is structured in fields. Here, we will learn about the several types of data that can be stored in fields, and how to add them to a model.

Getting ready

This recipe assumes that you have an instance ready with the `my_module` addon module available, as described in *Chapter 3*, *Creating Odoo Modules*.

How to do it...

The `my_module` addon module should already have a `models/library_book.py` defining a basic Model. We will edit it to add new fields:

1. Use the minimal syntax to add fields to the Library Books model:

```
from openerp import models, fields
class LibraryBook(models.Model):
    # ...
    short_name = fields.Char('Short Title')
    notes = fields.Text('Internal Notes')
    state = fields.Selection(
        [('draft', 'Not Available'),
         ('available', 'Available'),
         ('lost', 'Lost')],
        'State')
    description = fields.Html('Description')
    cover = fields.Binary('Book Cover')
```

```
out_of_print = fields.Boolean('Out of Print?')
date_release = fields.Date('Release Date')
date_updated = fields.Datetime('Last Updated')
pages = fields.Integer('Number of Pages')
reader_rating = fields.Float(
    'Reader Average Rating',
    (14, 4),  # Optional precision (total, decimals),
)
```

2. All these fields support a few common attributes. As an example, we could edit the preceding `pages` field to add them:

```
pages = fields.Integer(
    string='Number of Pages',
    default=0,
    help='Total book page count',
    groups='base.group_user',
    states={'cancel': [('readonly', True)]},
    copy=True,
    index=False,
    readonly=False,
    required=False,
    company_dependent=False,
)
```

3. The `Char` fields support a few specific attributes. As an example, we can edit the `short_name` field to add them:

```
short_name = fields.Char(
    string='Short Title',
    size=100,  # For Char only
    translate=False,  # also for Text fields
)
```

4. The HTML fields also have specific attributes:

```
description = fields.Html(
    string='Description',
    # optional:
    sanitize=True,
    strip_style=False,
    translate=False,
)
```

Upgrading the module will make these changes effective in the Odoo model.

How it works...

Fields are added to models by defining an attribute in its Python class. The non-relational field types available are as follows:

- `Char` for string values.

- `Text` for multi-line string values.

- `Selection` for selection lists. This has a list of values and description pairs. The value that is selected is what gets stored in the database, and it can be a string or an integer.

- `Html` is similar to the Text field, but is expected to store rich text in the HTML format.

- `Binary` fields store binary files, such as images or documents.

- `Boolean` stores `True`/`False` values.

- `Date` stores date values. The ORM handles them in the string format, but they are stored in the database as dates. The format used is defined in `openerp.fields.DATE_FORMAT`.

- `Datetime` for date-time values. They are stored in the database in a naive date time, in UTC time. The ORM represents them as a string and also in UTC time. The format used is defined in `openerp.fields.DATETIME_FORMAT`.

- `Integer` fields need no further explanation.

- `Float` fields store numeric values. The precision can optionally be defined with a total number of digits and decimal digits pairs.

- `Monetary` can store an amount in a certain currency; it is also explained in another recipe.

The first step in the recipe shows the minimal syntax to add each field type. The field definitions can be expanded to add other optional attributes, as shown in step 2.

Here is an explanation for the field attributes used:

- `string` is the field's title, used in UI view labels. It actually is optional; if not set, a label will be derived from the field name by adding title case and replacing underscores with spaces.

- `size` only applies to `Char` fields and is the maximum number of characters allowed. In general, it is advised not to use it.

- `translate` when set to `True`, makes the field translatable; it can hold a different value depending on the user interface language.

- `default` is the default value. It can also be a function that is used to calculate the default value. For example, `default=_compute_default`, where `_compute_default` is a method defined on the model before the field definition.

- `help` is an explanation text displayed in the UI tooltips.

- ▶ `groups` makes the field available only to some security groups. It is a string containing a comma-separated list of XML IDs for security groups. This is addressed in more detail in *Chapter 10, Access Security*.

- ▶ `states` allows the user interface to dynamically set the value for the `readonly`, `required`, and `invisible` attributes, depending on the value of the `state` field. Therefore, it requires a `state` field to exist and be used in the form view (even if it is invisible).

- ▶ `copy` flags if the field value is copied when the record is duplicated. By default, it is `True` for non-relational and `Many2one` fields and `False` for `One2many` and computed fields.

- ▶ `index`, when set to `True`, makes for the creation of a database index for the field, allowing faster searches. It replaces the deprecated `select=1` attribute.

- ▶ The `readonly` flag makes the field read-only by default in the user interface.

- ▶ The `required` flag makes the field mandatory by default in the user interface.

- ▶ The `sanitize` flag is used by HTML fields and strips its content from potentially insecure tags.

- ▶ `strip_style` is also an HTML field attribute and has the sanitization to also remove style elements.

- ▶ The `company_dependent` flag makes the field store different values per company. It replaces the deprecated `Property` field type.

There's more...

The `Selection` field also accepts a function reference instead of a list, as its "selection" attribute. This allows for dynamically generated lists of options. You can see an example of this in the *Add dynamic relations using Reference fields* recipe, where a selection attribute is also used.

The `Date` and `Datetime` field objects expose a few utility methods that can be convenient.

For `Date`, we have the following:

- ▶ `fields.Date.from_string(string_value)` parses the string into a date object.
- ▶ `fields.Date.to_string(date_value)` represents the `Date` object as a string.
- ▶ `fields.Date.today()` returns the current day in string format.
- ▶ `fields.Date.context_today(record)` returns the current day in string format according to the timezone of the record's (or recordset) context.

For `Datetime`, we have the following:

- `fields.Datetime,from_string(string_value)` parses the string into a `datetime` object.

- `fields.Datetime,to_string(datetime_value)` represents the `datetime` object as a string.

- `fields.Datetime,now()` returns the current day and time in string format. This is appropriate to use for default values.

- `fields.Datetime,context_timestamp(record, value)` converts a `value` naive date-time into a timezone-aware date-time using the timezone in the context of `record`. This is not suitable for default values.

Other than basic fields, we also have relational fields: `Many2one`, `One2many`, and `Many2many`. These are explained in the *Add relational fields to a model* recipe.

It's also possible to have fields with automatically computed values, defining the computation function with the `compute` field attribute. This is explained in the *Adding computed fields to a model* recipe.

A few fields are added by default in Odoo models, so we should not use these names for our fields. These are the `id` field, for the record's automatically generated identifier, and a few audit log fields, which are as follows:

- `create_date` is the record creation timestamp
- `create_uid` is the user that created the record
- `write_date` is the last recorded edit timestamp
- `write_uid` is the user that last edited the record

The automatic creation of these log fields can be disabled by setting the `_log_access=False` model attribute.

Another special column that can be added to a model is `active`. It should be a Boolean flag allowing for mark records as inactive. Its definition looks like this:

```
active = fields.Boolean('Active', default=True)
```

By default, only records with `active` set to `True` are visible. To have them retrieved, we need to use a domain filter with `[('active', '=', False)]`. Alternatively, if the `'active_test': False` value is added to the environment Context, the ORM will not filter out inactive records.

Using a float field with configurable precision

When using float fields, we may want to let the end user configure the precision that is to be used. The **Decimal Precision Configuration** module addon provides this ability.

We will add a **Cost Price** field to the Library Book model, with a user-configurable number of digits.

Getting ready

We will reuse the `my_module` addon module from *Chapter 3, Creating Odoo Modules.*

How to do it...

We need to install the `decimal_precision` module, add a "Usage" entry for our configuration, and then use it in the model field:

1. Make sure the Decimal Accuracy module is installed; select **Apps** from the top menu, remove the default filter, search for the **Decimal Precision Configuration** app, and install it if it's not already installed:

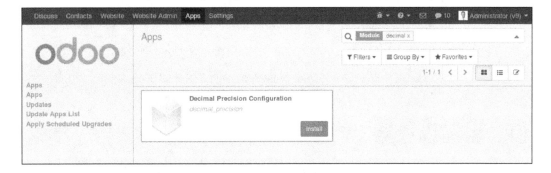

2. Activate the **Developer Mode** in the **About** dialog box, available within the **?** icon in the menu bar at the top. This will enable the **Settings | Technical** menu.

3. Access the Decimal Precision configurations. To do this, open the **Settings** top menu and select **Technical | Database Structure | Decimal Accuracy**. We should see a list of the currently defined settings.

4. Add a new configuration, setting **Usage** to **Book Price** and choosing the
   Digits precision:

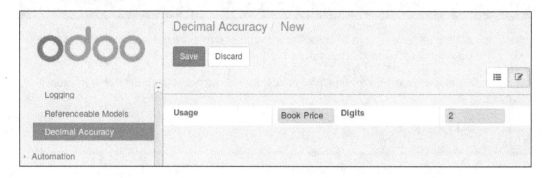

5. Add the new dependency to the __openerp__.py manifest file. It should be similar
   to this:

```
{    'name': 'Chapter 03 code',
     'depends': ['base', 'decimal_precision],
     'data': ['views/library_book.xml'] }
```

6. To add the model field using this decimal precision setting, edit the models/
   library_book.py file by adding the following:

```
from openerp.addons import decimal_precision as dp
# ...
class LibraryBook(models.Model):
    # ...
    cost_price = fields.Float(
        'Book Cost', dp.get_precision('Book Price))
```

How it works...

The get_precision() function looks up the name in the Decimal Accuracy **Usage** field
and returns a tuple representing 16-digit precision with the number of decimals defined
in the configuration.

Using this function in the field definition, instead of having it hardcoded, allows the end user
to configure it according to his needs.

Adding a monetary field to a Model

Odoo has special support for monetary values related to a currency. Let's see how to use it in a Model.

 The Monetary field was introduced in Odoo 9.0 and is not available in previous versions. If you are using Odoo 8.0, the float field type is your best alternative.

Getting ready

We will reuse the `my_module` addon module from *Chapter 3, Creating Odoo Modules*.

How to do it...

The monetary field needs a complementary currency field to store the currency for the amounts.

The `my_module` already has a `models/library_book.py` defining a basic Model. We will edit this to add the needed fields:

1. Add the field to store the currency that is to be used:

```
class LibraryBook(models.Model):
    # ...
    currency_id = fields.Many2one(
        'res.currency', string='Currency')
```

2. Add the monetary field to store our amount:

```
class LibraryBook(models.Model):
    # ...
    retail_price = fields.Monetary(
        'Retail Price',
        # optional: currency_field='currency_id',
        )
```

Now, upgrade the addon module, and the new fields should be available in the Model. They won't be visible in views until they are added to them, but we can confirm their addition by inspecting the Model fields in **Settings | Technical | Database Structure | Models**.

How it works...

Monetary fields are similar to Float fields, but Odoo is able to represent them correctly in the user interface since it knows what their currency is through a second field for that purpose.

This currency field is expected to be named `currency_id`, but we can use whatever field name we like as long as it is indicated using the `currency_field` optional parameter. You might like to know that the decimal precision for the amount is taken from the currency definition (the `decimal_precision` field of the `res.currency` model).

Adding relational fields to a Model

Relations between Odoo Models are represented by relational fields. We can have three different types of relations: many-to-one, one-to-many, and many-to-many. Looking at the Library Books example, we see that each book can have one Publisher, so we can have a many-to-one relation between books and publishers.

Looking at it from the Publishers point of view, each Publisher can have many Books. So, the previous many-to-one relation implies a one-to-many reverse relation.

Finally, there are cases where we can have a many-to-many relation. In our example, each book can have several (many) Authors. And inversely, each Author can have written many books. Looking at it from either side, this is a many-to-many relation.

Getting ready

We will reuse the `my_module` addon module from *Chapter 3, Creating Odoo Modules*.

How to do it...

Odoo uses the Partner model, `res.partner`, to represent persons, organizations, and addresses. So, we should use it for authors and publishers. We will edit the `models/library_book.py` file to add these fields:

1. Add to `Library Books` the many-to-one field for the book's publisher:

    ```python
    class LibraryBook(models.Model):
        # ...
        publisher_id = fields.Many2one(
            'res.partner', string='Publisher',
            # optional:
            ondelete='set null',
            context={},
            domain=[],
            )
    ```

2. To add the one-to-many field for a publisher's books, we need to extend the partner model. For simplicity, we will add that to the same Python file:

```
class ResPartner(models.Model):
    _inherit = 'res.partner'
    book_ids = fields.One2many(
        'library.book', 'publisher_id',
        string='Published Books')
```

3. The many-to-many relation between books and authors was already created, but let's revisit it:

```
class LibraryBook(models.Model):
    # ...
    author_ids = fields.Many2many(
        'res.partner', string='Authors')
```

4. The same relation, but from authors to books, should be added to the Partner model:

```
class ResPartner(models.Model):
    # ...
    book_ids = fields.Many2many(
        'library.book',
        string='Authored Books',
        # relation='library_book_res_partner_rel'  # optional
        )
```

Now, upgrade the addon module, and the new fields should be available in the Model. They won't be visible in views until they are added to them, but we can confirm their addition by inspecting the Model fields in **Settings | Technical | Database Structure | Models**.

How it works...

Many-to-one fields add a column to the database table of the model storing the database ID of the related record. At the database level, a foreign key constraint will also be created for it, ensuring that the stored IDs are a valid reference to a record in the related table. No database index is created for these relation fields, but this should often be considered; it can be done by adding the attribute `index=True`.

We can see that there are four more attributes we can use for many-to-one fields:

The `ondelete` attribute determines what happens when the related record is deleted. For example, what happens to Books when their Publisher record is deleted? The default is `'set null'`, setting an empty value on the field. It can also be `'restrict'`, which prevents the related record from being deleted, or `'cascade'`, which causes the linked record to also be deleted.

The last two (`context` and `domain`) are also valid for the other relational fields. They are mostly meaningful on the client side and at the model level act just as default values to be used in the client-side views.

- ▸ `context` adds variables to the client context when clicking through the field to the related record's view. We can, for example, use it to set default values on that view.
- ▸ `domain` is a search filter used to limit the list of related records available for selection when choosing a value for our field.

Both context and domain are explained in more detail in *Chapter 8, Backend Views*.

One-to-many fields are the reverse of many-to-one relations, and although they are added to models just like other fields, they have no actual representation in the database. They are instead programmatic shortcuts and enable views to represent these lists of related records.

Many-to-many relations also don't add columns in the tables for the models. This type of relation is represented in the database using an intermediate relation table, with two columns to store the two related IDs. Adding a new relation between a Book and an Author creates a new record in the relation table with the ID for the Book and the ID for the Author.

Odoo automatically handles the creation of this relation table. The relation table name is, by default, built using the name of the two related models plus a `_rel` suffix. But, we can override it using the `relation` attribute. A case to keep in mind is when the two table names are large enough for the automatically generated database identifiers to exceed the PostgreSQL limit of 63 characters.

As a rule of thumb, if the names of the two related tables exceed 23 characters, you should use the `relation` attribute to set a shorter name. In the next section, we will go into more detail on this.

There's more...

The `Many2one` fields support an additional `auto_join` attribute. It is a flag that allows the ORM to use SQL joins on this field. Because of this, it bypasses the usual ORM control such as user access control and record access rules. On a specific case, it can solve a performance issue, but it is advised to avoid using it.

We have seen the shortest way to define the relational fields. For completeness, these are the attributes specific to this type of field:

The `One2many` field attributes are as follows:

- `comodel_name`: This is the target model identifier and is mandatory for all relational fields, but it can be defined position-wise without the keyword
- `inverse_name`: This applies only to `One2many` and is the field name in the target model for the inverse `Many2one` relation
- `limit`: This applies to `One2many` and `Many2many` and sets an optional limit on the number of records to read that are used at the user interface level

The `Many2many` field attributes are as follows:

- `comodel_name`: (as defined earlier)
- `relation`: This is the name to use for the table supporting the relation, overriding the automatically defined name
- `column1`: This is the name for the `Many2one` field in the relational table linking to this model
- `column2`: This is the name for the `Many2one` field in the relational table linking to the `comodel`

For `Many2many` relations, in most cases the ORM will take perfect care of the default values for these attributes. It is even capable of detecting inverse `Many2many` relations, detecting the already existing `relation` table and appropriately inverting the `column1` and `column2` values.

But there are two cases where we need to step in and provide our own values for these attributes. One is the case where we need more than one `Many2many` relation between the same two models. For this to be possible, we must provide ourselves with a `relation` table name that is different from the first relation. The other case is when the database names of the related tables are long enough for the automatically generated relation name to exceed the 63 character PostgreSQL limit for database object names.

The relation table's automatic name is `<model1>_<model2>_rel`. But this relation table also creates an index for its primary key with the following identifier:

```
<model1>_<model2>_rel_<model1>_id_<model2>_id_key
```

It also needs to meet the 63 characters limit. So, if the two table names combined exceed a total of 63 characters, you will probably have trouble meeting the limits and will need to manually set the `relation` attribute.

Adding a hierarchy to a Model

Hierarchies are represented using model relations with itself; each record has a parent record in the same model and also has many child records. This can be achieved by simply using many-to-one relations between the model and itself.

But Odoo also provides improved support for this type of field using the **Nested set model** (https://en.wikipedia.org/wiki/Nested_set_model). When activated, queries using the child_of operator in their domain filters will run significantly faster.

Staying with the Library Books example, we will build a hierarchical category tree that could be used to categorize books.

Getting ready

We will reuse the my_module addon module from *Chapter 3, Creating Odoo Modules*.

How to do it...

We will add a new Python file, models/library_book_categ.py, for the category tree, shown as follows:

1. To have the new Python code file loaded, add this line to models/__init__.py:

```python
from . import library_book_categ
```

2. To create the Book Category model with the parent and child relations, create the models/library_book_categ.py file with the following:

```python
# -*- coding: utf-8 -*-
from openerp import models, fields, api
class BookCategory(models.Model):
    _name = 'library.book.category'
    name = fields.Char('Category')
    parent_id = fields.Many2one(
        'library.book.category',
        string='Parent Category',
        ondelete='restrict',
        index=True)
    child_ids = fields.One2many(
        'library.book.category', 'parent_id',
        string='Child Categories')
```

3. To enable the special hierarchy support, also add the following:

```
_parent_store = True
parent_left = fields.Integer(index=True)
parent_right = fields.Integer(index=True)
```

4. To add a check preventing looping relations, add the following line to the model:

```
@api.constrains('parent_id')
def _check_hierarchy(self):
    if not self._check_recursion():
        raise models.ValidationError(
            'Error! You cannot create recursive categories.')
```

Finally, a module upgrade should make these changes effective.

How it works...

Steps 1 and 2 create the new model with hierarchic relations. The Many2one relation adds a field to reference the parent record. For faster child record discovery, this field is indexed in the database using the index=True parameter. The parent_id field must have ondelete set to either 'cascade' or 'restrict'.

At this point, we have all that is required to have a hierarchic structure. But there are a few more additions we can make to enhance it.

The One2many relation does not add any additional fields to the database but provides a shortcut to access all the records with this record as their parent.

In step 3, we activate the special support for hierarchies. This is useful for high-read but low-write instructions, since it brings faster data browsing at the expense of costlier write operations. It is done by adding two helper fields, parent_left and parent_right, and setting the model attribute to _parent_store=True. When this attribute is enabled, the two helper fields will be used to store data in searches in the hierarchic tree.

By default, it is assumed that the field for the record's Parent is called parent_id, but a different name can be used. In that case, the correct field name should be indicated using the additional model attribute _parent_name. The default is as follows:

```
_parent_name = 'parent_id'
```

Step 4 is advised in order to prevent cyclic dependencies in the hierarchy— that is, having a record both in the ascending and descending trees. This is dangerous for programs that navigate through the tree, since they can get into an infinite loop. The models.Model provides a utility method for this (_check_recursion) that we have reused here.

There's more...

The technique shown here should be used for "static" hierarchies, which are read and queried often but seldom updated. Book categories are a good example, since the Library will not be continuously creating new categories, but readers will often be restricting their searches to a category and all its children categories. The reason for this lies in the implementation of the Nested Set Model in the database, which requires an update of the `parent_left` and `parent_right` columns (and the related database indexes) for all records whenever a category is inserted, removed, or moved. This can be a very expensive operation, especially when multiple editions are being performed in parallel transactions.

If you are dealing with a very dynamic hierarchical structure, the standard `parent_id` and `child_ids` relations can result in better performance.

Adding constraint validations to a Model

Models can have validations preventing them from entering undesired conditions. Two different types of constraint can be used: the ones checked at the database level and the ones checked at the server level.

Database level constraints are limited to the constraints supported by PostgreSQL. The most commonly used are the `UNIQUE` constraints, but `CHECK` and `EXCLUDE` constraints can also be used. If these are not enough for our needs, we can use Odoo server level constraints, written in Python code.

We will use the Library Book model created in *Chapter 3, Creating Odoo Modules,* and add a couple of constraints to it. We will add a database constraint preventing duplicate book titles, and a Python model constraint preventing release dates in the future.

Getting ready

We will reuse the `my_module` addon module from *Chapter 3, Creating Odoo Modules*.

We expect it to contain at least the following:

```
# -*- coding: utf-8 -*-
from openerp import models, fields
class LibraryBook(models.Model):
    _name = 'library.book'
    name = fields.Char('Title', required=True)
    date_release = fields.Date('Release Date')
```

How to do it...

We will edit the `LibraryBook` class in the `models/library_book_categ.py` Python file:

1. To create the database constraint, add a model attribute:

```
class LibraryBook(models.Model):
    # ...
    _sql_constraints = [
        ('name_uniq',
         'UNIQUE (name)',
         'Book title must be unique.')
        ]
```

2. To create the Python code constraint, add a `model` method:

```
from openerp import api
class LibraryBook(models.Model):
    # ...
    @api.constrains('date_release')
    def _check_release_date(self):
        for r in self:
            if r.date_release > fields.Date.today():
                raise models.ValidationError(
                    'Release date must be in the past')
```

After these changes are made to the code file, an addon module upgrade and server restart are needed.

How it works...

The first step has a database constraint created on the model's table. It is enforced at the database level. The `_sql_constraints` model attribute accepts a list of constraints to create. Each constraint is defined by a three element tuple; they are listed as follows:

▶ A suffix to use for the constraint identifier. In our example, we used `name_uniq` and the resulting constraint name is `library_book_name_uniq`.

▶ The SQL to use in the PostgreSQL instruction to alter or create the database table.

▶ A message to report to the user when the constraint is violated.

As mentioned earlier, other database table constraints can be used. Note that column constraints, such as `NOT NULL`, can't be added this way. For more information on PostgreSQL constraints in general and table constraints in particular, take a look at `http://www.postgresql.org/docs/9.4/static/ddl-constraints.html`.

In the second step, we added a method to perform a Python code validation. It is decorated with @api.constrains, meaning that it should be executed to run checks when one of the fields in the argument list is changed. If the check fails, a ValidationError exception should be raised.

 The _constraints model attribute is still available but has been deprecated since version 8.0. Instead, we should use methods with the new @api.constrains decorator.

Adding computed fields to a Model

Sometimes, we need to have a field that has a value calculated or derived from other fields in the same record or in related records. A typical example is the total amount that is calculated by multiplying a unit price with a quantity. In Odoo models, this can be achieved using computed fields.

To show how computed fields work, we will add one to the Library Books model to calculate the days since the book's release date.

It is also possible to make computed fields editable. We will also implement this in our example.

Getting ready

We will reuse the my_module addon module from *Chapter 3, Creating Odoo Modules*.

How to do it...

We will edit the models/library_book.py code file to add a new field and the methods supporting its logic:

1. Start by adding the new field to the Library Books model:

```
class LibraryBook(models.Model):
    # ...
    age_days = fields.Float(
        string='Days Since Release',
        compute='_compute_age',
        inverse='_inverse_age',
        search='_search_age',
        store=False,
        compute_sudo=False,
    )
```

2. Next, add the method with the value computation logic:

```
# ...
from openerp import api  # if not already imported
from openerp.fields import Date as fDate
# ...
class LibraryBook(models.Model):
    # …
    @api.depends('date_release')
    def _compute_age(self):
        today = fDate.from_string(fDate.today())
        for book in self.filtered('date_release'):
            delta = (fDate.from_string(book.date_release -
                    today)
            book.age_days = delta.days
```

3. To add the method implementing the logic to write on the computed field, use the
    following code:

```
from datetime import timedelta as td
# ...
class LibraryBook(models.Model):
    # …
    def _inverse_age(self): today =
    fDate.from_string(fDate.today())
        for book in self.filtered('date_release'):
            d = td(days=book.age_days) - today
            book.date_release = fDate.to_string(d)
```

4. To implement the logic allowing you to search on the computed field, use the
    following code:

```
# from datetime import timedelta as td
class LibraryBook(models.Model):
    # …
    def _search_age(self, operator, value):
        today = fDate.from_string(fDate.today())
        value_days = td(days=value)
        value_date = fDate.to_string(today - value_days)
        return [('date_release', operator, value_date)]
```

An Odoo restart followed by a module upgrade should be needed to correctly activate these
new additions.

How it works...

The definition of a computed field is the same as the one for a regular field, except that a `compute` attribute is added to specify the name of the method to use for its computation.

The similarity can be deceptive, since computed fields are internally quite different from regular fields. Computed fields are dynamically calculated at runtime, and unless you specifically add that support yourself, they are not writeable or searchable.

The computation function is dynamically calculated at runtime, but the ORM uses caching to avoid inefficiently recalculating it every time its value is accessed. So, it needs to know what other fields it depends on, using the `@depends` decorator to detect when its cached values should be invalidated and recalculated.

 Make sure that the `compute` function always sets a value on the computed field. Otherwise, an error will be raised. This can happen when you have `if` conditions in your code that sometimes fail to set a value on the computed field, and can be tricky to debug.

Write support can be added by implementing the `inverse` function; it uses the value assigned to the computed field to update the origin fields. Of course, this only makes sense for simpler calculations; nevertheless, there are still cases where it can be useful. In our example, we make it possible to set the book release date by editing the **Days Since Release** computed field.

It is also possible to make searchable a non-stored computed field by setting the `search` attribute to the method name to use (similar to `compute` and `inverse`).

However, this method is not expected to implement the actual search. Instead, it receives as parameters the operator and value used to search on the field and is expected to return a domain with the replacement search conditions to use. In our example, we translate a search of the **Days Since Release** field into an equivalent search condition on the **Release Date** field.

The optional `store=True` flag makes the field stored in the database. In this case, after being computed, the field values are stored in the database, and from there on, they are retrieved like regular fields instead of being recomputed at runtime. Thanks to the `@api.depends` decorator, the ORM will know when these stored values need to be recomputed and updated. You can think of it as a persistent cache. It also has the advantage of making the field usable for search conditions, sorting and grouping by operations, without the need to implement the `search` method.

The `compute_sudo=True` flag is to be used in those cases where the computations need to be done with elevated privileges. This can be the case when the computation needs to use data that may not be accessible to the end user.

Exposing Related fields stored in other models

When reading data from the server, Odoo clients can only get values for the fields available in the model being queried. Client-side code can't use dot notation to access data in the related tables like server-side code can.

But those fields can be made available there by adding them as related fields. We will do this to make the publisher's city available in the Library Book model.

Getting ready

We will reuse the `my_module` addon module from *Chapter 3, Create Odoo Modules*.

How to do it...

Edit the `models/library_book.py` file to add the new "related" field:

1. Make sure that we have a field for the book Publisher:

```
class LibraryBook(models.Model):
    # ...
    publisher_id = fields.Many2one(
        'res.partner', string='Publisher')
```

2. Now, add the related field for the Publisher's city:

```
# class LibraryBook(models.Model):
    # ...
    publisher_city = fields.Char(
        'Publisher City',
        related='publisher_id.city')
```

Finally, we need to upgrade the addon module for the new fields to be available in the Model.

How it works...

Related fields are just like regular fields, but they have the additional attribute, `related`, with a string for the separated chain of fields to traverse.

In our case, we access the Publisher related record through `publisher_id`, and then read its `city` field. We can also have longer chains, such as `publisher_id.country_id.country_code`.

There's more...

Related fields are in fact computed fields. They just provide a convenient shortcut syntax to read field values from related models. As a computed field, this means that the `store` attribute is also available to them. As a shortcut, they also have all the attributes from the referenced field, such as `name`, `translatable`, `required`, and so on.

Additionally, they support a `related_sudo` flag similar to `compute_sudo`; when set to `True`, the field chain is traversed without checking user access rights.

Adding dynamic relations using Reference fields

With relational fields, we need to decide beforehand the relation's target model (or comodel). But sometimes, we may need to leave that decision to the user and first choose the model we want and then the record we want to link to.

With Odoo, this can be achieved using Reference fields.

Getting ready

We will reuse the `my_module` addon module from *Chapter 3, Creating Odoo Modules.*

How to do it...

Edit the `models/library_book.py` file to add the new related field:

1. We first add a helper method to dynamically build the list of selectable target models:

```
from openerp import models, fields, api
class LibraryBook(models.Model):
    # …
    @api.model
    def _referencable_models(self):
        models = self.env['res.request.link'].search([])
        return [(x.object, x.name) for x in models]
```

2. Then, we add the Reference field and use the previous function to provide the list of selectable models:

```
ref_doc_id = fields.Reference(
    selection='_referencable_models',
    string='Reference Document')
```

Since we are changing the model's structure, a module upgrade is needed to activate these changes.

How it works...

Reference fields are similar to many-to-one fields, except that they allow the user to select the model to link to.

The target model is selectable from a list provided by the `selection` attribute. The `selection` attribute must be a list of two element tuples, where the first is the model internal identifier, and the second is a text description for it.

Here is an example:

```
[('res.users', 'User'), ('res.partner', 'Partner')]
```

However, rather than providing a fixed list, we can use a model list configurable by end users. That is the purpose of the built-in **Referenceable Models** available in the **Settings | Technical | Database Structure** menu option. This model's internal identifier is `res.request.link`.

Our recipe started with providing a function to browse all the Model records that can be referenced to dynamically build a list to be provided to the `selection` attribute. Although both forms are allowed, we declared the function name inside quotes, instead of a direct reference to the function without quotes. This is more flexible, and for example, allows for the referenced function to be defined only later in the code, which is something that is not possible when using a direct reference.

The function needs the `@api.model` decorator because it operates on the model level, not on the recordset level.

 While this feature looks nice, it comes with a significant execution overhead. Displaying the reference fields for a large number of records, for instance, in a list view, can create heavy database loads as each value has to be looked up in a separate query. It is also unable to take advantage of database referential integrity like regular relation fields can.

Adding features to a Model using inheritance

One of the most important Odoo features is the ability of module addons extending features defined in other module addons without having to edit the code of the original feature. This might be to add fields or methods, or modify existing fields, or extend existing methods to perform additional logic.

It is the most frequently used method of inheritance and is referred to by the official documentation as **traditional inheritance** or **classical inheritance**.

We will extend the built in Partner model to add it to a computed field with the authored book count. This involves adding a field and a method to an existing model.

Getting ready

We will reuse the `my_module` addon module from *Chapter 3, Creating Odoo Modules*.

How to do it...

We will be extending the built-in Partner model. We should do this in its own Python code file, but to keep the explanation as simple we can, we will reuse the `models/library_book.py` code file:

1. First, we make sure the `authored_book_ids` inverse relation is in the Partner model and add the computed field:

```
class ResPartner(models.Model):
    _inherit = 'res.partner'
    _order = 'name'
    authored_book_ids = fields.Many2many(
        'library.book', string='Authored Books')
    count_books = fields.Integer(
        'Number of Authored Books',
        compute='_compute_count_books'
        )
```

2. Next, add the method needed to compute the book count:

```
# ...
from openerp import api  # if not already imported
# class ResPartner(models.Model):
    # ...
    @api.depends('authored_book_ids')
    def _compute_count_books(self):
        for r in self:
            r.count_books = len(r.authored_book_ids)
```

Finally, we need to upgrade the addon module for the modifications to take effect.

How it works...

When a model class is defined with the `_inherit` attribute, it adds modifications to the inherited model rather than replacing it.

This means that fields defined in the inheriting class are added or changed on the parent model. At the database layer, it is adding fields on the same database table.

Fields are also incrementally modified. This means that if the field already exists in the super class, only the attributes declared in the inherited class are modified; the other ones are kept as in the parent class.

Methods defined in the inheriting class replace the method in the parent class. So, unless they include a call to the parent's version of the method, we will lose features. Because of this, when we want to add logic to existing methods, they should include a statement with `super` to call its version in the parent class. This is discussed in more detail in *Chapter 5, Basic Server Side Business Log*.

There's more...

With the `_inherit` traditional inheritance, it's also possible to copy the parent model's features into a completely new model. This is done by simply adding a `_name` model attribute with a different identifier. Here is an example:

```
class LibraryMember(models.Model):
    _inherit = 'res.partner'
    _name = 'library.member'
```

The new model has its own database table with its own data totally independent from the `res.partner` parent model. Since it still inherits from the Partner model, any later modifications to it will also affect the new model.

In the official documentation, this is called **prototype inheritance**, but in practice, it is seldom used. The reason is that delegation inheritance usually answers to that need in a more efficient way, without the need to duplicate data structures. For more information on it, you can refer to the *Use Delegation inheritance to copy features to another Model* recipe.

Using Abstract Models for reusable Model features

Sometimes, there is a particular feature that we want to be able to add to several different models. Repeating the same code in different files is bad programming practice, so it would be nice to be able to implement it once and be able to reuse it many times.

Abstract models allow us to just create a generic model that implements some feature that can then be inherited by regular models in order to make that feature available in them.

As an example, we will implement a simple `Archive` feature. It adds the `active` field to the model (if it doesn't exist already) and makes available an archive method to toggle the `active` flag. This works because `active` is a magic field; if present in a model by default, the records with `active=False` will be filtered out from queries.

We will then add it to the Library Book model.

Getting ready

We will reuse the `my_module` addon module from *Chapter 3*, *Creating Odoo Modules*.

How to do it...

The archive feature would certainly deserve its own addon module, or at least its own Python code file. But to keep the explanation as simple as possible, we will cram it into the `models/library_book.py` file:

1. Add the abstract model for the archive feature. It must be defined in the `Library Book` model, where it will be used:

```
class BaseArchive(models.AbstractModel):
    _name = 'base.archive'
    active = fields.Boolean(default=True)

    def do_archive(self):
        for record in self:
            record.active = not record.active
```

2. Now, we will edit the `Library Book` model to inherit the Archive model:

```
class LibraryBook(models.Model):
    _name = 'library.book'
    _inherit = ['base.archive']
    # ...
```

An upgrade to the addon module is needed for the changes to be activated.

How it works...

An Abstract model is created by a class based on `models.AbstractModel` instead of the usual `models.Model`. It has all the attributes and capabilities of regular models; the difference is that the ORM will not create an actual representation for it in the database. So, it can have no data stored in it. It serves only as a template for a reusable feature that is to be added to regular models.

Our Archive abstract model is quite simple; it just adds the `active` field and a method to toggle the value of the `active` flag, which we expect to later be used via a button on the user interface.

When a model class is defined with the `_inherit` attribute, it inherits the attribute methods of those classes, and what is defined in our class adds modifications to these inherited features.

The mechanism at play here is the same as that for a regular model extension (as per the *Add features to a Model using inheritance* recipe). You may have noticed that here, `_inherit` uses a list of model identifiers instead of a string with one model identifier. In fact, `_inherit` can have both forms. Using the list form allows us to inherit from multiple (usually Abstract) classes. In this case, we are inheriting just one, so a text string would be fine. A list was used instead to underline that a list can be used.

There's more...

A noteworthy built-in abstract model is `ir.needaction_mixin`. It allows for records to signal that a user action is needed on them and is widely used together with the Social Network messaging features.

Another widely used abstract model is `mail.thread`, provided by the `mail` (Discuss) addon module. It enables, on models, the message features that power the message wall seen at the bottom of many forms.

Other than `AbstractModel`, a third model type is available: `models.TransientModel`.

It has database representation like `models.Model`, but the records created there are supposed to be temporary and regularly purged by a server-scheduled job. Other than that, Transient models work just like regular models.

They are useful for more complex user interactions known as wizards, for example, to request the user some input to then run a process or a report. In *Chapter 6, Advanced Server Side Development Techniques*, we explore how to use them for advanced user interaction.

Using Delegation inheritance to copy features to another Model

Traditional inheritance using `_inherit` performs in-place modification to extend the model's features.

But there are cases where rather than modifying an existing model, we want to create a new model based on an existing one to leverage the features it already has. This is one with Odoo's **delegation inheritance** that uses the model attribute, `_inherits` (note the additional s).

Traditional inheritance is quite different than the concept in object-oriented programming. Delegation inheritance in turn is similar in that a new model can be created to include the features from a parent model. It also supports polymorphic inheritance, where we inherit from two or more other models.

We have a library with books. It's about time for our library to also have members. For a library member, we need all the identification and address data found in the Partner model, and we also want it to keep some information regarding the membership: a start date, termination date, and card number.

Adding those fields to the Partner model is not the best solution since they will be not be used for Partners that are not members. It would be great to extend the Partner model to a new model with some additional fields.

Getting ready

We will reuse the my_module addon module from *Chapter 3*, *Creating Odoo Modules*.

How to do it...

The new Library Member model should be in its own Python code file, but to keep the explanation as simple as possible, we will reuse the models/library_book.py file:

1. Add the new model, inheriting from res.partner:

```
# from openerp import models, fields  # if not done yet
class LibraryMember(models.Model):
    _name = 'library.member'
    _inherits = {'res.partner': 'partner_id'}
    partner_id = fields.Many2one(
        'res.partner',
        ondelete='cascade')
```

2. Next, we add the fields that are specific to Library Members:

```
# class LibraryMember(models.Model):
    # ...
    date_start = fields.Date('Member Since')
    date_end = fields.Date('Termination Date')
    member_number = fields.Char()
```

Now, we should upgrade the addon module to have the changes activated.

How it works...

The `_inherits` model attribute sets the parent models that we want to inherit from. In this case, just one: `res.partner`. Its value is a key-value dictionary where the keys are the inherited models, and the values are the field names used to link to them. These are `Many2one` fields that we must also define in the model. In our example, `partner_id` is the field that will be used to link with the `Partner` parent model.

To better understand how it works, let's look at what happens on the database level when we create a new Member:

- A new record is created in the `res_partner` table
- A new record is created in the `library_member` table
- The `partner_id` field of the `library_member` table is set to the `id` of the `res_partner` record that is created for it

The Member record is automatically linked to a new Partner record. It's just a many-to-one relation, but the delegation mechanism adds some magic so that the Partner's fields are seen as if belonging to the Member record, and a new Partner record is also automatically created with the new Member.

You might like to know that this automatically created Partner record has nothing special about it. It's a regular Partner, and if you browse the Partner model, you will be able to find that record (without the additional Member data, of course). All Members are at the same time Partners, but only some Partners are also Members.

So, what happens if you delete a Partner record that is also a Member? You decide by choosing the `ondelete` value for the relation field. For `partner_id`, we used `cascade`. This means that deleting the Partner would also delete the corresponding Member. We could have used the more conservative setting `restrict` to forbid deleting the Partner while it has a linked Member. In this case, only deleting the Member would work.

It's important to note that delegation inheritance only works for fields and not for methods. So, if the Partner model has a `do_something()` method, the Members model will not automatically inherit it.

There's more...

A noteworthy case of delegation inheritance is the Users model, `res.users`. It inherits from Partners (`res.partner`). This means that some of the fields that you can see on the User are actually stored in the Partner model (notably the `name` field). When a new User is created, we also get a new automatically created Partner.

We should also mention that traditional inheritance with `_inherit` can also copy features into a new model, although in a less efficient way. This was discussed in the *Add features to a Model using inheritance* recipe.

5
Basic Server Side Development

In this chapter, we will cover the following topics:

- Defining model methods and use the API decorators
- Reporting errors to the user
- Obtaining an empty recordset for a different model
- Creating new records
- Updating values of recordset records
- Searching for records
- Combining recordsets
- Filtering recordsets
- Traversing recordset relations
- Extending the business logic defined in a model
- Extending write() and create()
- Customizing how records are searched

Introduction

In *Chapter 4, Application Models*, we have seen how to declare or extend business models in custom modules. The recipes in that chapter cover writing methods for computed fields as well as methods to constrain the values of fields. This chapter focuses on the basics of server side development in Odoo—method definitions, recordset manipulation, and extending inherited methods.

Defining model methods and use the API decorators

The model classes defining custom data models declare fields for the data processed by the model. They can also define custom behavior by defining methods on the model class.

In this recipe, we will see how to write a method that can be called by a button in the user interface, or by some other piece of code in our application. This method will act on `LibraryBooks` and perform the required actions to change the state of a selection of books.

Getting ready

This recipe assumes you have an instance ready, with the `my_module` addon module available, as described in *Chapter 3, Creating Odoo Modules*. You will need to add a state field to the `LibraryBook` model defined as follows:

```
from openerp import models, fields, api
class LibraryBook(models.Model):
    # [...]
    state = fields.Selection([('draft', 'Unavailable'),
                              ('available', 'Available'),
                              ('borrowed', 'Borrowed'),
                              ('lost', 'Lost')],
                             'State')
```

Please refer to *Chapter 4, Adding data fields to a Model* for more clarity.

How to do it...

For defining a method on `LibraryBook` to allow changing the state of a selection of books, you need to add the following code to the model definition:

1. Add a helper method to check whether a state transition is allowed:

    ```
    @api.model
    def is_allowed_transition(self, old_state, new_state):
        allowed= [('draft', 'available'),
                  ('available', 'borrowed'),
                  ('borrowed', 'available'),
                  ('available', 'lost'),
                  ('borrowed', 'lost'),
                  ('lost', 'available')]
        return (old_state, new_state) in allowed
    ```

2. Add a method to change the state of some books to a new one passed as an argument:

```
@api.multi
def change_state(self, new_state):
    for book in self:
        if book.is_allowed_transition(book.state,
                                      new_state):
            book.state = new_state
        else:
            continue
```

How it works...

The code in the recipe defines two methods. They are normal Python methods, having `self` as their first argument and can have additional arguments as well.

The methods are decorated with **decorators** from the `openerp.api` module. These decorators are there to ensure the conversion of calls made using the **old** or **traditional** API to the **new** API. The old API is used by the remote procedure call (RPC) protocol of the web client and by modules that have not yet been ported to the new API. A key part of this conversion is the creation of an execution **environment** stored in `self.env`; it contains the following:

- `self.env.cr`: This is a database cursor
- `self.env.user`: This is the user executing the action
- `self.env.context`: This is **context**, which is a Python dictionary containing various information such as the language of the user, his configured time zone, and other specific keys that can be set at run time by the actions of the user interface

When writing a new method, you will generally be using `@api.multi`. In addition to the creation of the environment, this decorator tells the RPC layer to initialize `self` using the record IDs supplied in the RPC argument `ids`. In such methods, `self` is a recordset that can refer to an arbitrary number of database records.

The `@api.model` decorator is similar but is used on methods for which only the model is important, not the contents of the recordset, which is not acted upon by the method. The concept is similar to Python's `@classmethod` decorator (but we generally cannot use this in Odoo models because we need access to `self.env` and other important instance attributes).

The `@api.model` and `@api.multi` decorators also have specific meaning when ensuring the compatibility of your addon module with other modules still using the "old API". You will find more information on this in the *Porting old API code to the new API* recipe in *Chapter 6, Advanced Server Side Development Techniques*.

Here is an example code snippet called `change_state()`:

```
# returned_book_ids is a list of book ids to return
books = self.env['library.book']
books.browse(returned_book_ids).change_state('available')
```

When `change_state()` is called, `self` is a (possibly empty) recordset containing records of the `library.book` model. The body of the `change_state()` method loops over `self` to process each book in the recordset. Looping on `self` looks strange at first, but you will get used to this pattern very quickly.

Inside the loop, `change_state()` calls `is_allowed_transition()`. The call is made using the local variable `book`, but it could have been made on any recordset for the `library.book` model, including, for example, `self`, since `is_allowed_transition()` is decorated with `@api.model`. If the transition is allowed, `change_state()` assigns the new state to the book by assigning a value to the attribute of the recordset. This is only valid on recordsets of length `1`, which is guaranteed to be the case when iterating over `self`.

There's more...

There are some important factors that are worth understanding.

Hiding methods from the RPC interface

In the old API, methods with a name prefixed by an underscore are not exposed through the RPC interface and are therefore not callable by the web client. This is still the case with the new API, which also offers another way to make a method unavailable to the RPC interface; if you don't put an `@api.model` or `@api.multi` decorator on it (or on one of the decorators mentioned in the *Porting old API code to the new API* recipe in *Chapter 6, Advanced Server Side Development Techniques*), then the method will neither be callable by extensions of the model using the traditional API nor via RPC.

The @api.one decorator

You may encounter the `@api.one` decorator while reading source code. In Odoo 9.0, **this decorator is deprecated** because its behavior can be confusing—at first glance, and knowing of `@api.multi`, it looks like this decorator allows the method to be called only on recordsets of size 1, but it does not. When it comes to recordset length, `@api.one` is similar to `@api.multi`, but it does a `for` loop on the recordset outside the method and aggregates the returned value of each iteration of the loop in a list, which is returned to the caller. Avoid using it in your code.

See also

In *Chapter 8, Backend Views*, refer to the *Adding buttons to form* recipe to learn how to call such a method from the user interface.

You will find additional information on the decorators defined in `openerp.api` in the recipe from *Chapter 6, Advanced Server Side Development Techniques: Porting old API code to the new API*.

Reporting errors to the user

During method execution, it is sometimes necessary to abort the processing because an error condition was met. This recipe shows how to do this so that a helpful error message is displayed to the user when a method which writes a file to disk encounters an error.

Getting ready

To use this recipe, you need a method, which can have an abnormal condition. We will use the following one:

```
import os
from openerp import models, fields, api

class SomeModel(models.Model):
    data = fields.Text('Data')

    @api.multi
    def save(self, filename):
        path = os.path.join('/opt/exports', filename)
        with open(path, 'w') as fobj:
            for record in self:
                fobj.write(record.data)
                fobj.write('\n')
```

This method can fail because of permission issues, or a full disk, or an illegal name, which would cause an `IOError` or an `OSError` exception to be raised.

How to do it...

To display an error message to the user when an error condition is encountered, you need to take the following steps:

1. Add the following import at the beginning of the Python file:

   ```
   from openerp.exceptions import UserError
   ```

2. Modify the method to catch the exception raised and raise a `UserError` exception:

   ```
   @api.multi
   def save(self, filename):
       if '/' in filename or '\\' in filename:
   ```

```
            raise UserError('Illegal filename %s' % filename)
        path = os.path.join('/opt/exports', filename)
        try:
            with open(path, 'w') as fobj:
                for record in self:
                    fobj.write(record.data)
                    fobj.write('\n')
        except (IOError, OSError) as exc:
            message = 'Unable to save file: %s' % exc
            raise UserError(message)
```

How it works...

When an exception is raised in Python, it propagates up the call stack until it is processed. In Odoo, the RPC layer that answers the calls made by the web client catches all exceptions and, depending on the exception class, it will trigger different possible behaviors on the web client.

Any exception not defined in `openerp.exceptions` will be handled as an Internal Server Error (**HTTP status 500**), with the stack trace. A `UserError` will display an error message in the user interface. The code of the recipe changes the `OSError` to a `UserError` to ensure the message is displayed in a friendly way. In all cases, the current database transaction is rolled back.

Of course, it is not required to catch an exception with a `try..except`, construct to raise a `UserError` exception. It is perfectly OK to test for some condition, such as the presence of illegal characters in a filename, and to raise the exception when that test is `True`. This will prevent further processing of the user request.

There's more...

There are a few more exception classes defined in `openerp.exceptions`, all deriving the base legacy `except_orm` exception class. Most of them are only used internally, apart from the following:

- ▶ `Warning`: In Odoo 8.0, `openerp.exceptions.Warning` played the role of `UserError` in 9.0. It is now deprecated because the name was deceptive (it is an error, not a warning) and it collided with the Python built-in `Warning` class. It is kept for backward compatibility only and you should use `UserError` in 9.0.

- ▶ `ValidationError`: This exception is raised when a Python constraint on a field is not respected. In *Chapter 4, Application Models*, refer to the *Adding constraint validations to a Model* recipe for more information.

Obtaining an empty recordset for a different model

When writing Odoo code, the methods of the current model are available via `self`. If you need to work on a different model, it is not possible to directly instantiate the class of that model—you need to get a recordset for that model to start working.

This recipe shows how to get an empty recordset for any model registered in Odoo inside a model method.

Getting ready

This recipe will reuse the setup of the library example in the addon module `my_module`.

We will write a small method in the `library.book` model searching for all `library.members`. To do this, we need to get an empty recordset for `library.members`.

How to do it...

To get a recordset for `library.members` in a method of `library.book`, you need to take the following steps:

1. In the `LibraryBook` class, write a method called `get_all_library_members`:

```
class LibraryBook(models.Model):
    # ...
    @api.model
    def get_all_library_members(self):
        # ...
```

2. In the body of the method, use the following code:

```
library_member_model = self.env['library.member']
return library_member_model.search([])
```

How it works...

At start up, Odoo loads all the modules and combines the various classes deriving from `Model` and defining or extending a given model. These classes are stored in the Odoo **registry** indexed by name. The **environment** in `self.env` provides a shortcut access to the registry by emulating a Python dictionary; if you know the name of the model you're looking for, `self.env[model_name]` will get you an empty recordset for that model. Moreover, the recordset will share the environment of `self`.

The call to `search()` is explained in the *Searching for records* recipe later.

See also

The *Changing the user performing an action* and *Calling a method with a modified enviroment* recipes in *Chapter 6, Advanced Server Side Development Techniques*, deal with modifying `self.env` at runtime.

Creating new records

A frequent need when writing business logic methods is to create new records. This recipe explains how to create records of the `res.partner` model, which is defined in Odoo's `base` addon module. We will create a new partner representing a company, with some contacts.

Getting ready

You need to know the structure of the models for which you want to create a record, especially their names and types as well as any constraints existing on these fields (for example, whether some of them are mandatory). The `res.partner` model defined in Odoo has a very large number of fields, and to keep things simple, we will only use a few of these. Moreover, the model definition in Odoo uses the old API. To help you follow the recipe, here is a port of the model definition we will be using for the new API:

```
class ResPartner(models.Model):
    _name = 'res.partner'
    name = fields.Char('Name', required=True)
    email = fields.Char('Email')
    date = fields.Date('Date')
    is_company = fields.Boolean('Is a company')
    parent_id = fields.Many2one('res.partner', 'Related Company')
    child_ids = fields.One2many('res.partner', 'parent_id',
                                'Contacts')
```

How to do it...

In order to create a partner with some contacts, you need to take the following steps:

1. Inside the method that needs to create a new partner, get the current date formatted as a string expected by `create()`:

    ```
    today_str = fields.Date.context_today()
    ```

2. Prepare a dictionary of values for the fields of the first contact:

    ```
    val1 = {'name': u'Eric Idle',
            'email': u'eric.idle@example.com'
            'date': today_str}
    ```

3. Prepare a dictionary of values for the fields of the second contact:

```
val2 = {'name': u'John Cleese',
        'email': u'john.cleese@example.com',
        'date': today_str}
```

4. Prepare a dictionary of values for the fields of the company:

```
partner_val = {
    'name': u'Flying Circus',
    'email': u'm.python@example.com',
    'date': today_str,
    'is_company': True,
    'child_ids': [(0, 0, val1),
                  (0, 0, val2),
                  ]
}
```

5. Call the `create()` method to create the new records:

```
record = self.env['res.partner'].create(partner_val)
```

How it works...

To create a new record for a model, we can call the `create(values)` method on any recordset related to the model. This method returns a new recordset of length 1 containing the new record, with fields values specified in the `values` dictionary.

In the dictionary:

▸ Text field values are given with Python strings (preferably Unicode strings).

▸ `Float` and `Integer` field values are given using Python floats or integers.

▸ `Boolean` field values are given, preferably using Python booleans or integer.

▸ Date (resp. `Datetime`) field values are given as Python strings. Use `fields.Date.to_string()` (resp. `fields.Datetime.to_string()`) to convert a Python `datetime.date` (resp. `datetime.datetime`) object to the expected format.

▸ `Binary` field values are passed as a Base64 encoded string. The `base64` module from the Python standard library provides methods such as `encodestring(s)` to encode a string in Base64.

▸ `Many2one` field values are given with an integer, which has to be the database ID of the related record.

▶ One2many and Many2many fields use a special syntax. The value is a list containing tuples of three elements, as follows:

Tuple	Effect
(0, 0, dict_val)	Create a new record that will be related to the main record
(6, 0, id_list)	Create a relation between the record being created and existing records, whose IDs are in the Python list id_list
	Caution: When used on a One2many, this will remove the records from any previous relation

In the recipe, we create the dictionaries for two contacts in the company we want to create, and then we use these dictionaries in the child_ids entry of the dictionary for the company being created, using the (0, 0, dict_val) syntax explained previously.

When create() is called in step 5, three records are created:

▶ One for the main partner company, which is returned by create

▶ One for each of the two contacts, which are available in record.child_ids

There's more

If the model defined some **default values** for some fields, nothing special needs to be done; create() will take care of computing the default values for the fields not present in the supplied dictionary.

On the other hand, **onchange methods** are *not* called by create(), because they are called by the web client during the initial edition of the record. Some of these methods compute default values for fields related to a given field. When creating records by hand you have to do the work yourself, either by providing explicit values or by calling the onchange methods. The *Calling onchange methods on the server side* recipe in *Chapter 6, Advanced Server Side Development Techniques* explains how to do this.

Updating values of recordset records

Business logic often means updating records by changing the values of some of their fields. This recipe shows how to add a contact for a partner and modify the date field of the partner as we go.

Getting ready

This recipe will be using the same simplified `res.partner` definition as the *Creating new records* recipe previously. You may refer to this simplified definition to know the fields.

The `date` field of `res.partner` has no defined meaning in Odoo. In order to illustrate our purpose, we will use this to record an activity date on the partner, so creating a new contact should update the date of the partner.

How to do it...

To update a partner, you can write a new method called `add_contact()` defined like this:

```
@api.model
def add_contacts(self, partner, contacts):
    partner.ensure_one()
    if contacts:
        partner.date = fields.Date.context_today()
        partner.child_ids |= contacts
```

How it works...

The method starts by checking whether the partner passed as an argument contains exactly one record by calling `ensure_one()`. This method will raise an exception if this is not the case and the processing will abort. This is needed, as we cannot add the same contacts to several partners at the same time.

Then the method checks that the `contacts` recordset is not empty, because we don't want to update the `date` of the partner if we are not modifying it.

Finally, the method modifies the values of the attributes of the partner record. Since `child_ids` is a One2many relation, its value is a recordset. We use `|=` to compute the union of the current contacts of the partner and the new contacts passed to the method. See the following recipe, *Combining recordsets*, for more information on these operators.

Note that no assumption is made on `self`. This method could be defined on any model class.

There's more...

There are three options available if you want to write new values to the fields of records.

Option 1 is the one explained in the recipe, and it works in all contexts—assigning values directly on the attribute representing the field of the record. It is not possible to assign a value to all recordset elements in one go, so you need to iterate on the recordset, unless you are certain that you are only handling a single record.

Option 2 is to use the `update()` method by passing a dictionary mapping field names to the values you want to set. This also only works for recordsets of length 1. It can save some typing when you need to update the values of several fields at once on the same record. Here is step 2 of the recipe, rewritten to use this option:

```
@api.model
def add_contacts(self, partner, contacts):
    partner.ensure_one()
    if contacts:
        today = fields.Date.context_today()
        partner.update(
            {'date': today,
             'child_ids': partner_child_ids | contacts}
        )
```

Option 3 is to call the `write()` method, passing a dictionary mapping field names to the values you want to set. This method works for recordsets of arbitrary size and will update all records with the specified values in one single database operation when the two previous options perform one database call per record and per field. However, it has some limitations:

- It does not work if the records are not yet present in the database (see *Writing onchange methods* in *Chapter 6*, *Advanced Server Side Development Techniques* for more information on this)

- It requires using a special format when writing relational fields, similar to the one used by the `create()` method

Tuple	Effect
`(0, 0, dict_val)`	This creates a new record that will be related to the main record.
`(1, id, dict_val)`	This updates the related record with the specified ID with the supplied values.
`(2, id)`	This removes the record with the specified ID from the related records and deletes it from the database.
`(3, id)`	This removes the record with the specified ID from the related records. The record is not deleted from the database.
`(4, id)`	This adds an existing record with the supplied ID to the list of related records.
`(5, )`	This removes all the related records, equivalent to calling `(3, id)` for each related id.
`(6, 0, id_list)`	This creates a relation between the record being updated and the existing record, whose IDs are in the Python list `id_list`.

At the time of this writing, the official documentation is outdated and mentions that the operation numbers 3, 4, 5, and 6 are not available on One2many fields, which is no longer true. However, some of these may not work with One2many fields, depending on constraints on the models; for instance, if the reverse Many2one relation is required, then operation 3 will fail because it would result in an unset Many2one relation.

Searching for records

Searching for records is also a common operation in business logic methods. This recipe shows how to find all the Partner companies and their contacts by company name.

Getting ready

This recipe will be using the same simplified res.partner definition as the *Creating new records* recipe previously. You may refer to this simplified definition to know the fields.

We will write the code in a method called find_partners_and_contact(self, name).

How to do it...

In order to find the partners, you need to perform the following steps:

1. Get an empty recordset for res.partner:

    ```
    @api.model
    def find_partners_and_contacts(self, name):
        partner = self.env['res.partner']
    ```

2. Write the search domain for your criteria:

    ```
    domain = ['|',
              '&',
              ('is_company', '=', True),
              ('name', 'like', name),
              '&',
              ('is_company', '=', False),
              ('parent_id.name', 'like', name)
              ]
    ```

3. Call the search() method with the domain and return the recordset:

    ```
    return partner.search(domain)
    ```

How it works...

Step 1 defines the method. Since we are not using the contents of `self`, we decorate it with `@api.model`, but this is not linked to the purpose of this recipe. Then, we get an empty recordset for the `res.partner` model because we need it to search `res.partner` records.

Step 2 creates a search domain in a local variable. Often you'll see this creation inlined in the call to search, but with complex domains, it is a good practice to define it separately.

For a full explanation of the **search domain** syntax, please refer to the *Defining filters on record lists: Domain* recipe in *Chapter 8, Backend Views*.

Step 3 calls the `search()` method with the domain. The method returns a recordset containing all records matching the domain, which can then be further processed. In the recipe, we call the method with just the domain, but the following keyword arguments are also supported:

- ▸ `offset=N`: This is used to skip the `N` first records that match the query. This can be used together with `limit` to implement pagination or to reduce memory consumption when processing a very large number of records. It defaults to `0`.

- ▸ `limit=N`: return at most `N` records. By default, there is no limit.

- ▸ `order=sort_specification`: This is used to force the order on the returned recordset. By default, the order is given by the `_order` attribute of the model class.

- ▸ `count=boolean`: If `True`, this returns the number of records instead of the recordset. It defaults to `False`.

 We recommend using the `search_count(domain)` method rather than `search(domain, count=True)`, as the name of the method conveys the behavior in a much clearer way; both will give the same result.

There's more...

We said that the `search()` method returned all the records matching the domain. This is not completely true. The method ensures that only records to which the user performing the search has access are returned. Additionally, if the model has a `boolean` field called **active** and no term of the search domain is specifying a condition on that field, then an implicit condition is added by search to only return `active=True` records. So if you expect a search to return something but you only get empty recordsets, be sure to check the value of the `active` field (if present) and to check for **record rules**.

See the recipe *Calling a method with a different context* in *Chapter 6, Advanced Server Side Development Techniques* for a way to not have the implicit `active = True` condition added. See the *Limit record access using record rules* recipe in *Chapter 10, Accessing Security* for more information about record level access rules.

If for some reason you find yourself writing raw SQL queries to find record IDs, be sure to use `self.env['`*record.model*`'].search([('id', 'in', tuple(ids)).ids` after retrieving the IDs to make sure that security rules are applied. This is especially important in **multicompany** Odoo instances where record rules are used to ensure proper discrimination between companies.

Combining recordsets

Sometimes, you will find that you have obtained recordsets which are not exactly what you need. This recipe shows various ways of combining them.

Getting ready

To use this recipe, you need to have two or more recordsets for the same model.

How to do it...

Here is the way to achieve common operations on recordsets:

1. To merge two recordsets into one while preserving their order, use the following operation:

    ```
    result = recordset1 + recordset2
    ```

2. To merge two recordsets into one ensuring that there are no duplicates in the result, use the following operation:

    ```
    result = recordset1 | recordset2
    ```

3. To find the records that are common to two recordsets, use the following operation:

    ```
    result = recordset1 & recordset2
    ```

How it works...

The class for recordsets implements various Python operator redefinitions, which are used here. Here is a summary table of the most useful Python operators that can be used on recordsets:

Operator	Action performed
R1 + R2	This returns a new recordset containing the records from R1 followed by the records from R2. This can generate duplicate records in the recordset.
R1 - R2	This returns a new recordset consisting of the records from R1, which are not in R2. The order is preserved.

Operator	Action performed
R1 & R2	This returns a new recordset with all the records that belong to both R1 and R2 (intersection of recordsets). The order is *not* preserved here.
R1 | R2	This returns a new recordset with the records belonging to either R1 or R2 (union of recordsets). The order is *not* preserved, but there are no duplicates.
R1 == R2	True if both recordsets contain the same records.
R1 <= R2 R1 in R2	True if all records in R1 are also in R2. Both syntaxes are equivalent.
R1 >= R2 R2 in R1	True if all records in R2 are also in R1. Both syntaxes are equivalent.
R1 != R2	True if R1 and R2 do not contain the same records.

There are also in-place operators +=, -=, &=, and |=, which modify the left-hand operand instead of creating a new recordset. These are very useful when updating a record's One2many or Many2many fields. See the *Updating values of recordset records* recipe previously for an example.

There's more...

The sorted() method will sort the records in a recordset. Called without arguments, the _order attribute of the model will be used. Otherwise, a function can be passed to compute a comparison key in the same fashion as the Python built-in sorted(sequence, key) function. The reverse keyword argument is also supported.

Note about performance

When the default _order parameter of the model is used, the sorting is delegated to the database and a new SELECT function is performed to get the order. Otherwise, the sorting is performed by Odoo. Depending on what is being manipulated, and on the size of the recordsets, there can be some important performance differences.

Filtering recordsets

In some cases, you already have a recordset, but you need to operate only on some records. You can, of course, iterate on the recordset, checking for the condition on each iteration and acting depending on the result of the check. It can be easier, and in some cases, more efficient to construct a new recordset containing only the interesting records and calling a single operation on that recordset.

This recipe shows how to use the filter() method to extract a recordset from another one.

Getting ready

We will reuse the simplified `res.partner` model shown in the *Create new records* recipe previously. This recipe defines a method to extract partners having an e-mail address from a supplied recordset.

How to do it...

In order to extract records with an e-mail address from a recordset, you need to perform the following steps:

1. Define the method accepting the original recordset:

   ```
   @api.model
   def partners_with_email(self, partners):
   ```

2. Define an inner predicate function:

   ```
   def predicate(partner):
       if partner.email:
           return True
       return False
   ```

3. Call `filter()` as follows:

   ```
   return partners.filter(predicate)
   ```

How it works...

The implementation of the `filter()` method of recordsets creates an empty recordset in which it adds all the records for which the predicate function evaluates to `True`. The new recordset is finally returned. The order of records in the original recordset is preserved.

The preceding recipe used a named internal function. For such simple predicates, you will often find an anonymous lambda function used:

```
@api.model
def partners_with_email(self, partners):
    return partners.filter(lambda p: p.email)
```

Actually, to filter a recordset based on the fact that one attribute is *truthy* in the Python sense, you can use `partners.filter('email')`.

There's more...

Keep in mind that `filter()` operates in the memory. If you are trying to optimize the performance of a method on the critical path, you may want to use a search domain or even move to SQL, at the cost of readability.

Traversing recordset relations

When working with a recordset of length 1, the various fields are available as record attributes. Relational attributes (`One2many`, `Many2one`, and `Many2many`) are also available with values that are recordsets too. When working with recordsets with more than one record, the attributes cannot be used.

This recipe shows how to use the `mapped()` method to traverse recordset relations; we will write two methods performing the following operations:

▸ Retrieving the e-mails of all contacts of a single partner company passed as an argument

▸ Retrieving the various companies to which some contact partners are related

Getting ready

We will be reusing the simplified Partner model shown in the *Create new records* recipe of this chapter.

How to do it...

To write the partner manipulation methods, you need to perform the following steps:

1. Define a method called `get_email_addresses()`:

   ```
   @api.model
   def get_email_addresses(self, partner):
       partner.ensure_one()
   ```

2. Call `mapped()` to get the e-mail addresses of the contacts of the partner:

   ```
   return partner.mapped('child_ids.email')
   ```

3. Define a method called `get_companies()`:

   ```
   @api.model
   def get_companies(self, partners):
   ```

4. Call `mapped()` to get the different companies of the partners:

   ```
   return partners.mapped('parent_id')
   ```

How it works...

In step 1, we call `ensure_one()` to make sure we have a single partner. This is not required for the recipe, as `mapped()` works very well on recordsets of arbitrary size. However, it is mandated by the specification of the method we are writing, as we don't want to retrieve contacts from multiple companies by mistake.

In step 2 and step 4, we call the `mapped(path)` method to traverse the fields of the recordset; `path` is a string containing field names separated by dots. For each field in the path, `mapped()` produces a new recordset containing all the records related by this field to all elements in the current recordset and then applies the next element in the path on that new recordset. If the last field in the path is a relational field, `mapped()` will return a recordset; otherwise, a Python list is returned.

The `mapped()` method has two remarkable properties:

- ▸ If the path is a single scalar field name, then the returned list is in the same order as the processed recordset.

- ▸ If the path contains a relational field, then order is not preserved, but duplicates are removed from the result.

 This second property is very useful in a method decorated with `@api.multi` where you want to perform an operation on all the records pointed by a `Many2many` field of all records in `self`, but need to make sure that the action is performed only once (even if two records of self share the same target record).

There's more...

When using `mapped()`, keep in mind that it operates in the memory inside the Odoo server by repeatedly traversing relations and therefore making SQL queries, which may not be efficient; however, the code is terse and expressive. If you are trying to optimize a method on the critical path of the performance of your instance, you may want to rewrite the call to `mapped()` and express it as a `search()` with the appropriate domain, or even move to SQL (at the cost of readability).

The `mapped()` method can also be called with a function as argument. In this case, it returns a list containing the result of the function applied to each record of `self`, or the union of the recordsets returned by the function, if the function returns a recordset.

See also

▸ The *Search for records* recipe

▸ The *Executing raw SQL queries* recipe In *Chapter 6, Advanced Server Side Development Techniques*

Extending the business logic defined in a Model

When defining a model that extends another model, it is often necessary to customize the behavior of some methods defined on the original model. This is a very easy task in Odoo, and one of the most powerful features of the underlying framework.

We will demonstrate this by extending a method that creates records to add a new field in the created records.

Getting ready

If you want to follow the recipe, make sure you have the `my_module` addon from *Chapter 3, Creating Odoo Modules*, with the loan wizard defined in the *Writing a wizard to guide the user* recipe from *Chapter 6, Advanced Server Side Development Techniques*.

Create a new addon module called `library_loan_return_date` that depends on `my_module`. In this module, extend the `library.book.loan` model as follows:

```
class LibraryBookLoan(models.Model):
    _inherit = 'library.book.loan'
    expected_return_date = fields.Date('Due for', required=True)
```

Extend the `library.member` model as follows:

```
class LibraryMember(models.Model):
    _inherit = 'library.member'
    loan_duration = fields.Integer('Loan duration',
                                   default=15,
                                   required=True)
```

Since the `expected_return_date` field is required and no default is provided, the wizard to record loans will cease functioning because it does not provide a value for that field when it creates loans.

How to do it...

To extend the business logic in the `library.loan.wizard` model, you need to perform the following steps:

1. In `my_module`, modify the method `record_loans()` in the `LibraryLoanWizard` class. The original code is in the *Writing a wizard to guide the user* recipe in *Chapter 6, Advanced Server Side Development Techniques*. The new version is:

```
@api.multi
def record_loans(self):
    for wizard in self:
        books = wizard .book_ids
        loan = self.env['library.book.loan']
        for book in wizard.book_ids:
            values = self._prepare_loan(book)
            loan.create(values)
@api.multi
def _prepare_loan(self, book):
    return {'member_id': self.member_id.id,
            'book_id': book.id}
```

2. In `library_loan_return_date`, create a class which extends `library.loan.wizard` and defines the `_prepare_loan` method as follows:

```
from datetime import timedelta
from openerp import models, fields, api
class LibraryLoanWizard(models.TransientModel):
    _inherit = 'library.load.wizard'

    def _prepare_loan(self, book):
        values = super(LibraryLoanWizard,
                        self
                      )._prepare_loan(book)
        loan_duration = self.member_id.loan_duration
        today_str = fields.Date.context_today()
        today = fields.Date.from_string(today_str)
        expected = today + timedelta(days=loan_duration)
        values.update(
            {'expected_return_date':
                fields.Date.to_string(expected)}
        )
        return values
```

How it works...

In step 1, we refactor the code from the *Writing a wizard to guide the user* recipe in *Chapter 6, Advanced Server Side Development Techniques*, to use a very common and useful coding pattern to create the `library.book.loan` records: the creation of the dictionary of values is extracted in a separate method rather than hardcoded in the method calling `create()`. This eases extending the addon module in case new values have to be passed at creation time, which is exactly the case we are facing.

Step 2 then does the extension of the business logic. We define a model that extends `library.loan.wizard` and redefines the `_prepare_loan()` method. The redefinition starts by calling the implementation from the parent class:

```
values = super(LibraryLoanWizard, self)._prepare_loan(book)
```

In the case of Odoo models, the parent class is not what you'd expect by looking at the Python class definition. The framework has dynamically generated a class hierarchy for our recordset, and the parent class is the definition of the model from the modules on which we depend. So the call to `super()` brings back the implementation of `library.loan.wizard` from `my_module`. In this implementation, `_prepare_loan()` returns a dictionary of values with `'member_id'` and `'book_id'`. We update this dictionary by adding the `'expected_return_date'` key before returning it.

There's more...

In this recipe, we chose to extend the behavior by calling the normal implementation and modifying the returned result *afterwards*. It is also possible to perform some actions *before* calling the normal implementation, and of course, we can also do both.

However, what we saw in this recipe is that it is harder to change the behavior of the middle of a method. We had to refactor the code to extract an extension point to a separate method and override this new method in the extension module.

 You may be tempted to completely rewrite a method. Always be very cautious when doing so—if you do not call the `super()` implementation of your method, you are breaking the extension mechanism and potentially breaking addons for which their extension of the same method will never be called. Unless you are working in a controlled environment, in which you know exactly which addons are installed and you've checked that you are not breaking them, avoid doing this. And if you have to, be sure to document what you are doing in a very visible way.

What can you do before and after calling the original implementation of the method? Lots of things, including (but not limited to):

- ▶ Modifying the arguments that are passed to the original implementation (before)
- ▶ Modifying the context that is passed to the original implementation (before)
- ▶ Modifying the result that is returned by the original implementation (after)
- ▶ Calling another method (before, after)
- ▶ Creating records (before, after)
- ▶ Raising a `UserError` to cancel the execution in forbidden cases (before, after)
- ▶ Splitting `self` in smaller recordsets, and calling the original implementation on each of the subsets in a different way (before)

Extending write() and create()

The *Extending the business logic defined in a Model* recipe showed how to extend methods defined on a model class. If you think about it, methods defined on the parent class of the model are also part of the model. This means that all the base methods defined on `models.Model` (actually on `models.BaseModel`, which is the parent class of `models.Model`) are also available and can be extended.

This recipe shows how to extend `create()` and `write()` to control access to some fields of the records.

Getting ready

We will extend on the library example from the `my_module` addon module in *Chapter 3, Creating Odoo Modules.*

You will also need the security groups defined in *Chapter 10, Accessing Security* in the *Creating security Groups and assigning them to Users* recipe and the access rights defined in the *Adding security access to models* recipe from the same chapter.

Modify the file `security/ir.model.access.csv` to give write access to library users to books:

```
id,name,model_id:id,group_id:id,perm_read,perm_write,perm_create,perm_
unlink
access_library_book_user,library.book.user,model_library_book,base.
group_user,1,1,0,0
access_library_book_admin,library.book.admin,model_library_book,base.
group_system,1,0,0,0
```

Add a field `manager_remarks` to the `library.book` model. We want only members of the `Library Managers` group to be able to write to that field:

```
class LibraryBook(models.Model):
    _name = 'library.book'
    manager_remarks = fields.Text('Manager Remarks')
```

How to do it...

In order to prevent users who are not members of the **Library Managers** group from modifying the value of `manager_remarks`, you need to perform the following steps:

1. Extend the `create()` method like this:

```
@api.model
@api.returns('self', lambda rec: rec.id)
def create(self, values):
    if not self.user_has_groups(
            'library.group_library_manager'):
        if 'manager_remarks' in values:
            raise exceptions.UserError(
                'You are not allowed to modify '
                'manager_remarks'
            )
    return super(LibraryBook, self).create(values)
```

2. Extend the `write()` method as follows:

```
@api.multi
def write(self, values):
    if not self.user_has_groups(
            'library.group_library_manager'):
        if 'manager_remarks' in values:
            raise exceptions.UserError(
                'You are not allowed to modify '
                'manager_remarks'
            )
    return super(LibraryBook, self).write(values)
```

3. Extend the `fields_get()` method as follows:

```
@api.model
def fields_get(self,
               allfields=None,
               write_access=True,
               attributes=None):
    fields = super(LibraryBook, self).fields_get(
```

```
    allfields=allfields,
        write_access=write_access,
        attributes=attributes
    )
    if not self.user_has_groups(
            'library.group_library_manager'):
        if 'manager_remarks' in fields:
            fields['manager_remarks']['readonly'] = True
```

How it works...

Step 1 redefines the create() method. It uses a decorator we have not seen so far, @api.returns.

> This decorator maps the returned value from the new API to the old API, which is expected by the RPC protocol. In this case, the RPC calls to create expect the database id for the new record to be created, so we pass the @api.returns decorator an anonymous function, which fetches the id from the new record returned by our implementation. It is also needed if you want to extend the copy() method. Do not forget it when extending these methods if the base implementation uses the old API or you will crash with hard to interpret messages.

Before calling the base implementation of create(), our method uses the user_has_groups() method to check whether the user belongs to the group library.group_library_manager (this is the XML ID of the group). If it is not the case and a value is passed for manager_remarks, a UserError exception is raised preventing the creation of the record. This check is performed before the base implementation is called.

Step 2 does the same thing for the write() method; before writing, we check the group and the presence of the field in the values to write and raise UserError if there is a problem.

Step 3 is a small bonus; the fields_get() method is used by the web client to query for the fields of the model and their properties. It returns a Python dictionary mapping field names to a dictionary of field attributes, such as the display string or the help string. What interests us is the readonly attribute, which we force to True if the user is not a library manager. This will make the field read only in the web client, which will avoid unauthorized users from trying to edit it only to be faced with an error message.

> Having the field set to read-only in the web client does not prevent RPC calls from writing it. This is why we extend create() and write().

There's more...

When extending `write()`, note that before calling the `super()` implementation of `write()`, `self` is still unmodified. You can use this to compare the current values of the fields to the ones in the values dictionary.

In the recipe, we chose to raise an exception, but we could have also removed the offending field from the values dictionary and silently skipped updating that field in the record:

```
@api.multi
def write(self, values):
    if not self.user_has_groups(
            'library.group_library_manager'):
        if 'manager_remarks' in values:
            del values['manager_remarks']
    return super(LibraryBook, self).write(values)
```

After calling `super().write()`, if you want to perform additional actions, you have to be wary of anything that can cause another call to `write()`, or you will create an infinite recursion loop. The workaround is to put a marker in the context to be checked to break the recursion:

```
class MyModel(models.Model):
    @api.multi
    def write(self, values):
        super(MyModel, self).write(values)
        if self.env.context.get('MyModelLoopBreaker'):
            return
        self = self.with_context(MyModelLoopBreaker=True)
        self.compute_things() # can cause calls to writes
```

Customizing how records are searched

The *Defining the Model representation and order* recipe in *Chapter 3, Creating Odoo Modules* introduced the `name_get()` method, which is used to compute a representation of the record in various places, including in the widget used to display `Many2one` relations in the web client.

This recipe shows how to allow searching for a book in the `Many2one` widget by title, author, or ISBN by redefining `name_search`.

Getting ready

For this recipe, we will be using the following model definition:

```
class LibraryBook(models.Model):
    _name = 'library.book'
    name = fields.Char('Title')
    isbn = fields.Char('ISBN')
    author_ids = fields.Many2many('res.partner', 'Authors')

    @api.model
    def name_get(self):
        result = []
        for book in self:
            authors = book.author_ids.mapped('name')
            name = u'%s (%s)' % (book.title,
                                 u', '.join(authors))
            result.append((book.id, name))
        return result
```

When using this model, a book in a `Many2one` widget is displayed as **Book Title (Author1, Author2...)**. Users expect to be able to type in an author's name and find the list filtered according to this name, but this will not work as the default implementation of `name_search` only uses the attribute referred to by the `_rec_name` attribute of the model class, in our case, `'name'`. As a service to the advanced users, we also want to allow filtering by ISBN number.

How to do it...

In order to allow searching `library.book` either by book title, one of the authors, or ISBN, you need to define the `_name_search()` method in the `LibraryBook` class as follows:

```
    @api.model
    def _name_search(self, name='', args=None, operator='ilike',
                     limit=100, name_get_uid=None):
        args = [] if args is None else args.copy()
        if not(name == '' and operator == 'ilike'):
            args += ['|', '|',
                     ('name', operator, name),
                     ('isbn', operator, name),
                     ('author_ids.name', operator, name)
                     ]
        return super(LibraryBook, self)._name_search(
            name='', args=args, operator='ilike',
            limit=limit, name_get_uid=name_get_uid)
```

How it works...

The default implementation of `name_search()` actually only calls the `_name_search()` method, which does the real job. This `_name_search()` method has an additional argument, `name_get_uid`, which is used in some corner cases to compute the results using `sudo()`.

We pass most of the arguments that we receive unchanged to the `super()` implementation of the method:

- ▸ `name` is a string containing the value the user has typed so far
- ▸ `args` is either `None` or a search domain used as a prefilter for the possible records (it can come from the domain parameter of the `Many2one` relation for instance)
- ▸ `operator` is a string containing the match operator. Generally, you will have `'ilike'` or `'='`
- ▸ `limit` is the maximum number of rows to retrieve
- ▸ `name_get_uid` can be used to specify a different user when calling `name_get()` in the end to compute the strings to display in the widget

Our implementation of the method does the following:

1. It generates a new empty list if `args` is `None`, or makes a copy of `args` otherwise. We make a copy to avoid our modifications to the list having side effects on the caller.

2. Then, we check whether `name` is not an empty string or if `operator` is not `'ilike'`. This is to avoid generating a dumb domain `[('name', ilike, '')]` that does not filter anything. In that case, we jump straight to the call to the `super()` implementation.

3. If we have a `name`, or if the `operator` is not `'ilike'`, then we add some filtering criteria to `args`. In our case, we add clauses that will search for the supplied name in the title of the books, or in their ISBN, or in the authors' names.

4. Finally, we call the `super()` implementation with the modified domain in `args` and forcing `name` to `''` and `operator` to `ilike`. We do this to force the default implementation of `_name_search()` to not alter the domain it receives, so the one we specified is to be used.

There's more...

We mentioned in the introduction that this method is used in the `Many2one` widget. For completeness, it is also used in the following parts of Odoo:

- Proposals in the search widget
- When using the `in` operator on `One2many` and `Many2many` fields in the domain
- To search for records in the `many2many_tags` widget
- To search for records in the CSV file import

See also

The *Define the Model Representation and Order* recipe in *Chapter 3, Creating Odoo Modules* presents how to define the `name_get()` method, which is used to create a text representation of a record.

The *Defining filters on record lists: Domain* recipe in *Chapter 8, Backend Views* provides more information about search domain syntax.

6

Advanced Server Side Development Techniques

In this chapter, we will see how to:

- ► Change the user performing an action
- ► Call a method with a modified context
- ► Execute raw SQL queries
- ► Write a wizard to guide the user
- ► Define onchange methods
- ► Call onchange methods on the server side
- ► Port old API code to the new API

Introduction

In *Chapter 5, Basic Server Side Development*, we saw how to write methods on a model class, how to extend methods from inherited models, and how to work with recordsets. This chapter deals with more advanced topics such as working with the environment of a recordset and working with onchange methods.

Change the user performing an action

When writing business logic code, you may have to perform some actions with a different security context. A typical case is performing an action with the rights of the Administrator, who bypasses security checks.

This recipe shows how to let normal users modify the phone number of a company by using `sudo()`.

Getting ready

We will be working on records of the `res.company` model. By default, only members of the **Administration/Access Rights** user group can modify records of `res.company`, but in our case, we need to provide an access point to change only the phone number to users who are not necessarily members of that group.

How to do it...

In order to let normal users modify the phone number of a company, you need to perform the following steps:

1. Define a model extending the `res.company` model:

```
class ResCompany(models.Model):
    _inherit = 'res.company'
```

2. Add a method called `update_phone_number()`:

```
@api.multi
def update_phone_number(self, new_number):
```

3. In the method, ensure we are acting on a single record:

```
self.ensure_one()
```

4. Modify the user of the environment:

```
company_as_superuser = self.sudo()
```

5. Write the new phone number:

```
company_as_superuser.phone = new_number
```

How it works...

In step 4, we call `self.sudo()`. This method returns a new recordset with a new **environment** in which the user is not the same as the one in `self`. When called without an argument, `sudo()` will link the Odoo **superuser**, Administrator, to the environment. All method calls via the returned recordset are made with the new environment, and therefore with superuser privileges.

If you need a specific user, you can pass either a recordset containing that user or the database `id` of the user. The following snippet allows you to search books that are visible, using the `public` user:

```
public_user = self.env.ref('base.public_user')
public_book = self.env['library.book'].sudo(public_user)
```

Caution when using sudo()

There is no traceability of the action; the author of the last modification of the company in our recipe will be Administrator, not the user originally calling `update_phone_number`.

The community addon, `base_suspend_security`, found at `https://github.com/OCA/server-tools/` can be used to work around this limitation.

There is more...

When using `sudo()` without an argument, you set the user of the context to the Odoo superuser. This superuser bypasses all the security rules of Odoo, both the **access control lists** and the **record rules**. By default, this user also has a `company_id` field set to the main company of the instance (the one with id `1`). This can be problematic in a **multi company** instance:

- ▶ If you are not careful, new records created in this environment will be linked to the company of the superuser

- ▶ If you are not careful, records searched in this environment may be linked to any company present in the database, which means that you may be leaking information to the real user, or worse, you may be silently corrupting the database by linking together records belonging to different companies

Using `sudo()` also involves creating a new `Environment` instance. This environment will have an initially empty recordset cache, and that cache will evolve independently from the cache of `self.env`. This can cause spurious database queries. In any case, you should avoid creating new environment inside loops, and try to move these environment creations to the outmost possible scope.

See also

▶ The *Obtain an empty recordset for a model* recipe in *Chapter 5, Basic Server Side Development*, explains what the environment is.

Call a method with a modified context

The context is part of the environment of a recordset. It is used to pass information such as the timezone or the language of the user from the user interface as well as contextual parameters specified in actions. A number of methods in the standard addons use the context to adapt their behavior to these values. It is sometimes necessary to modify the context on a recordset to get the desired results from a method call or the desired value for a computed field.

This recipe shows how to read the stock level for all `product.product` models in a given `stock.location`.

Getting ready

This recipe uses the `stock` and `product` addons. For our purposes, here is a simplified version of the `product.product` model:

```
class product.product(models.Model):
    _name = 'product.product'
    name = fields.Char('Name', required=True)
    qty_available = fields.Float('Quantity on Hand',
                             compute='_product_available')
    def _product_available(self):
        """if context contains a key 'location' linked to a
        database id, then the stock available is computed within
        that location only. Otherwise the stock of all internal
        locations is computed"""
        pass  # read the real source in addons/stock/product.py :)
```

We intentionally don't provide the implementation of the computation and we skipped a few other keys that are looked for in the context in order to focus on the recipe.

How to do it...

In order to compute the stock levels in a given location for all the products, you need to perform the following steps:

1. Create a model class extending `product.product`:

```
class ProductProduct(models.Model):
    _inherit = 'product.product'
```

2. Add a method called `stock_in_location()`:

    ```
    @api.model
    def stock_in_location(self, location):
    ```

3. In the method, get a `product.product` recordset with a context modified as follows:

    ```
    product_in_loc = self.with_context(
        location=location.id,
        active_test=False
    )
    ```

4. Search all products:

    ```
    all_products = product_in_loc.search([])
    ```

5. Create an array with the product name and stock level of all products present in the specified location:

    ```
    stock_levels = []
    for product in all_products:
        if product.qty_available:
            stock_levels.append((product.name,
                                 product.qty_available))
    return stock_levels
    ```

How it works...

Step 3 calls `self.with_context()` with some keyword arguments. This returns a new version of `self` (which is a `product.product` recordset) with the keys added to the current **context**. We are adding two keys:

▶ `location`: This one is mentioned in the docstring of the `product.product` method computing the `qty_available` field.

▶ `active_test`: When this key is present and linked to the `False` value, the `search()` method does not automatically add `('active', '=', True)` to the search domain. Using this ensures that in step 4, we get all products, including the disabled ones.

When we read the value of `product.qty_available` in step 5, the computation of that field is made using only the specified stock location.

There's more...

It is also possible to pass a dictionary to `self.with_context()`, in which case the dictionary is used as the new context, overwriting the current one. So step 3 could also have been written like this:

```
new_context = self.env.context.copy()
new_context.update({'location': location.id,
                    'active_test': False})
product_in_loc = self.with_context(new_context)
```

Using `with_context()` involves creating a new `Environment` instance. This **environment** will have an initially empty recordset cache, and that cache will evolve independently of the cache of `self.env`. This can cause spurious database queries. In any case, you should avoid creating new environments inside loops and try to move these environment creations to the outmost possible scope.

See also

▸ The *Obtain an empty recordset for a model* recipe in *Chapter 5, Basic Server Side Development*, explains what the environment is

▸ The *Passing parameters to forms and actions: Context* recipe in *Chapter 8, Backend Views*, explains how to modify the context in action definitions

▸ The *Search for records* recipe in *Chapter 5, Basic Server Side Development*, explains active records

Execute raw SQL queries

Most of the time, you can perform the operations you want using the `search()` method. However, sometimes, you need more—either you cannot express what you want using the domain syntax, for which some operations are tricky if not downright impossible, or your query requires several calls to `search()`, which ends up being inefficient.

This recipe shows you how to use raw SQL queries to read `res.partner` records grouped by country.

Getting ready

We will be using a simplified version of the `res.partner` model:

```
class ResPartner(models.Model):
    _name = 'res.partner'
    name = fields.Char('Name', required=True)
```

```
email = fields.Char('Email')
is_company = fields.Boolean('Is a company')
parent_id = fields.Many2one('res.partner', 'Related Company')
child_ids = fields.One2many('res.partner', 'parent_id',
                                'Contacts')
country_id = fields.Many2one('res.country', 'Country')
```

How to do it...

To write a method that returns a dictionary that contains the mapped names of countries to a recordset of all active partners from that country, you need to perform the following steps:

1. Write a class extending res.partner:

```
class ResPartner(models.Model):
    _inherit = 'res.partner'
```

2. Add a method called partners_by_country():

```
@api.model:
def partners_by_country(self):
```

3. In the method, write the following SQL query:

```
sql = ('SELECT country_id, array_agg(id) '
        'FROM res_partner '
        'WHERE active=true AND country_id IS NOT NULL '
        'GROUP BY country_id')
```

4. Execute the query:

```
self.env.cr.execute(sql)
```

5. Iterate over the results of the query to populate the result dictionary:

```
country_model = self.env['res.country']
result = {}
for country_id, partner_ids in self.env.cr.fetchall():
    country = country_model.browse(country_id)
    partners = self.search(
        [('id', 'in', tuple(partner_ids))]
    )
    result[country] = partners
return result
```

How it works...

In step 3, we declare an SQL `SELECT` query. It uses the `id` field and the `country_id` foreign key, which refers to the `res_country` table. We use a `GROUP BY` statement so that the database does the grouping by `country_id` for us, and the `array_agg` aggregation function. This is a very useful PostgreSQL extension to SQL that puts all the values for the group in an array, which Python maps to a list.

Step 4 calls the `execute()` method on the database cursor stored in `self.env.cr`. This sends the query to PostgreSQL and executes it.

Step 5 uses the `fetchall()` method of the cursor to retrieve a list of rows selected by the query. From the form of the query we executed, we know that each row will have exactly two values, the first being `country_id` and the other one, the list of `ids` for the partners having that country. We loop over these rows and create recordsets from the values, which we store in the result dictionary.

There's more...

The object in `self.env.cr` is a thin wrapper around a `psycopg2` cursor. The following methods are the ones you will want to use most of the time:

- `execute(query, params)`: This executes the SQL `query` with the parameters marked as `%s` in the query substituted with the values in params, which is a tuple

 Warning: never do the substitution yourself, as this can make the code vulnerable to SQL injections.

- `fetchone()`: This returns one row from the database, wrapped in a tuple (even if there is only one column selected by the query)
- `fetchall()`: This returns all the rows from the database as a list of tuples
- `fetchalldict()`: This returns all the rows from the database as a list of dictionaries mapping column names to values

Be very careful when dealing with raw SQL queries:

- You are bypassing all the security of the application. Be sure to call `search([('id', 'in', tuple(ids)])` with any list of `ids` you are retrieving to filter out records to which the user has no access to.
- Any modification you are making is bypassing the constraints set by the addon modules, except the `NOT NULL`, `UNIQUE`, and `FOREIGN KEY` constraints, which are enforced at the database level. So are any computed field recomputation triggers, so you may end up corrupting the database.

See also

▸ For access rights management, see *Chapter 10, Access Security*.

Write a wizard to guide the user

In the *Use Abstract Models for reusable Model features* recipe in *Chapter 4, Application Models*, the base class `models.TransientModel` was introduced; this class shares a lot with normal `Models` except that the records of **transient models** are periodically cleaned up in the database, hence the name *transient*. These are used to create **wizards** or dialog boxes, which are filled in the user interface by the users and generally used to perform actions on the persistent records of the database.

This recipe extends the code from *Chapter 3, Creating Odoo Modules,* by creating a wizard to record the borrowing of books by a library member.

Getting ready

If you want to follow the recipe, make sure you have the `my_module` addon module from *Chapter 3, Creating Odoo Modules*.

We will also use a simple model to record book loans:

```
class LibraryBookLoan(models.Model):
    _name = 'library.book.loan'
    book_id = fields.Many2one('library.book', 'Book',
                              required=True)
    member_id = fields.Many2one('library.member', 'Borrower',
                                required=True)
    state = fields.Selection([('ongoing', 'Ongoing'),
                              ('done', Done')],
                             'State',
                             default='ongoing', required=True)
```

How to do it...

To add a wizard for recording borrowed books to the addon module, you need to perform the following steps:

1. Add a new transient model to the module with the following definition:

```
class LibraryLoanWizard(models.TransientModel):
    _name = 'library.loan.wizard'
    member_id = fields.Many2one('library.member', 'Member')
    book_ids = fields.Many2many('library.book', 'Books')
```

2. Add the callback method performing the action on the transient model. Add the following code to the `LibraryLoanWizard` class:

```python
@api.multi
def record_loans(self):
    for wizard in self:
        member = wizard.member_id
        books = wizard.book_ids
        loan = self.env['library.book.loan']
        for book in wizard.book_ids:
            loan.create({'member_id': member.id,
                         'book_id': book.id})
```

3. Create a form view for the model. Add the following view definition to the module views:

```xml
<record id='library_loan_wizard_form' model='ir.ui.view'>
  <field name='name'>library loan wizard form view</field>
  <field name='model'>library.loan.wizard</field>
  <field name='arch' type='xml'>
    <form string="Borrow books">
      <sheet>
        <group>
          <field name='member_id'/>
        </group>
        <group>
          <field name='book_ids'/>
        </group>
      <sheet>
      <footer>
        <button name='record_loans'
                string='OK'
                class='btn-primary'
                type='object'/>
        or
        <button string='Cancel'
                class='btn-default'
                special='cancel'/>
      </footer>
    </form>
  </field>
</record>
```

4. Create an action and a menu entry to display the wizard. Add the following declarations to the module menu file:

```xml
<act_window id="action_wizard_loan_books"
            name="Record Loans"
```

```
                res_model="library.loan.wizard"
                view_mode="form"
                target="new"
                />
    <menuitem id="menu_wizard_loan_books"
              parent="library_book_menu"
              action="action_wizard_loan_books"
              sequence="20"
              />
```

How it works...

Step 1 defines a new model. It is no different from other models, apart from the base class, which is `TransientModel` instead of `Model`. Both `TransientModel` and `Model` share a common base class called `BaseModel`, and if you check the source code of Odoo, you will see that 99 percent of the work is in `BaseModel` and that both `Model` and `TransientModel` are almost empty.

The only things that change for `TransientModel` records are as follows:

▶ Records are periodically removed from the database so the tables for transient models don't grow up in size over time

▶ You cannot define access rules on `TransientModels`. Anyone is allowed to create a record, but only the user who created a record can read it and use it.

▶ You must not define `One2many` fields on a `TransientModel` that refer to a normal model, as this would add a column on the persistent model linking to transient data. Use `Many2many` relations in this case. You can of course define `Many2one` and `One2many` fields for relations between transient models.

We define two fields in the model, one to store the member borrowing the books and one to store the list of books being borrowed. We could add other scalar fields to record a scheduled return date, for instance.

Step 2 adds the code to the wizard class that will be called when the button defined in step 3 is clicked on. This code reads the values from the wizard and creates `library.book.loan` records for each book.

Step 3 defines a view for our wizard. Please refer to the *Document-style forms* recipe in *Chapter 8*, *Backend Views*, for details. The important point here is the button in the footer: the type attribute is set to `'object'`, which means that when the user clicks on the button, the method with the name specified by the name attribute of the button will be called.

Step 4 makes sure we have an entry point for our wizard in the menu of the application. We use `target='new'` in the action so that the form view is displayed as a dialog box over the current form. Please refer to the *Add a Menu Item and Window Action* recipe in *Chapter 8, Backend Views*, for details.

There's more...

Here are a few tips to enhance your wizards.

Using the context to compute default values

The wizard we are presenting requires the user to fill in the name of the member in the form. There is a feature of the web client we can use to save some typing. When an action is executed, the **context** is updated with some values that can be used by wizards:

Key	Value
`active_model`	This is the name of the model related to the action. This is generally the model being displayed on screen.
`active_id`	This indicates that a single record is active, and provides the ID of that record.
`active_ids`	If several records were selected, this will be a list with the IDs (this happens when several items are selected in a tree view when the action is triggered. In a form view, you get [`active_id`]).
`active_domain`	An additional domain on which the wizard will operate.

These values can be used to compute default values of the model, or even directly in the method called by the button. To improve on the recipe example, if we had a button displayed on the form view of a `library.member` model to launch the wizard, then the context of the creation of the wizard would contain `{'active_model': 'library.member', 'active_id': <member id>}`. In that case, you could define the `member_id` field to have a default value computed by the following method:

```
def _default_member(self):
    if self.context.get('active_model') == 'library.member':
        return self.context.get('active_id', False)
```

Wizards and code reuse

In step 2, we could have dispensed with the `for wizard in self` loop, and assumed that `len(self)` is 1, possibly adding a call to `self.ensure_one()` at the beginning of the method, like this:

```
@api.multi
def record_borrows(self):
    self.ensure_one()
```

```
    member = self.member_id
    books = self.book_ids
    member.borrow_books(books)
```

We recommend using the version in the recipe though, because it allows reusing the wizard from other parts of the code by creating records for the wizard, putting them in a single recordset (see the *Combine recordsets* recipe in *Chapter 5*, *Basic Server Side Development*, to see how to do this) and then calling `record_loans()` on the recordset. Granted, here the code is trivial and you don't really need to jump through all those hoops to record that some books were borrowed by different members. However, in an Odoo instance, some operations are much more complex, and it is always nice to have a wizard available that does "the right thing." When using such wizards, be sure to check the source code for any possible use of the `active_model` / `active_id` / `active_ids` keys from the context, in which case, you need to pass a custom context (see the *Call a method with a modified context* recipe previously for how to do this).

Redirecting the user

The method in step 2 does not return anything. This will cause the wizard dialog to be closed after the action is performed. Another possibility is to have the method return a dictionary with the fields of an `ir.action`. In this case, the web client will process the action as if a menu entry had been clicked on by the user. For instance, if we wanted to display the form view of the member who has just borrowed the books, we could have written the following:

```
@api.multi
def record_borrows(self):
    for wizard in self:
        member = wizard.member_id
        books = wizard.book_ids
        member.borrow_books(books)
    member_ids = self.mapped('member_id').ids
    action = {
        'type': 'ir.action.act_window',
        'name': 'Borrower',
        'res_model': 'library.member',
        'domain': [('id', '=', member_ids)],
        'view_mode': 'form,tree',
    }
    return action
```

This builds a list of members who has borrowed books from this wizard (in practice, there will only be one such member, when the wizard is called from the user interface) and creates a dynamic action, which displays the members with the specified IDs.

This trick can be extended by having a wizard (with several steps to be performed one after the other), or depending on some condition from the preceding steps, by providing a **Next** button that calls a method defined on the wizard. This method will perform the step (maybe using a hidden field and storing the current step number), update some fields on the wizard, and return an action that will redisplay the same updated wizard and get ready for the next step.

Define onchange methods

When writing Odoo models, it is often the case that some fields are interrelated. We have seen how to specify constraints between fields in the *Add constraint validations to a Model* recipe in *Chapter 4, Application Models*. This recipe illustrates a slightly different concept—**onchange methods** are called when a field is modified in the user interface to update the values of other fields of the record in the web client, usually in a form view.

We will illustrate this by providing a wizard similar to the one defined in the preceding recipe, *Write a wizard to guide the user*, but which can be used to record loan returns. When the member is set on the wizard, the list of books is updated to the books currently borrowed by the member. While we are demonstrating onchange methods on a `TransientModel`, these features are also available on normal `Models`.

Getting ready

If you want to follow the recipe, make sure you have the `my_module` addon from *Chapter 3, Creating Odoo Modules*, with the *Write a wizard to guide the user* recipe's changes applied.

You will also want to prepare your work by defining the following transient model for the wizard:

```python
class LibraryReturnsWizard(models.TransientModel):
    _name = 'library.returns.wizard'
    member_id = fields.Many2one('library.member', 'Member')
    book_ids = fields.Many2many('library.book', 'Books')
    @api.multi
    def record_returns(self):
        loan = self.env['library.book.loan']
        for rec in self:
            loans = loan.search(
                [('state', '=', 'ongoing'),
                 ('book_id', 'in', rec.book_ids.ids),
                 ('member_id', '=', rec.member_id.id)]
            )
            loans.write({'state': 'done'})
```

Finally, you will need to define a view, an action, and a menu entry for the wizard. This is left as an exercise.

How to do it...

To automatically populate the list of books to return when the user is changed, you need to add an onchange method in the `LibraryReturnsWizard` step with the following definition:

```
@api.onchange('member_id')
def onchange_member(self):
    loan = self.env['library.book.loan']
    loans = loan.search(
        [('state', '=', 'ongoing'),
         ('member_id', '=', self.member_id.id)]
    )
    self.book_ids = loans.mapped('book_id')
```

How it works...

An onchange method uses the `@api.onchange` decorator, which is passed the names of the fields that change and thus will trigger the call to the method. In our case, we say that whenever `member_id` is modified in the user interface, the method must be called.

In the body of the method, we search the books currently borrowed by the member, and we use an attribute assignment to update the `book_ids` attribute of the wizard.

 The `@api.onchange` decorator takes care of modifying the view sent to the web client to add an `on_change` attribute to the field. This used to be a manual operation in the "old API".

There's more...

The basic use of onchange methods is to compute new values for fields when some other fields are changed in the user interface, as we've seen in the recipe.

Inside the body of the method, you get access to the fields displayed in the current view of the record, but not necessarily all the fields of the model. This is because onchange methods can be called while the record is being created in the user interface _before_ it is stored in the database! Inside an onchange method, `self` is in a special state, denoted by the fact that `self.id` is not an integer, but an instance of `openerp.models.NewId`. Therefore, you must not make any changes to the database in an onchange method, because the user may end up canceling the creation of the record, which would not roll back any changes made by the onchanges called during the edition. To check for this, you can use `self.env.in_onchange()` and `self.env.in_draft()`—the former returns `True` if the current context of execution is an onchange method and the latter returns `True` if `self` is not yet committed to the database.

Additionally, onchange methods can return a Python dictionary. This dictionary can have the following keys:

- warning: The value must be another dictionary with the keys title and message respectively containing the title and the content of a dialog box, which will be displayed when the onchange method is run. This is useful for drawing the attention of the user to inconsistencies or to potential problems.

- domain: The value must be another dictionary mapping field names to domains. This is useful when you want to change the domain of a One2many field depending on the value of another field.

For instance, suppose we have a fixed value set for expected_return_date in our library.book.loan model, and we want to display a warning when a member has some books that are late. We also want to restrict the choice of books to the ones currently borrowed by the user. We can rewrite the onchange method as follows:

```python
@api.onchange('member_id')
def onchange_member(self):
    loan = self.env['library.book.loan']
    loans = loan.search(
        [('state', '=', 'ongoing'),
         ('member_id', '=', self.member_id.id)]
    )
    self.book_ids = loans.mapped('book_id')
    result = {
        'domain': {'book_ids': [
                        ('id', 'in', self.book_ids.ids)]
                  }
    }
    late_domain = [
        ('id', 'in', loans.ids),
        ('expected_return_date', '<', fields.Date.today())
    ]
    late_loans = loans.search(late_domain)
    if late_loans:
        message = ('Warn the member that the following '
                   'books are late:\n')
        titles = late_loans.mapped('book_id.name')
        result['warning'] = {
            'title': 'Late books',
            'message': message + '\n'.join(titles)
        }
    return result
```

Call onchange methods on the server side

The *Create new records* and *Update values of a recordset record* recipes in *Chapter 5, Basic Server Side Development*, mentioned that these operations did not call onchange methods automatically. Yet in a number of cases it is important that these operations are called because they update important fields in the created or updated record. Of course, you can do the required computation yourself, but this is not always possible as the onchange method can be added or modified by a third-party addon module installed on the instance that you don't know about.

This recipe explains how to call the onchange methods on a record by manually playing the onchange method before creating a record.

Getting ready

We will reuse the settings from the preceding recipe, *Write onchange methods*. The action will take place in a new method of `library.member` called `return_all_books(self)`.

How to do it...

In this recipe, we will manually create a record of the `library.returns.wizard` model, and we want the onchange method to compute the returned books for us. To do this, you need to perform the following steps:

1. Create the method `return_all_books` in the `LibraryMember` class:

```
@api.multi
def return_all_books(self):
    self.ensure_one
```

2. Get an empty recordset for `library.returns.wizard`:

```
wizard = self.env['library.returns.wizard']
```

3. Prepare the values to create a new wizard record:

```
values = {'member_id': self.id, book_ids=False}
```

4. Retrieve the onchange specifications for the wizard:

```
specs = wizard._onchange_spec()
```

5. Get the result of the onchange method:

```
updates = wizard.onchange(values, ['member_id'], specs)
```

6. Merge these results with the values of the new wizard:

```
value = updates.get('value', {})
for name, val in value.iteritems():
```

```
            if isinstance(val, tuple):
                value[name] = val[0]
        values.update(value)
```

7. Create the wizard:

```
        record = wizard.create(values)
```

How it works...

For an explanation of step 1 to step 3, please refer to the recipe *Create new records* in *Chapter 5, Basic Server Side Development*.

Step 4 calls the _onchange_spec method on the model, passing no argument. This method will retrieve the updates that are triggered by the modification of which other field. It does this by examining the form view of the model (remember, onchange methods are normally called by the web client).

Step 5 calls the onchange(values, field_name, field_onchange) method of the model with 3 arguments:

- ▶ values: The list of values we want to set on the record. You need to provide a value for all the fields you expect to be modified by the onchange method. In the recipe, we set book_ids to False for this reason.

- ▶ field_name: A list of fields for which we want to trigger the onchange methods. You can pass an empty list, and it will use the fields defined in values. However, you will often want to specify that list manually to control the order of evaluation, in case different fields can update a common field.

- ▶ field_onchange: The onchange specifications that were computed in step 4. This method finds out which onchange methods must be called and in what order and returns a dictionary, which can contain the following keys:
    - ❏ value: This is a dictionary of newly computed field values. This dictionary only features keys that are in the values parameter passed to onchange(). Note that Many2one fields are mapped to a tuple containing (id, display_name) as an optimization for the web client.
    - ❏ warning: This is a dictionary containing a warning message that the web client will display to the user.
    - ❏ domain: This is a dictionary mapping field names to new validity domains.

Generally, when manually playing onchange methods, we only care about what is in value.

Step 6 updates our initial values dictionary with the values computed by the onchange. We process the values corresponding to `Many2one` fields to only keep the `id`. To do so, we take advantage of the fact that these fields are only those whose value is returned as a tuple.

Step 7 finally creates the record.

There's more...

If you need to call an onchange method after modifying a field, the code is the same. You just need to get a dictionary for the values of the record, which can be obtained by using `values = dict(record._cache)` after modifying the field.

See also

 ▸ The *Create new records* and *Update values of recordset records* recipes in *Chapter 5, Basic Server Side Development*

Port old API code to the new API

Odoo has a long history and the so-called "traditional" or "old" API has been in use for a very long time. When designing the "new" API in Odoo 8.0, time was taken to ensure that the APIs would be able to coexist, because it was foreseen that porting the huge codebase to the new API would be a huge effort. So you will probably come across addon modules using the traditional API. When migrating them to the current version of Odoo, you may want to port them to the new API.

This recipe explains how to perform this translation. It can also serve as an aide memoire when you need to extend a module that uses the traditional API with the new API.

Getting ready

Let's port the following addon module code developed with the traditional API:

```
from datetime import date, timedelta
from openerp.osv import orm, fields
from openerp.tools import _, DEFAULT_SERVER_DATE_FORMAT as DATE_FMT

class library_book(orm.Model):
    _name = 'library.book'
    _columns = {
        'name': fields.char('Name', required=True),
```

```
            'author_ids': field.many2many('res.partner'),
    }

class library_member(orm.Model):
    _name = 'library.member'
    _inherits = {'res.partner': 'partner_id'}

    _columns = {
        'partner_id': fields.many2one('res.partner',
                                      'Partner',
                                      required=True),
        'loan_duration': fields.integer('Loan duration',
                                        required=True),
        'date_start': fields.date('Member since'),
        'date_end': fields.date('Expiration date'),
        'number': fields.char('Number', required=True),
    }

    _defaults = {
        'loan_duration': 10,
    }

    def on_change_date_end(self, cr, uid, date_end, context=None):
        date_end = date.strptime(date_end, DATE_FMT)
        today = date.today()
        if date_end <= today:
            return {
                'value': {'loan_duration': 0},
                'warning': {
                    'title': 'expired membership',
                    'message': "This member's membership " \
                               "has expired",
                },
            }

    def borrow_books(self, cr, uid, ids, book_ids, context=None):
        if len(ids) != 1:
            raise orm.except_orm(
                _('Error!'),
                _('It is forbidden to loan the same books '
                  'to multiple members.'))
        loan_obj = self.pool['library.book.loan']
        member = self.browse(cr, uid, ids[0], context=context)
        for book_id in book_ids:
```

```
        val = self._prepare_loan(
            cr, uid, member, book_id, context=context
        )
        loan_id = loan_obj.create(cr, uid, val,
            context=context)

    def _prepare_loan(self, cr, uid,
                      member, book_id,
                      context=None):
        return {'book_id': book_id,
                'member_id': member.id,
                'duration': member.loan_duration}


class library_book_loan(orm.Model):
    _name = 'library.book.loan'

    def _compute_date_due(self, cr, uid, ids,
                          fields, arg, context=None):
        res = {}
        for loan in self.browse(cr, uid, ids, context=context):
            start_date = date.strptime(loan.date, DATE_FMT)
            due_date = start_date + timedelta(days=loan.duration)
            res[loan.id] = due_date.strftime(DATE_FMT)
        return res

    _columns = {
        'book_id': fields.many2one('library.book', required=True),
        'member_id': fields.many2one('library.member',
                                     required=True),
        'state': fields.selection([('ongoing', 'Ongoing'),
                                   ('done', 'Done')],
                                  'State', required=True),
        'date': fields.date('Loan date', required=True),
        'duration': fields.integer('Duration'),
        'date_due': fields.function(
            fnct=_compute_date_due,
            type='date',
            store=True,
            string='Due for'),
    }

    def _default_date(self, cr, uid, context=None):
```

```
        return date.today().strftime(DATE_FMT)

    _defaults = {
        'duration': 15,
        'date': _default_date,
    }
```

The module, of course, defined some views. Most of them will need no change, so we won't show them. The only one relevant in this recipe is the `library.member` form view. Here is the relevant excerpt for that view:

```
<record id='library.member_form_view' model='ir.ui.view'>
  <field name='model'>library.member</field>
  <field name='arch' type='xml'>
    <!-- [...] -->
    <field name='date_end'
           on_change='on_change_date_end(date_end)'/>
    <!-- [...] -->
  </field>
</record>
```

How to do it...

To port this module code to the new API, you need to perform the following steps:

1. Copy the original source file to make a backup.

2. In the new file, modify the module imports as follows:

   ```
   from datetime import date, timedelta
   from openerp import models, fields, api, exceptions
   from openerp.tools import _
   ```

3. Modify the class definitions to the new API base classes, and rename the classes to use CamelCase:

   ```
   class LibraryBook(models.Model):
       _name = 'library.book'


   class LibraryMember(models.Model):
       _name = 'library.member'
       _inherits = {'res.partner': 'partner_id'}


   class LibraryBookLoan(models.Model):
       _name = 'library.book.loan'
   ```

4. Migrate the `_columns` definitions to attribute declaration of fields in the `LibraryBook` class:

   ❏ The `_columns` keys become class attributes

   ❏ The names of the field types get capitalized

```
class LibraryBook(models.Model):
    _name = 'library.book'

    name = fields.Char('Name', required=True)
    author_ids = field.Many2many('res.partner')
```

 Don't forget to remove the commas at the ends of the lines.

5. Do the same thing for `LibraryMember`, taking care to move `_defaults` declarations to the field definition:

```
class LibraryMember(models.Model):
    # [...]

    partner_id = fields.Many2one('res.partner',
                                 'Partner',
                                 required=True)
    loan_duration = fields.Integer('Loan duration',
                                   default=10,
                                   required=True)
    date_start = fields.Date('Member since')
    date_end = fields.Date('Expiration date')
    number = fields.Char('Number', required=True)
```

6. Migrate the column's definition of the `LibraryBookLoan` class, changing the type of the `function` field to `fields.Date`:

```
class LibraryBookLoan(models.Model):
    # [...]

    book_id = fields.Many2one('library.book', required=True)
    member_id = fields.Many2one('library.member',
                                required=True)
    state = fields.Selection([('ongoing', 'Ongoing'),
                              ('done', 'Done')],
                             'State', required=True)
    date = fields.Date('Loan date', required=True,
                       default=_default_date)
```

```
       duration = fields.Integer('Duration', default=15)
       date_due = fields.Date(
           compute='_compute_date_due',
           store=True,
           string='Due for'
       )
```

7. In the `LibraryBookLoan` class, migrate the definition of the `_compute_date_due` function to the new API:

   ❏ Remove all the arguments except `self`

   ❏ Add an `@api.depends` decorator

   ❏ Change the body of the method to use the new computed field protocol (see the *Add computed fields to a Model* recipe in *Chapter 4, Application Models*, for details):

```
# in class LibraryBookLoan
   @api.depends('start_date', 'due_date')
   def _compute_date_due(self):
       for loan in self:
           start_date = fields.Date.from_string(loan.date)
           due_date = start_date + timedelta(days=loan.duration)
           loan.date_due = fields.Date.to_string(due_date)
```

8. In the `LibraryBookLoan` class, migrate the definition of the `_default_date` function:

   ❏ The function definition must be moved before the field declaration

   ❏ The new prototype only has one argument, `self` (see the *Add data fields to a Model* recipe in *Chapter 4, Application Models*, for details):

```
# in class LibraryBookLoan, before the fields definitions
   def _default_date(self):
       return fields.Date.today()
```

9. Rewrite the `borrow_books` and `_prepare_loan` methods in the `LibraryMember` class:

   ❏ Add an `@api.multi` decorator

   ❏ Remove the arguments `cr, uid, ids, context`

   ❏ Port the code to the new API (see the various recipes in this chapter for details)

   ❏ Replace the `orm.except_orm` exception with `UserError`:

```
# in class LibraryMember
   @api.multi
   def borrow_books(self, book_ids):
```

```
        if len(self) != 1:
            raise exceptions.UserError(
                _('It is forbidden to loan the same books '
                  'to multiple members.')
            )
        loan_model = self.env['library.book.loan']
        for book in self.env['library.book'].browse(book_ids):
            val = self._prepare_loan(book)
            loan = loan_model.create(val)
    @api.multi
    def _prepare_loan(self, book)
        self.ensure_one()
        return {'book_id': book.id,
                'member_id': self.id,
                'duration': self.loan_duration}
```

10. Port the `on_change_date_end` method in the `LibraryMember` class:

    ❑ Add an `@api.onchange` decorator

    ❑ Port the code to the new API (see the *Write onchange methods* recipe in this chapter for details):

```
# in LibraryMember
    @api.onchange('date_end')
    def on_change_date_end(self):
        date_end = fields.Date.from_string(self.date_end)
        today = date.today()
        if date_end <= today:
            self.loan_duration = 0
            return {
                'warning': {
                    'title': 'expired membership',
                    'message': "Membership has expired",
                },
            }
```

11. Edit the `library.member` form's view definition and remove the `on_change` attribute in the `date_end` field:

```
<record id='library.member_form_view' model='ir.ui.view'>
  <field name='model'>library.member</field>
  <field name='arch' type='xml'>
    <!-- [...] -->
    <field name='date_end'/>
    <!-- [...] -->
  </field>
</record>
```

How it works

Step 1 changes the imports. The old API lives in the `openerp.osv` package, which we change to use `openerp.models`, `openerp.fields`, `openerp.api`, and `openerp.exceptions`. We also drop the import of `DEFAULT_SERVER_DATE_FORMAT`, because we will use the helper methods on `fields.Date` to perform `datetime` / string conversions.

Step 2 changes the base classes of the models. Depending on the age of the code you are migrating, you may need to replace the following:

- ▸ `osv.osv`, `osv.Model` or `orm.Model` with `models.Model`
- ▸ `osv.osv_memory`, `osv.TransientModel`, or `orm.TransientModel` with `models.TransientModel`

The usual class attributes such as `_name`, `_order`, `_inherit`, `_inherits`, and so on are unchanged.

Steps 3 to 8 deal with the migration of the field's definitions. The `_columns` dictionaries mapping field names to field definitions in the old API are migrated to class attributes.

 When doing so, don't forget to remove the commas following each field definition in the dictionary, otherwise the attribute value will be a 1-element tuple, and you will get errors. You also get a warning log line for these.

The field classes in `openerp.fields` usually have the same name as their counterparts in `openerp.osv.fields`, but capitalized (`openerp.osv.fields.char` becomes `openerp.fields.Char`). Default values are moved from the `_defaults` class attribute to a default parameter in the type declaration:

```
_columns = {
    'field1': fields.char('Field1'),
    'field2': fields.integer('Field2'),
}
_defaults = {
    'field2': 42,
}
```

Now the preceding code is modified to the following:

```
field1 = fields.Char('Field1')
field2 = fields.Integer('Field2', default=42)
```

The biggest change is for function fields. The old API uses `fields.function` defined with a `type` parameter giving the type of the column. The new API uses a field of the expected type, defined with a `compute` parameter, which gives the method used to compute the field:

```
_columns = {
    'field3': fields.function(
        _compute_field3,
        arg=None,
        fnct_inv=_store_field3,
        fnct_inv_arg=None,
        type='char',
        fnct_search=_search_field3,
        store=trigger_dict,
        multi=keyword
    ),
}
```

Now the preceding code is modified to the following:

```
field3 = fields.Char('Field1'
                     compute='_compute_field3',
                     inverse='_store_field3',
                     search='_search_field3',
                     store=boolean)
```

The `trigger_dict` in the old API is replaced with `@api.depends` decorators, and there is no need for the `multi` parameter in the new API, as the `compute` method can update several fields sharing the same compute parameter value. See the *Add Computed Fields to a Model* recipe in *Chapter 4, Application Models*, for more detailed information.

Step 9 migrates the business logic methods. The decorator to use on the method defines the parameter conversions, which are to be used to map the arguments. You need to choose them carefully because this can break modules using the old API extending the ported module. The same advice is valid if you need to extend a model defined using the old API with the new API. Here are the most common cases, with `<args>` denoting additional arbitrary arguments and keyword arguments:

Old API prototype	New API prototype
`def m(self, cr, uid, ids, <args>,` `context=None)`	`@api.multi` `def m(self, <args>)`
`def m(self, cr, uid, <args>, context=None)`	`@api.model` `def m(self, <args>)`
`def m(self, cr, <args>)`	`@api.cr` `def m(self, <args>)`

Old API prototype	New API prototype
`def m(self, cr, uid, <args>)`	`@api.cr_uid`
	`def m(self, <args>)`

Finally, steps 10 and 11 migrate the onchange method. Things have changed quite a bit between the two versions of the API; in the traditional API, onchange methods are declared in the view definitions by using an attribute `on_change` on the `<field>` element with a value describing the call to be performed when the field is edited. In the new API, this declaration is not necessary because the framework dynamically generates it in the view by analyzing the methods decorated with `@api.onchange`.

7
Debugging and Automated Testing

In this chapter, we will cover the following topics:

- ▶ Producing server logs to help debug methods
- ▶ Using the Odoo shell to interactively call methods
- ▶ Using the Python debugger to trace method execution
- ▶ Writing tests for your module using YAML
- ▶ Writing tests for your module using Python unit tests
- ▶ Running server tests
- ▶ Using the Odoo Community Association maintainer quality tools

Introduction

We saw in *Chapter 5, Basic Server Side Business Logic,* how to write model methods to implement the logic of our module. However, a responsible developer not only writes the implementation but also provides automated tests for this implementation. The recipes in this chapter cover the debugging and testing of server side methods.

Producing server logs to help debug methods

Server logs are helpful when trying to figure out what has been happening at runtime before a crash. They can also be added to provide additional information when debugging an issue. This recipe shows how to add logging to an existing method.

Getting ready

We will add some logging statements to the following method, which saves the stock levels of products to a file:

```
from os.path import join
from openerp import models, api, exceptions
EXPORTS_DIR = '/srv/exports'

class ProductProduct(models.Model):
    _inherit = 'product.product'
    @api.model
    def export_stock_level(self, stock_location):
        products = self.with_context(
            location=stock_location.id
        ).search([])
        products = products.filtered('qty_available')
        fname = join(EXPORTS_DIR, 'stock_level.txt')
        try:
            with open(fname, 'w') as fobj:
                for prod in products:
                    fobj.write('%s\t%f\n' % (prod.name,
                                             prod.qty_available))
        except IOError:
            raise exceptions.UserError('unable to save file')
```

How to do it...

In order to get some logs when this method is being executed, perform the following steps:

1. At the beginning of the code, import the `logging` module:

   ```
   import logging
   ```

2. Before the definition of the model class, get a logger for the module:

   ```
   _logger = logging.getLogger(__name__)
   ```

3. Modify the code of the `export_stock_level()` method as follows:

   ```
   @api.model
   def export_stock_level(self, stock_location):
       _logger.info('export stock level for %s',
                    stock_location.name)
       products = self.with_context(
           location=stock_location.id).search([])
       products = products.filtered('qty_available')
   ```

```
_logger.debug('%d products in the location',
                len(products))
fname = join(EXPORTS_DIR, 'stock_level.txt')
try:
    with open(fname, 'w') as fobj:
        for prod in products:
            fobj.write('%s\t%f\n' % (prod.name,
                prod.qty_available))
except IOError:
    _logger.exception(
        'Error while writing to %s in %s',
        'stock_level.txt', EXPORTS_DIR)
    raise exceptions.UserError('unable to save
                                file')
```

How it works...

Step 1 imports the module `logging` from the Python standard library. Odoo uses this module to manage its logs.

Step 2 sets up a logger for the Python module. We use a common idiom in Odoo by using the `__name__` automatic variable for the logger name and calling the logger `_logger`.

 The `__name__` variable is set automatically by the Python interpreter at module import time and its value is the full name of the module. Since Odoo does a little trick with the imports, the addon modules are seen by Python as belonging to the `openerp.addons` Python package. So if the code of the recipe is in `my_module/models/book.py`, `__name__` will be `openerp.addons.my_module.models.book`.

By doing this, we get two benefits:

- The global logging configuration set on the `openerp` logger is applied to our logger, because of the hierarchical structure of loggers in the `logging` module
- The logs will be prefixed with the full module path, which is a great help when trying to find where a given log line is produced

Step 3 uses the logger to produce log messages. Available methods for this are (by increasing log level) `debug`, `info`, `warning`, `error`, and `critical`. All these methods accept a message in which you can have % substitutions and additional arguments to be inserted in the message. You should *not* do the % substitution yourself; the logging module is smart enough to perform this operation *only if the log has to be produced*. If you are running with log level of `INFO`, then `DEBUG` logs will avoid doing the substitution.

Another useful method shown in the recipe is `_logger.exception()`, which can be used in an exception handler. The message will be logged with a level of `ERROR` and the stack trace is also printed in the application log.

There's more...

You can control the **logging level** of the application from the command line or from the configuration file. There are two main ways of doing this:

- To control the log level globally, you can use the `--log-level` command line option. See *Chapter 2*, *Managing Odoo Server Instances*, for more information.

- To set the log level for a given logger, you can use `--log-handler=prefix:level`. In this case, `prefix` is a piece of the path of the logger name, and `level` is one of DEBUG, INFO, WARNING, ERROR, or CRITICAL. If you omit `prefix`, then you set the default level for all loggers. For instance, to set the logging level of `my_module` loggers to DEBUG and keep the default log level for the other addons, you can start Odoo like this:

  ```
  $ python odoo.py --log-handler=openerp.addons.my_module:DEBUG
  ```

- It is possible to specify `--log-handler` multiple times on the command line.

- You can also configure the **log handler** in the configuration file of your Odoo instance. In that case, you can use a comma-separated list of `prefix:level` pairs. For example, the following line is a sane configuration for minimal logging output, still keeping the most important messages: we keep error messages by default, except for messages produced by `werkzeug` for which we only want critical messages, and `openerp.service.server` for which we keep info level messages (this includes the notification of server start up):

  ```
  log_handler = :ERROR,werkzeug:CRITICAL,openerp.service.server:INFO
  ```

Using the Odoo shell to interactively call methods

The Odoo web interface is meant for end users, although the developer mode unlocks a number of powerful features. However, testing and debugging through the web interface is not the easiest way to do things, as you need to manually prepare data, navigate in the menus to perform actions, and so on. The Odoo shell is a **command-line interface**, which you can use to issue calls. This recipe shows how to start the Odoo shell and perform actions such as calling a method inside the shell.

Getting ready

We will reuse the same code as in the previous recipe to produce server logs to help debug methods; this enables the `product.product` model to add a new method. We assume that you have an instance with the addon installed available. In the recipe, we expect that you have an Odoo configuration file for this instance called `project.conf`.

How to do it...

In order to call the `export_stock_level()` method from the Odoo shell, you need to perform the following steps:

1. Start the Odoo shell specifying your project configuration file:

    ```
    $ odoo/odoo.py shell -c project.conf --log-level=error
    ```

2. Check for error messages, and read the information text displayed before the usual Python command-line prompt:

    ```
    env: <openerp.api.Environment object at 0x7fbc244e3a90>
    openerp: <module 'openerp' from '/home/cookbook/odoo/openerp/__
    init__.pyc'>
    self: res.users(1,)
    Python 2.7.9 (default, Mar  1 2015, 12:57:24)
    [GCC 4.9.2] on linux2
    Type "help", "copyright", "credits" or "license" for more
    information.
    (Console)
    >>>
    ```

3. Get a recordset for `product.product`:

    ```
    >>> product = env['product.product']
    ```

4. Get the main stock location record:

   ```
   >>> location_stock = env.ref('product.stock_location_stock')
   ```

5. Call the `export_stock_level()` method:

   ```
   >>> product.export_stock_level(location_stock)
   ```

6. Commit the transaction before exiting:

   ```
   >>> env.cr.commit()
   ```

7. Exit the shell by pressing *Ctrl+D*.

How it works...

Step 1 uses `odoo.py shell` to start the Odoo shell. All the usual command line arguments are available. We use `-c` to specify a project configuration file and `--log-level` to reduce the verbosity of the logs. When debugging, you may want to have a logging level of DEBUG only for some specific addons.

Before providing you with a Python command-line prompt, `odoo.py shell` starts an Odoo instance that does not listen on the network and initializes some global variables, which are mentioned in the output:

- `env` is an environment connected to the database specified on the command line or in the configuration file.

- `openerp` is the `openerp` package imported for you. You get access to all the Python modules within that package so you can do what you want.

- `self` is a recordset of `res.users` containing a single record for the Odoo super user (Administrator), which is linked to the environment `env`.

Step 3 and 4 use `env` to get an empty recordset and find a record by XML ID. Step 5 calls the method on the `product.product` recordset. These operations are identical to what you would use inside a method, with the small difference that we use `env` and not `self.env` (although we could have both as they are identical). See *Chapter 5*, *Basic Server Side Development*, for more information on what is available.

Step 6 commits the database transaction. This is not strictly necessary here because we did not modify any record in the database, but if we had done so and wanted these changes to persist, this is necessary—when you use Odoo through the web interface, each RPC call runs in its own database transaction and Odoo manages these for you. When running in the shell mode, this no longer happens and you have to call `env.cr.commit()` or `env.cr.rollback()` yourself. Otherwise, when you exit the shell, any transaction in progress is automatically rolled back. When testing, this is fine, but if you use the shell, for example, to script the configuration of an instance, don't forget to commit your work!

Using the Python debugger to trace method execution

Sometimes, application logs are not enough to figure out what is going wrong. Fortunately, we have the Python **debugger** available to us. This recipe shows how to insert a break point in a method and trace the execution by hand.

Getting ready

We will be reusing the `export_stock_level()` method shown in the two previous recipes. Be sure to have a copy at hand.

How to do it...

In order to trace the execution of `export_stock_level()` with `pdb`, follow the following steps:

1. Edit the code of the method, and insert the line highlighted here:

```
def export_stock_level(self, stock_location):
    import pdb; pdb.set_trace()
    products = self.with_context(
        location=stock_location.id
    ).search([])
    fname = join(EXPORTS_DIR, 'stock_level.txt')
    try:
        with open(fname, 'w') as fobj:
            for prod in products.filtered('qty_available'):
                fobj.write('%s\t%f\n' % (
                    prod.name, prod.qty_available))
    except IOError:
        raise exceptions.UserError('unable to save file')
```

2. Run the method. We will use the Odoo shell, as explained in the *Use the Odoo shell to interactively call methods* recipe previously:

```
$ odoo.py shell -c project.cfg --log-level=error
[...]
>>> product = env['product.product']
>>> location_stock = env.ref('product.stock_location_stock')
>>> product.export_stock_level(location_stock)
> /home/cookbook/stock_level/models.py(16)export_stock_level()
-> products = self.with_context(
(Pdb)
```

3. At the (Pdb) prompt, issue the `args` (shortcut a) command to get the values of the arguments passed to the method:

```
(Pdb) a
self = product.product()
stock_location = stock.location(12,)
```

4. Enter the `list` command to check where in the code you are standing:

```
(Pdb) list
def export_stock_level(self, stock_location):
    import pdb; pdb.set_trace()
    products = self.with_context(
        location=stock_location.id
    ).search([])
    fname = join(EXPORTS_DIR, 'stock_level.txt')
    try:
        with open(fname, 'w') as fobj:
            for prod in products.filtered('qty_available'):
                fobj.write('%s\t%f\n' % (prod.name,
                                         prod.qty_available))
```

5. Enter the `next` command three times to walk through the first lines of the method. You may also use `n`, which is a shortcut:

```
(Pdb) next
> /home/cookbook/stock_level/models.py(17)export_stock_level()
-> location=stock_location.id
(Pdb) n
> /home/cookbook/stock_level/models.py(18)export_stock_level()
-> ).search([])
(Pdb) n
> /home/cookbook/stock_level/models.py(19)export_stock_level()
-> fname = join(EXPORTS_DIR, 'stock_level.txt')
(Pdb) n
> /home/cookbook/stock_level/models.py(20)export_stock_level()
-> try:
```

6. Use the p command to display the values of the `products` and `fname` variables:

```
(Pdb) p products
product.product(67, 14, 12, 6, 7, 8, 17, 18, 13, 55, 15, 10, 11,
64, 31, 23, 42, 30, 29, 53, 56, 63, 62, 43, 61, 35, 51, 26, 24,
25, 39, 40, 45, 34, 32, 33, 57, 65, 28, 27, 38, 16, 19, 49, 5, 36,
37, 44, 21, 22, 20, 59, 52, 66, 58, 54, 60, 46, 41, 47, 48, 50, 3,
```

```
    2, 1, 4)
    (Pdb) p fname
    '/srv/exports/stock_level.txt'
```

7. Change the value of `fname` to point to the `/tmp` directory:

    ```
    (Pdb) !fname = '/tmp/stock_level.txt'
    ```

8. Use the `return` (shortcut `r`) command to execute the current function to its end:

    ```
    (Pdb) return
    --Return--
    > /home/afayolle/work/OdooCookbook/project1/stock_level/models.
    py(22)export_stock_level()->None
    -> for product in products.filtered('qty_available'):
    ```

9. Use the `cont` (shortcut `c`) command to resume execution of the program:

    ```
    (Pdb) c
    >>>
    ```

How it works...

In step 1, we hardcode a break point in the source code of the method by calling the `set_trace()` method of the `pdb` module from the Python standard library. When this method is executed, the normal flow of the program stops, and you get a `(Pdb)` prompt in which you can enter `pdb` commands.

Step 2 calls the `stock_level_export()` method using the shell mode. It is also possible to restart the server normally and to use the web interface to generate a call to the method you need to trace by clicking on the appropriate elements of the user interface.

When you need to manually step through some code using the Python debugger, here are a few tips that will make your life easier:

- ▶ Reduce the logging level to avoid having too many log lines polluting the output of the debugger. Starting at the ERROR level is generally fine. You may want to enable some specific loggers with a higher verbosity, which you can do by using the `--log-handler` command line option (see the preceding recipe, *Produce server logs to help debug methods*).

- ▶ Run the server with `--workers=0` to avoid any multiprocessing issues that could cause the same break point to be reached twice in two different processes.

- ▶ Run the server with `--max-cron-threads=0` to disable the processing of `ir.cron` periodic tasks, which otherwise may trigger while you are stepping through the method, producing unwanted logs and side effects.

Steps 3 to 8 use several `pdb` commands to step through the execution of the method. Here is a summary of the main commands of `pdb`. Most of them are also available using the first letter as a shortcut. We indicate this by having the optional letters between parenthesis:

- `h(elp)`: This displays help on the `pdb` commands.
- `a(rgs)`: This shows the value of the arguments of the current function/methods.
- `l(ist)`: This displays the source code being executed by chunks of 11 lines, initially centered on the current line. Successive calls will move further in the source code file. Optionally, you can pass two integers, `start` and `end`, specifying the region to display.
- `p`: This prints a variable.
- `pp`: This pretty-prints a variable (useful with lists and dictionaries).
- `w(here)`: This shows the call stack, with the current line at the bottom and the Python interpreter at the top.
- `u(p)`: This moves up one level in the call stack.
- `d(own)`: This moves down one level in the call stack.
- `n(ext)`: This executes the current line of code and then stops.
- `s(tep)`: This is to step inside the execution of a method call.
- `r(eturn)`: This resumes the execution of the current method until it returns.
- `c(ont)`: This resumes the execution of the program until the next break point is hit.
- `b(reak) <args>`: This creates a new break point, and displays its identifier. `args` can be one of the following:
  - `<empty>`: This lists all break points
  - `line_number`: This breaks at the specified line in the current file
  - `filename:line_number`: This breaks at the specified line of the specified file (which is searched for in the directories of `sys.path`)
  - `function_name`: This breaks at the first line of the specified function
- `tbreak <args>`: This is similar to `break` but the break point will be canceled after it has been reached, so successive execution of the line won't trigger it twice.
- `disable bp_id`: This disables a breakpoint by ID.
- `enable bl_id`: This enables a disabled breakpoint by ID.
- `j(ump) lineno`: The next line to execute will be the one specified. This can be used to rerun or to skip some lines.
- `(!) statement`: This executes a Python statement. The `!` character can be omitted if the command does not look like a `pdb` command; for instance, you need it if you want to set the value of a variable named `a`, because `a` is the shortcut for the `args` command.

There's more...

In the recipe, we inserted a `pdb.set_trace()` statement to break into `pdb`. We can also start `pdb` directly from within the Odoo shell, which is very useful when you cannot easily modify the code of the project by using `pdb.runcall()`. This function takes a method as the first argument and the arguments to pass to the function as the next arguments. So inside the Odoo shell, you do this:

```
>>> import pdb
>>> product = env['product.product']
>>> location_stock = env.ref('stock.stock_location_stock')
>>> pdb.runcall(product.export_stock_level, location_stock)
> /home/cookbook/odoo/openerp/api.py(235)wrapper()
-> if '_ids' in self.__dict__:
(Pdb)
```

Notice that in this case you do not end up in the `export_stock_level()` method but in the `wrapper()` function from `openerp.api`. This is part of the implementation of the `@api.model` decorator we set on `expert_stock_level()` and you will encounter lots of these in your `pdb` sessions when stepping inside method calls. You can either manually walk through the decorators or add breakpoints inside the source code of the methods.

If you choose to step manually, you will need to use next until you the line calling `new_api()` and step inside that call:

```
(Pdb) n
> /home/cookbook/odoo/openerp/api.py(236)wrapper()
-> return new_api(self, *args, **kwargs)
(Pdb) s
--Call--
> /home/cookbook/stock_level/models.py(13)export_stock_level()
-> @api.model
(Pdb) n
> /home/cookbook/stock_level/models.py(15)export_stock_level()
-> products = self.with_context(
```

If you'd rather add a breakpoint, check the file name and line number and use the break command like this:

```
(Pdb) b /home/cookbook/stock_level/models.py:15
Breakpoint 1 at /home/cookbook/stock_level/models.py:15
(Pdb) cont
```

```
> /home/cookbook/stock_level/models.py(15)export_stock_level()
-> products = self.with_context(
(Pdb)
```

Notice that we had to use the full path to the file because it is not in a directory inside `sys.path`.

In this recipe, we focused on the Python debugger from the Python standard library, `pdb`. It is very useful to know this tool because it is guaranteed to be available on any Python distribution. There are other Python debuggers available, such as `ipdb` (`https://pypi.python.org/pypi/ipdb`) and `pudb` (`https://pypi.python.org/pypi/pudb`), which can be used as drop-in replacements for `pdb`. They share the same API and most commands seen in this recipe are unchanged. And, of course, if you develop for Odoo using a Python IDE, you certainly have access to a debugger integrated with it.

See also

▶ For the full documentation of `pdb`, refer to `https://docs.python.org/2.7/library/pdb.html`

Writing tests for your module using YAML

Odoo supports different ways of writing addon module tests, YAML tests, and Python tests. In this recipe, we will see how to write **YAML tests** for the `my_module` methods we wrote in *Chapter 5*, *Basic Server Side Development*, in the recipe *Define Model methods and use the API decorators*.

Getting ready

This recipe assumes you have an instance ready with the code for the `my_module` module defined in *Chapter 3*, *Creating Odoo Modules*, and the code from the *Define Model methods and use the API decorators* recipe in *Chapter 5*, *Basic Server Side Development*.

How to do it...

In order to write YAML unit tests for `my_module`, you need to follow these steps:

1. Edit the `__openerp__.py` file of the module, and add the test's entry:

   ```
   {   # ...
       'test': ['test/test_books.yml']
   }
   ```

2. Create a `test` directory in `my_module`:

   ```
   $ mkdir test
   ```

3. Create a file called `test_books.yml` in the directory. Add a test description at the top:

   ```
   -

     Test LibraryBook.change_state
   ```

4. Add a step changing the current user to the demo user:

   ```
   -

     !context
       uid: 'base.user_demo'
   ```

5. Add a test step creating a book:

   ```
   -

     create book in draft state

   -

     !record {model: library.book, id: testbook}:
       - name: Test Book
       - state: draft
   ```

6. Add a step calling the `change_state` method:

   ```
   -

     call change_state to make book available

   -

     !python {model: library.book, id: testbook}: |
       self.change_state('available')
   ```

7. Add a step checking the successful result of the call:

   ```
   -

     !assert {model: library.book, id: testbook, string: wrong
   state}:
       - state == 'available'
   ```

8. Add a step calling the `change_state` method with a forbidden state:

   ```
   -

     try to call change_state to make book draft

   -

     !python {model: library.book, id: testbook}: |
       self.change_state('draft')
   ```

```
    -

    check the book is still available

    -

    !assert {model: library.book, id: testbook, string: wrong
state}:
      - state == 'available'
```

How it works...

The YAML files we are using here are the same as the ones used to load data files (see *Chapter 9, Module Data*), except that they are included in the test key of the __openerp__.py rather than in the data key. We add that key in step 1. They are therefore processed only when running the tests (see the *Running Server Tests* recipe in this chapter).

> Traditionally, YAML tests are added to the test/ subdirectory of the addon module, while Python unit tests live in the tests/ subdirectory.

Step 3 adds a description at the top of the test file in a YAML test node. Mind the indentation of the text, after the - delimiting a node. This description will be printed in the test log (at log level DEBUG).

Step 4 uses a !context YAML node to change the evaluation context used in the test. The most common use of this node is to modify the user used to run the test from the administrator to someone else by assigning a string containing the XML ID of the user to uid.

> It is always good practice, when writing tests, to have them run with a specific user, and in any case not with the administrator; this user bypasses all the security checks, so this will hide issues in your security rules.

Step 5 creates some test data using a !record YAML node. The YAML attributes, between braces, give the name of the model to be used and the XML ID to use for the new record.

> In all the YAML files, pay attention to the spacing, as the syntax is quite stringent; you need a single space after the commas, a single space before the opening brace, and the trailing colon has to be just after the closing brace.

Step 6 uses a !python YAML node to execute some Python code. The attributes specify the model to be used and the XML ID of the record. Inside the block, self is a recordset of the specified model containing a single record with the supplied XML ID.

YAML Syntax

Take note of the | character at the end of the !python node. It is used to denote a literal text node, in which whitespace is not processed. You need this for Python code where spacing is significant.

Inside the Python block, you may also use the following variables:

- `ref`: This is a function returning a recordset from an XML ID passed as a string

- `time`: This is the `time` module from the Python standard library

- `datetime`: This is the `datetime` type from the `datetime` module of the Python standard library

- `timedelta`: This is the `timedelta` type from the `datetime` module of the Python standard library

In step 7, we use an `!assert` YAML node to make assertions about the record. The attributes specify the model to use and on which XML ID the assertions must be checked. The string attribute is used in the error message if one of the checks in the node is not `True`.

See the following recipe, *Run server tests*, to see how to run the test.

There's more...

When `!assert` is not convenient for writing checks, for instance, if you don't have an XML ID for the record you want to check, you can use a `!python` block and the `assert` Python keyword. We could also rewrite the last check of the recipe like this:

```
    -
        try to call change_state to make book draft, check this has no
    effect
    -
    !python {model: library.book, id: testbook}: |
        self.change_state('draft')
        assert self.state == 'available', 'wrong state %s' % self.state
```

Writing tests for your module using Python unit tests

YAML is not the only way of writing tests with Odoo. If you are familiar with the Python unit testing tools, you will be pleased to know that these are also available within the Odoo framework. In this recipe, we will see how to write Python **unit tests** for the `my_module` methods we wrote in *Chapter 5, Basic Server Side Development*, in the recipe *Define Model methods and use the API decorators*.

Getting ready

This recipe assumes you have a instance ready with the code for the `my_module` module defined in *Chapter 3, Creating Odoo Modules*, and the code from *Chapter 5, Basic Server Side Development*, in the recipe *Define Model methods and use the API decorators*.

How to do it...

In order to write unit tests for the module, perform the following steps:

1. Create a subdirectory called `tests` inside the `addon` module directory:

    $mkdir my_module/tests

2. Create an `__init__.py` file in that directory with the following contents:

    ```
    from . import test_library
    ```

3. Create a `test_library.py` file in `tests/` subdirectory. Inside the `test_library.py file`, import the Odoo test base class:

    from openerp.test.common import TransactionCase

4. Create a `TestCase` class:

    class LibraryTestCase(TransactionCase):

5. Add a `setUp` method that creates a book:

    ```
    def setUp(self):
        super(LibraryTestCase, self).setUp()
        book_model = self.env['library.book'].sudo(
            self.ref('base.user_demo')
        )
        self.book = book_model.create(
    ```

```
        {'name': 'Test book',
         'state': 'draft',
         }
    )
```

6. Add a `test` method changing the state:

```
def test_change_draft_available(self):
    '''test changing state from draft to available'''
    self.book.change_state('available')
    self.assertEqual(self.book.state, 'available')
```

7. Add a second `test` method trying to make an illegal state change:

```
def test_change_available_draft_no_effect(self):
    '''test forbidden state change from available to draft'''
    self.book.change_state('available')
    self.book.change_state('draft')
    self.assertEqual(
        self.book.state,
        'available',
        'the state cannot change from available to %s' % \
        self.book.state
    )
```

How it works...

We create a Python subpackage in our module called `tests` and add a test module with a name starting with `test_`. This is the convention used by Odoo for **test discovery**.

In this file, we import the base test class, `TransactionCase`, from `openerp.test.common`. This class extends the `unittest.TestCase` class from the Python standard library to make it suitable for use in Odoo:

▶ The `setUp()` method initializes the `self.env` attribute, which you can use to perform the usual operations (see the recipes in *Chapter 5, Basic Server Side Development*)

▶ The `tearDown()` method rolls back the database transaction so that the tests are run in isolation

 If your test case redefines these two methods, be sure to call the `super()` implementation.

The tests are defined in methods named with a `test` prefix. The test runner will run then one after the other with a call to `setUp()` before each test method and a call to `tearDown()` after each. Inside the method, you can use all the usual assertion methods from `unittest.TestCase`. Here are the most commonly used ones:

Method	Checks that
`assertEqual(a, b)`	`a == b`
`assertNotEqual(a, b)`	`a != b`
`assertTrue(x)`	`bool(x) is True`
`assertFalse(x)`	`bool(x) is False`
`assertIn(a, b)`	`a in b`
`assertNotIn(a, b)`	`a not in b`
`assertRaises(exc, fun, *args, **kwargs)`	`fun(*args, **kwargs)` raises exc

All these methods except `assertRaises()` accept an optional `msg` argument, which will be displayed in the error message when the assertion is not true. Otherwise, a standard error message is used.

`assertRaises` is best used as a context manager. Suppose you want to test that modifying a record raises a `UserError` exception. You can write the following test:

```
class TestCase(TransactionCase):
    # setUp method defines self.record
    def testWriteRaisesUserError(self):
        with self.assertRaises(UserError):
            self.record.write({'some_field': some_value})
```

The test will succeed if the exception passed to `assertRaises` is generated by the block of code; otherwise it will fail.

For more information on unit tests in Python, please refer to the standard library documentation at `https://docs.python.org/2.7/library/unittest.html#test-cases`.

Note that in the `setUp()` method, we use `sudo()` to change the user in the environment of `self.book_model`. This ensures that the tests will not run using the administrator user, which bypasses the access rules and that the security rules we set up in our module are getting exercised.

See the following recipe, *Run server tests*, to see how to run the test.

There's more...

The module `openerp.test.common` defines several classes that can be used as base classes for test cases:

- ▶ `TransactionCase`: Each test method is run independently and the database transaction is rolled back after each. This means that any changes made in one test method are not seen by the other test methods. You can use the traditional `setUp()` and `tearDown()` methods to perform test initialization and cleanup.

- ▶ `SingleTransactionCase`: All the tests methods are run in the same transaction, which is only rolled back after the last method. If you need to perform initialization and cleanup for the test case, you need to extend the `setUpClass()` and `tearDownClass()` methods. Don't forget to decorate these with `@classmethod`, or you will get strange errors when calling the `super()` implementation.

- ▶ `SavePointCase`: It is an extension of `SingleTransactionCase` that creates a database `SAVEPOINT` before running test methods and restoring them after the test is run. The net effect is that you can run your tests in isolation as with `TransactionCase` without having to pay the price of a costly `setUp()` method recreating all the data between all tests—the initialization is performed in `setUpClass()` and we roll back the transaction to the saved state after each test.

The module also defines two decorators, `at_install(bool)` and `post_install(bool)`. By default, the tests for a given addon module are run just after the module is initialized, before initializing the next addon module; this corresponds to decorating the test methods with both `@at_install(True)` and `@post_install(False)`. Sometimes, you can need to change this. A typical case is the following: `module_a` and `module_b` both extend the same model, but they do not depend on one another. Both add a required field to the model `field_a` and `field_b` and provide a default value for that field. In the tests of these modules, new records are created. If both modules are installed when the tests are run, the tests will fail, whereas if only `module_a` or `module_b` is installed, the tests will pass. The reason is that if, for instance, `module_a` is loaded first, when the tests create a new record the default value for `field_b` is not computed because `module_b` is not loaded yet. However, the database `NOT NULL` constraint for `field_b` is present and will prevent the record from being created. A solution is to decorate the test methods of both modules with `@at_install(False)` and `@post_install(True)`, which will force the tests to be run after all modules have been initialized.

Running server tests

The two previous recipes showed how to write tests. Let's see how to run them! This recipe works for both YAML and Python unit tests.

Getting ready

We will be reusing the tests for the `my_module` module from one of the previous recipes. You will need an instance with the addon installed. In this recipe, we assume that the instance configuration file is in `project.cfg`.

How to do it...

To run the tests for my module addon, run the following command:

```
$ odoo/odoo.py -c project.cfg --test-enable --log-level=error --stop-
after-init -u my_module
```

How it works...

The key part in this recipe is the `--test-enable` command-line flag that tells Odoo to run the tests. The `--stop-after-init` flag will stop the instance after the tests have run and `-u` will update the specified module. When an update (or install) is performed in test mode, all the affected addon modules' tests are run (this includes dependencies automatically installed or reverse dependencies automatically updated; see the recipe *Install and upgrade local addon modules* in *Chapter 2, Managing Odoo Server Instances*, for more information on this).

 How do you know that the tests ran successfully? The exit status of Odoo will be equal to the number of failed tests, so if it is not 0, then at least one test has failed. You will get more information about the failures in the server log messages.

You can run the tests using the following log configuration: `--log-level=error --log-handler=openerp.modules.loading:INFO`. This allows to have information about the various tests' files to be processed but not the details of the logs of the operations, only the error messages.

There's more...

The main drawback of this way of running tests is that you have to run all the tests for a given addon module, even if you know that they all pass but the one you are trying to fix, and you also have to update the addon (which can be in itself a costly operation).

There is a way around this. If you want to run the tests in `my_module/tests/test_library.py`, you can use the following command:

```
$ odoo/odoo.py -c project.cfg --log-level=error --stop-after-init --test-file my_module/tests/test_library.py
```

This will run only the tests defined in that file, and it works too if you specify a file containing YAML tests. It will also skip updating the module, so it will not work if you have changed the model structure by adding new fields or modified the data files of the addon since the last time the module was updated.

> **One final note about tests:**
>
>
>
> Always be suspicious if your tests are not in error on the first run. There is a good chance this means you made a mistake. A typical goof is to forget to add the YAML test file in the `__openerp__.py` file, or to forget to import the test file in `tests/__init__.py`. It is always a good idea when tests are passing on the first run to force a failure, for instance, by adding `assert False` to the first line of a method and running them again.

Using the Odoo Community Association maintainer quality tools

The **Odoo Community Association** (**OCA**) manages a large number of Odoo projects using the GitHub infrastructure. The association projects use Travis CI for continuous integration. This recipe shows how you can use the maintainer QA tools developed by the community in your own GitHub repositories.

Getting ready

To use this recipe, you need to have a public GitHub repository with your modules. At the time of writing, the OCA tools expect that this repository contains several addons in subdirectories.

How to do it...

To integrate the OCA maintainer-quality-tools with your repository, you need to perform the following steps:

1. Connect to `https://travis-ci.org/`.

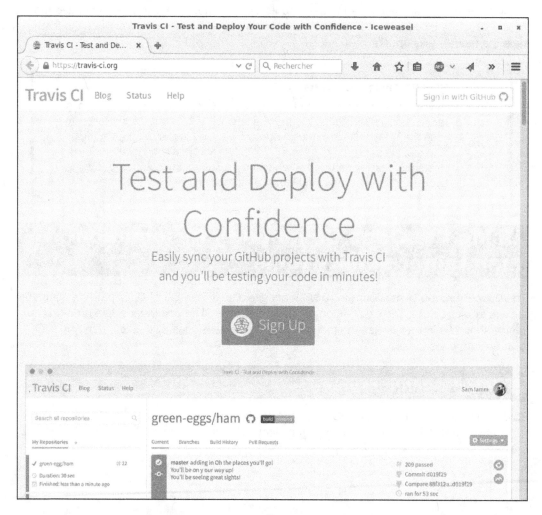

2. To sign in, choose **Sign in with Github**.

3. Click on your name in the top right corner to access to your profile's settings, as shown in the following screenshot:

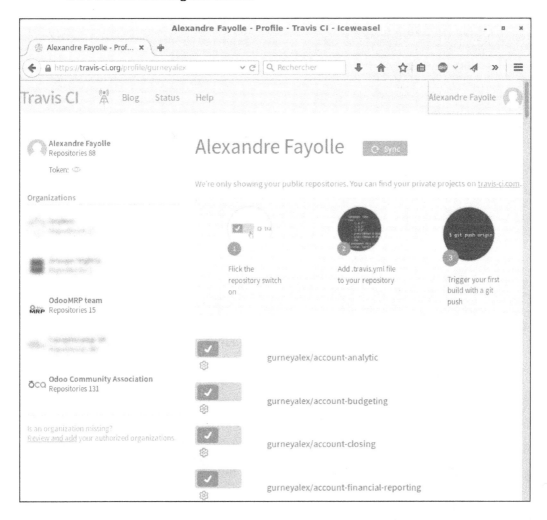

4. Click on the **Sync** button to load the information about all your public repositories in Travis. This can take a couple of minutes depending on how many repositories you have.

5. For all the repositories you want to use **Travis** on, enable them by toggling the grey cross to a green check mark.

6. You can click on the cogwheel to access each repository's settings, but the defaults are OK too.

7. Inside a local clone of your repository, create a file called `.travis.yml` with the following content:

```
language: python
sudo: false
cache:
  apt: true
  directories:
    - $HOME/.cache/pip
python:
  - "2.7"
addons:
  apt:
    packages:
      - expect-dev  # provides unbuffer utility
      - python-lxml  # because pip installation is slow
      - python-simplejson
      - python-serial
      - python-yaml
virtualenv:
  system_site_packages: true
env:
  global:
  - VERSION="9.0" TESTS="0" LINT_CHECK="0"
  matrix:
  - LINT_CHECK="1"
  - TESTS="1" ODOO_REPO="odoo/odoo"
  - TESTS="1" ODOO_REPO="OCA/OCB"
install:
  - git clone --depth=1 https://github.com/OCA/maintainer-quality-tools.git ${HOME}/maintainer-quality-tools
  - export PATH=${HOME}/maintainer-quality-tools/travis:${PATH}
  - travis_install_nightly
script:
  - travis_run_tests
after_success:
  - travis_after_tests_success
```

8. Commit the file and push it to GitHub:

```
$ git add .travis.yml
$ git commit -m "add travis configuration"
$ git push origin
```

9. Go to your `travis-ci.org` page and click on your project's name. You should see a first build in progress. If your code follows the OCA coding standard, it may even be green on the first run:

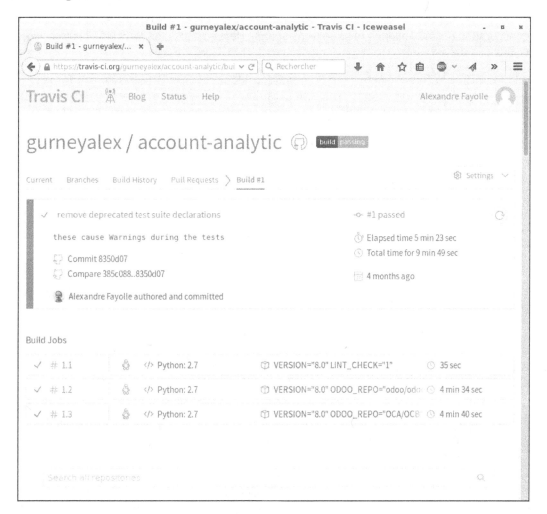

How it works...

When you enable Travis CI on a repository, Travis registers a hook on GitHub. By default, the hook will trigger a Travis CI build for each push to a branch of the repository and for each pull request. Pull requests are built on a temporary merge of the PR, to ensure that the merged branches pass the tests.

The Travis CI configuration file proposed here is fairly advanced and very close to the one found in the `sample_files` subdirectory of the maintainer-quality-tools project you can see at `https://github.com/OCA/maintainer-quality-tools` (we removed the transifex configuration used to manage module translations). Here's an explanation of the customized sections in the file:

- `addons`: This has nothing to do with Odoo addon modules. It's used to ask Travis to install some Ubuntu packages using distribution packages in the testing environment. This saves us from installing Python packages such as `python-lxml` from source, which takes a lot of time.

- `env`: This section defines environment variables and the build matrix. The maintainer quality tools use these environment variables to know what to test, and will run each `env` line in a separate test run:

  - `VERSION`: This is the Odoo version to test against.

  - `LINT_CHECK`: Use `0` for a build with no `flake8` or `Pylint` tests, and `1` otherwise. In the matrix, we set the first build to perform the lint check, as this is fast and we want rapid feedback if the coding standards are not met or if the linter finds errors.

  - `TESTS`: Use `0` for a build in which the module tests are not run; otherwise use `1`.

  - `ODOO_REPO`: This is the GitHub repository for Odoo to test against when `TESTS` is `1`. In the recipe, we set up a build against both the official `https://github.com/odoo/odoo` repository and the community backports repository `https://github.com/OCA/OCB`. If unset, only the official repository is used.

- `install`: This sections downloads `maintainer-quality-tools` in the build environment and calls the `travis_install_nightly` utility, which will set up Odoo in Travis for you.

- `script`: This section calls `travis_run_tests` from `maintainer-quality-tools`. This is the script in charge of checking the environment variables from the build matrix and performing the appropriate actions.

- `after_success`: After the tests in the script section have run successfully, the `travis_after_test_success` script is run. In the context of the recipe, this script will check the test coverage of the modules using `https://coveralls.io` and produce a report in the build.

8

Backend Views

In this chapter, we will cover the following topics:

- ▶ Adding a menu item and window action
- ▶ Having an action open a specific view
- ▶ Adding content and widgets to a form view
- ▶ Adding buttons to forms
- ▶ Passing parameters to forms and actions: Context
- ▶ Defining filters on record lists: Domain
- ▶ List views
- ▶ Search views
- ▶ Changing existing views: View inheritance
- ▶ Document-style forms
- ▶ Dynamic form elements using attrs
- ▶ Embedded views
- ▶ Kanban views
- ▶ Show kanban cards in columns according to their state
- ▶ Calendar and gantt views
- ▶ Graph and pivot views
- ▶ QWeb reports

Throughout this chapter, we will assume that you have a database with the base addon installed and an empty Odoo addon module where you add XML code from the recipes to a data file referenced in the addon's manifest. Refer to *Chapter 3, Creating Odoo Modules* for how to activate changes in your addon.

Introduction

This chapter covers all the UI elements that users are confronted with when they use anything other than the website part of Odoo. Historically, this basically was all of OpenERP, so also in an Odoo context, it is often just referred to as the web client. To be more specific, we will call this the **backend** as opposed to the website frontend.

Adding a menu item and window action

The most obvious way to make a new feature available to the users is by using a menu item. When you click on a menu item, something happens. This recipe walks you through how to define that something.

We will create a top level menu displaying a sub menu in the left hand menu bar, opening a list of all the customers.

This can also be done using the web user interface, via the settings menu, but we prefer to use XML data files since this is what we'll have to use when creating our addon modules.

How to do it...

In an XML data file of our addon module, perform the following steps:

1. Define an action to be executed:

    ```xml
    <act_window id="action_all_customers"
                name="All customers"
                res_model="res.partner"
                view_mode="tree,form"
                domain="[('customer', '=', True)]"
                context="{'default_customer': True}"
                limit="80" />
    ```

2. Create the menu structure:

    ```xml
    <menuitem id="menu_custom_toplevel"
              name="My custom menu" />
    <menuitem id="menu_custom_left"
    ```

```
            parent="menu_custom_toplevel"
            name="This will appear in the left bar" />
```

3. Refer to our action in menu:

```
<menuitem id="menu_all_customers"
            parent="menu_custom_left"
            action="action_all_customers"
            sequence="10"
            groups="" />
```

If we now upgrade the module, we will see a top level menu that opens a sub menu in the left menu bar. Clicking on that menu item will open a list of all the customers.

How it works...

The first XML element, `act_window`, declares a window action to display a list view with all the customers. We used the most important attributes:

- `name`: To be used as the title for the views opened by the action.

- `res_model`: This is the model to be used. We are using `res.partner`, where Odoo stores all the partners and addresses, including customers.

- `view_mode`: This lists the view types to make available. The default value is *tree, view*, making available the list and form views. Other possible choices are *kanban, graph, calendar*, and *gantt*, explained later in this chapter.

- `domain`: This is optional and allows you to set a filter on the records to be made available in the views. In this case, we want to limit the partners to only those that are customers. We will explain this in more detail in a dedicated recipe later.

- `context`: This can set values made available to the opened views, affecting their behavior. In our example, on new records we want the customer flag's default value to be `True`. This will be covered in more depth in another recipe.

- `limit`: This sets the default amount of records that can be seen on list views. It defaults to `80`.

Next we create the menu item hierarchy; from the top level menu to the clickable end menu item. The most important attributes for the `menuitem` element are:

- `name`: This is used as the text the menu items display. If your menu item links to an action you can leave this out, because in that case the action's name will be used.

- `parent` (`parent_id` if using the `record` element): This is the XML ID referencing the parent menu item. Items with no parent are top level menus.

- `action`: This is the XML ID referencing the action to be called. Only menu items without child elements are clickable, so this option is only effective in those cases.

- ▸ sequence: This is used to order sibling menu items.
- ▸ groups (groups_id with the record tag): This is an optional list of user groups that can access this menu item. If empty, it will be available to all the users.

Window actions automatically determine the view to be used by looking up views for the target model, with the intended type (form, tree, and so on) and picking the one with the lowest sequence number.

act_window and menuitem are convenient shortcut XML tags that hide what you're actually doing: You create a record of the models ir.actions.act_window and ir.ui.menu respectively.

> Be aware that names used with the menuitem shortcut may not map to the field names used when using a record element: parent should be parent_id and groups should be groups_id.

To build the menu, the web client reads all the records from ir.ui.menu and infers their hierarchy from the parent_id field. Menus are also filtered based on user permissions to models and groups assigned to menus and actions. When a user clicks a menu item, its action is executed.

There's more...

Window actions also support a target attribute to specify how the view is to be presented. Possible choices are:

- ▸ **current**: This is the default and opens the view in the web client main content area.
- ▸ **new**: This opens in a popup.
- ▸ **inline**: This makes most sense for forms. It opens a form in the edit mode but neither with the standard buttons to edit, create, or delete, nor with the **More** actions menu.
- ▸ **inlineview**: This is similar to inline, but opens in the read mode instead of edit.

The window action's view_type attribute is mostly obsolete by now. The alternative to the default **form** is **tree**, which causes the groups lists to render a hierarchical tree. Don't confuse this attribute with the view_mode attribute used and explained earlier, which actually decides which types of views are used.

There are also some additional attributes available for window actions that are not supported by the act_window shortcut tag. So to use them, we must use the record element with the following fields:

- ▸ **res_id**: If opening a form, you can have it open a specific record by setting its ID here. This can be useful for multi step wizards, or in cases when you often have to view/edit a specific record.

▸ **search_view_id**: This specifies a specific search view to use for the tree and graph views.

▸ **auto_search**: This is **True** by default. Set this to **False** if searching for your object is very time and/or resource consuming. This way, the user can review the search parameters and press **Search** when satisfied. With the default, the search is triggered immediately when the action is opened.

Keep in mind that the menu bar at the top and the menu to the left are all made up of the same stuff, the menu items. The only difference is that the items in the top bar don't have any parent menus, while the ones on the left bar have the respective menu item from the top bar as parent. In the left bar, the hierarchical structure is more obvious.

Also bear in mind that for design reasons, the first level menus in the left bar are rendered as a kind of header and standard Odoo doesn't assign an action to them very often. So even if you technically can assign an action to them, your users won't be used to click them and will probably be confused if you expect them to do so.

See also

You'll find a more detailed discussion of the XML ID reference mechanism in *Chapter 9, Module Data*. For now, just keep in mind that you can set references this way and – very importantly – that order matters. If the tags above were inverted, the addon containing this XML code wouldn't install because `menuitem` would refer to an unknown `action`.

> This can become a pitfall when you add new data files and new elements during your development process, because then the order in which you add those files and elements does not necessarily reflect the order they will be loaded in an empty database. Always check before deployment if your addon installs in an empty database.

The action type `ir.actions.act_window` is the most common one, but a menu can refer to any type of action. Technically, it is just the same if you link to a client action, a server action, or any other model defined in the **ir.actions.*** namespace. It just differs in what the backend makes out of the action.

If you need just a tiny bit more flexibility in the concrete action to be called, look into the server actions that return a window action in turn. If you need complete flexibility on what you present, look into the client actions (**ir.actions.client**) which allow you to have a completely custom user interface. But only do so as last resort as you lose a lot of Odoo's convenient helpers when using them.

Having an action open a specific view

Window actions automatically determine the view to be used, but sometimes we want an action to open a specific view.

We will create a basic form view for the partner model and make the window action specifically open it.

How to do it...

1. Define the partner minimal form view:

```
<record id="form_all_customers" model="ir.ui.view">
    <field name="name">All customers</field>
    <field name="model">res.partner</field>
    <field name="arch" type="xml">
        <form>
            <group>
                <field name="name" />
            </group>
        </form>
    </field>
</record>
```

2. Tell the action from the previous recipe to use it:

```
<record id="action_all_customers_form"
        model="ir.actions.act_window.view">
    <field name="act_window_id" ref="action_all_customers" />
    <field name="view_id" ref="form_all_customers" />
    <field name="view_mode">form</field>
    <field name="sequence">10</field>
</record>
```

Now if you open your menu and click some partner in the list, you should see the very minimal form we just defined.

How it works...

This time, we used the generic XML code for any type of record that is, the `record` element with the required attributes `id` and `model`. As earlier, the `id` attribute is an arbitrary string that must be unique for your addon. The `model` attribute refers to the name of the model you want to create. Given that we want to create a view, we need to create a record of model `ir.ui.view`. Within this element, you set fields as defined in the model you chose via the `model` attribute. For `ir.ui.view`, the crucial fields are `model` and `arch`. The `model` field contains the model you want to define a view for, while the `arch` field contains the definition of the view itself. We'll come to its contents in a short while.

The `name` field, while not strictly necessary, is helpful when debugging problems with views, so set it to some string that tells you what this view is intended to do. This field's content is not shown to the user, so you can fill in all the technical hints to yourself that you deem sensible. If you set nothing here, you'll get a default containing the model name and view type.

ir.actions.act_window.view

The second record we defined works in unison with `act_window` we defined previously. We know already that by setting the field `view_id` there, we can select which view is used for the first view mode. But given we set the field `view_mode` to the default *tree, form*, `view_id` would have to pick a tree view, but we want to set the form view, which comes second here.

If you find yourself in a situation like this, use the model `ir.actions.act_window.view`, which gives you fine grained control over which views to load for which view type. The first two fields defined here are an example of the generic way to refer to other objects; you keep the element's body empty but add an attribute called `ref` which contains the XML ID of the object you want to reference. So what happens here is that we refer to our action from the previous recipe in the `act_window_id` field, and refer to the view we just created in the `view_id` field. Then, though not strictly necessary, we add a sequence number to position this view assignment relatively to the other view assignments for the same action. This is only relevant if you assign views for different view modes by creating multiple `ir.actions.act_window.view` records.

Once you define the `ir.actions.act_window.view` records, they take precedence over what you filled in the action's `view_mode` field. So with only the above records, you won't see a list at all, but only a form. So you should add another `ir.actions.act_window.view` record pointing to a list view.

Adding content and widgets to a form view

The previous recipe showed how to pick a specific view for an action. Now we'll demonstrate how to make the form we defined previously more useful.

How to do it...

1. Define the form view basic structure:

```xml
<record id="form_all_customers" model="ir.ui.view">
  <field name="name">All customers</field>
  <field name="model">res.partner</field>
  <field name="arch" type="xml">
    <form>
      <!--form content goes here -->
    </form>
  </field>
</record>
```

2. To add a head bar, usually used for action buttons and stage pipeline, add inside the form:

```xml
<header>
  <button type="object"
          name="open_commercial_entity"
          string="Open commercial partner"
          class="oe_highlight" />
</header>
```

3. Add fields to the form, using group tags to visually organize them:

```xml
<group string="Content" name="my_content">
  <field name="name" />
  <field name="category_id" widget="many2many_tags" />
</group>
```

Now the form should display a top bar with a button and two vertically aligned fields.

How it works...

We'll look at the `arch` field of the `ir.ui.view` model. Here, everything that the user sees happens. First, note that views are defined in XML themselves, so you need to pass the attribute `type="xml"` for the arch field, otherwise the parser will be confused. It is also mandatory that your view definition contains well formed XML, otherwise you'll get in trouble when loading this snippet.

Now, we'll walk through the tags used previously and summarize the others that are available.

Form

When you define a form view, it is mandatory that the first element within the `arch` field is a `form` element. This fact is used internally to derive the record's `type` field, which is why you're not supposed to set this field. You'll see this a lot in legacy code though.

The `form` element can have two legacy attributes itself, which are `string` and `version`. In the previous versions of Odoo, those were used to decide on the title you saw in the breadcrumb and to differentiate between the forms written in pre-7.0 style and afterwards, but both can be considered obsolete by now. The title in the breadcrumb is now inferred from the model's `name_get` function, while the version is assumed to be 7.0 or above.

In addition to the elements listed next, you can use arbitrary HTML within the form tag. The algorithm is that every element unknown to Odoo is considered plain HTML and simply passed through to the browser. Be careful with that, as the HTML you fill in can interact with the HTML code the Odoo elements generate, which might distort the rendering.

Header

This element is a container for the elements that should be shown in a form's header, which is rendered as a gray bar. Usually, as in this example, you place action buttons here or a status bar if your model has a state field.

Button

The `button` element is used to allow the user to trigger an action. See the following recipe *Adding buttons to forms* for details.

Group

The `group` element is Odoo's main means for organizing content. Fields placed within a `group` element are rendered with their title, and all the fields within the same group are aligned so that there's also a visual indicator that they belong together. You can also nest the `group` elements; this causes Odoo to render the contained fields in adjacent columns.

In general, you should use this mechanism for all your fields and only revert to other methods (see next) when necessary.

If you assign the attribute `string` on a group, its content will be rendered as a heading for the group.

You should develop the habit of assigning a `name` to every logical group of fields too. This name is not visible to the user, but very helpful when we override views in the following recipes. Keep the name unique within a form definition to avoid confusion about which group you refer to.

Field

In order to actually show and manipulate data, your form should contain some `field` elements. They have one mandatory attribute `name`, which refers to the field's name in the model. So above, we offer the user to edit the partner's name and categories. If we only want to show one of them, without the user being able to edit the field, we set the attribute `readonly` to `1` or `True`. This attribute actually may contain a small subset of Python code, so `readonly="2>1"` would make the field read only too. The same applies to the attribute `invisible`, that you use to have the value read from the database, but not shown to the user. We'll see later in which situations we want to have that.

> Take care not to put the same field twice on your form. Odoo is not designed to support this, and the result will be that all but one of those fields will behave as if they were empty.

You must have noticed the attribute `widget` on the categories field. It defines how the data in the field is supposed to be presented to the user. Every type of field has its standard widget, so you don't have to explicitly choose a widget. But several types provide multiple ways of representation, in which case you might opt for something else than the default. As a complete list of available widgets would exceed the scope of this recipe, you'll have to resort to Odoo's source code to try them out and consult *Chapter 15, Web Client Development* for details on how to make your own.

General attributes

On most elements (this includes `group`, `field`, and `button`), you can set the attributes `attrs` and `groups`. While `attrs` is discussed next, the `groups` attribute gives you the possibility to show some elements only to the members of certain groups. Simply put the group's XML ID (separated by commas for multiple groups) in the attribute, and the element will be hidden for everyone who is not a member of at least one of the groups mentioned.

Other tags

There are situations where you might want to deviate from the strict layout groups prescribed. A good example is, if you want the `name` field of a record to be rendered as a heading, the field's label would interfere with the appearance. In this case, don't put your field into a `group` element, but for example, into the plain HTML `h1` element. Then before the `h1` element, put a `label` element with the `for` attribute set to your field name:

```
<label for="name" />
<h1><field name="name" /></h1>
```

This will be rendered with the field's content as a big heading, but the field's name only small above. That's basically what the standard partner form does.

If you need a line break within a group, use the `newline` element. It's always empty.

```
<newline />
```

Another useful element is the `footer` element. When you open a form as a popup, this is the good place to place the action buttons. It will be rendered as a gray bar too, analogous to the `header` element.

There's more...

Since form views are basically HTML with some extensions, Odoo also makes extensive use of CSS classes. Two very useful ones are `oe_read_only` and `oe_edit_only` – they cause elements with these classes applied to be visible only in read/view mode or only in edit mode. So to have the label visible only in edit mode:

```
<label for="name" class="oe_edit_only" />
```

Further, the `form` element can have attributes `create`, `edit`, and `delete`. If you set one of those to `false`, the corresponding action won't be available for this form. Without this being explicitly set, the availability of the action is inferred from the user's permissions. Note that this is purely for straightening the UI; don't use this for security.

See also

The widgets described earlier already offer a lot of functionality, but sooner or later you will encounter cases where they don't do exactly what you want. For defining your own widgets, refer to *Chapter 15, Web Client Development*.

Adding buttons to forms

We added a button in the previous form, but there are quite different types of buttons to use. This recipe will add another button; also put the following code in to the previous recipe's `header` element.

How to do it...

Add a button referring to an action:

```
<button type="action" name="%(base.action_partner_category_form)d"
string="Open partner categories" />
```

How it works...

The button's type attribute determines the semantics of the other fields, so we'll first look into the possible values:

▶ `action`: This makes the button call an action as defined in the **ir.actions.*** namespace. The `name` attribute needs to contain the action's database id, which you can conveniently look up with a python format string containing the XML ID of the action in question.

▶ `object`: This calls a method of the current model. The `name` attribute contains the function's name. The function should have the signature `@api.multi` and will act on the currently viewed record.

▶ `workflow`: This sends a workflow signal to the current record. The `name` attribute needs to contain the signal's name. Use the `states` attribute to make the workflow buttons only available in states where they actually do something, that is, in states that have transitions triggered by the signal in question.

The `string` attribute is used to assign the text the user sees.

There's more...

Use CSS classes `btn-primary` to render a button that is highlighted (currently blue) and `btn-default` to render a normal button. This is commonly used for the cancel buttons in wizards or to offer secondary actions in a visually unobtrusive way.

The call with a button of type **object** can return a dictionary describing an action, which will then be executed on the client side. This way you can implement multi screen wizards or just open some other record.

You can also have content within the `button` tag, replacing the `string` attribute. This is commonly used in button boxes as described in the recipe *Document style forms*.

Passing parameters to forms and actions: Context

Internally, every method in Odoo has access to a dictionary called **context** that is propagated from every action to the methods involved in delivering that action. The UI also has access to it and can be modified in various ways by setting values in the context. In this recipe, we'll explore some of the applications of this mechanism by toying with the language, default values, and implicit filters.

Getting ready

While not strictly necessary, this recipe will be more fun if you install the French language, in case you didn't start out with this language in the first place. Consult *Chapter 11, Internationalization*, for how to do this. If you have a French database, change **fr_FR** to some other language; **en_US** will do for English. Also, click the button **Not archived** on one of your customers in order to archive it and verify that this partner doesn't show up any more in the list.

How to do it...

1. Create a new action, very similar to the one from the first recipe:

```
<act_window id="action_all_customers_fr"
            name="Tous les clients"
            res_model="res.partner"
            domain="[('customer', '=', True)]"
            context="{'lang': 'fr_FR', 'default_lang': 'fr_FR',
                'active_test': False}" />
```

2. Add a menu that calls this action. This is left as an exercise for the reader.

When you open this menu, the views will show up in French, and if you create a new partner, she will have French as the preselected language. A less obvious difference is that you will also see the partner you deactivated earlier.

How it works...

The context dictionary is populated from several sources. First, some values from the current user's record (lang and tz, for the user's language and the user's timezone) are read, then there are addons that add keys for their own purposes. Further, the UI adds keys about which model and which record we're busy with at the moment (active_id, active_ids, active_model). And as seen previously, we can also add our own keys in actions. Those are merged together and passed to the underlying server functions, and also to the client side UI.

So by setting the lang context key, we force the display language to be French. You will note that this doesn't change the whole UI language, which is because only the list view that we open lies within the scope of this context. The rest of the UI was loaded already with another context that contained the user's original language. But if you open a record in this list view, it will be presented in French too, and if you open some linked record on the form or press a button that executes an action, the language will be propagated too.

By setting `default_lang`, we set a default value for every record created within the scope of this context. The general pattern is `default_$fieldname: my_default_value`, which enables you to set default values for the partners newly created in this case. Given that our menu is about customers, it might have made sense to also set `default_customer: True` to have the **Customer** field checked by default. But this is a model wide default for `res.partner` anyway, so this wouldn't have changed anything. For scalar fields, the syntax for this is as you would write it in Python code – string fields go in quotes, numbers just like that, and boolean fields are either `True` or `False`. For relational fields, the syntax is slightly more complicated – refer to *Chapter 9, Module Data*, for how to write those. Note that the default values set in the context override the default values set in the model definition, so you can have different default values in different situations.

The last key is `active_test`, which has very special semantics. For every model that has a field called **active**, Odoo automatically filters out the records where this field is `False`. This is why the partner where you unchecked this field disappeared from the list. By setting this key, we can suppress this behavior.

 This is useful for the UI in its own right, but even more useful in your Python code when you need to be sure some operation is applied to all the records, not just the active ones.

There's more...

While defining a context you have access to some variables, the most important one being `uid`, which evaluates to the current user's ID. You'll need this for setting the default filters (see the next recipe). Further, you have access to the *function* `context_today` and the *variable* `current_date`, where the first is a date object representing the current date as seen from the user's time zone and the latter the current date as seen in UTC, formatted as `YYYY-MM-DD`. For setting a default for a date field to the current date by default, use `current_date` and, for default filters, use `context_today()`.

Further, you can do some date calculations with a subset of Python's `datetime`, `time`, and `relativedelta` classes.

Why the repeated talk about 'a subset of Python'? For various technical reasons, domains have to be evaluated as well on the client side as on the server side. Server side evaluation existed earlier, there full Python was available (but is restricted by now too for security reasons). When client side evaluation was introduced, the best option in order not to break the whole system was to implement a part of Python in JavaScript. So there is a small JavaScript Python interpreter built into Odoo which works great for simple expressions, and that is usually enough.

Beware about variables in the context in conjunction with the `<act_window />` shortcut. Those are evaluated at installation time, which is nearly never what you want. If you need variables in your context, use `<record />` syntax.

The same way that we added some context keys in our action, we can do with buttons. This causes the function or action the button calls to be run in the context given and by now you know some of the tricks you can pull this way.

Most form element attributes that are evaluated as Python also have access to the context dictionary. The attributes `invisible` and `readonly` are such attributes. So in cases where you want an element to show up in a form sometimes, but not at other times, you set the `invisible` attribute to `context.get('my_key')`, and for actions that lead to the case where the field is supposed to be invisible, you set the context key `my_key: True`. Such a strategy enables you to adapt your form without having to rewrite it for different occasions.

You can also set a context on relational fields, which influences how the field is loaded. By setting the keys `form_view_ref` or `tree_view_ref` to the XML ID of a view, you can select a specific view for this field. This is necessary when you have multiple views of the same type for the same object. Without this key you get the view with the lowest sequence number, which might not always be desirable.

See also

One of the very useful applications of the context is to set default search filters as described in the recipe *Search views*.

Defining filters on record lists: Domain

We've already seen the first example of a domain in the first action, which was `[('customer', '=', True)]`. It is a very common use case when you need to display a subset of all available records from an action, or to allow only a subset of possible records to be the target of a many2one relation. The way to describe these filters in Odoo is called a domain. This recipe illustrates how to use such a domain to display a selection of partners.

How to do it...

To display a subset of partners from your action, you need to perform the following steps:

1. Add an action for non-French speaking customers:

```
<record id="action_my_customers" model="ir.actions.act_window">
    <field name="name">
        All customers who don't speak French
    </field>
    <field name="res_model">res.partner</field>
    <field name="domain">
        [('customer', '=', True), ('user_id', '=', uid), ('lang',
'!=', 'fr_FR')]
    </field>
</record>
```

2. Add an action for the customers who are customers or suppliers:

```
<record id="action_customers_or_suppliers"
        model="ir.actions.act_window">
    <field name="name">Customers or suppliers</field>
    <field name="res_model">res.partner</field>
    <field name="domain">
        ['|', ('customer', '=', True), ('supplier', '=', True)]
    </field>
</record>
```

3. Add menus that call this action. This is left as an exercise for the reader.

How it works...

The simplest form of a domain is a list of 3-tuples that contains a field name of the model in question as string in the first element, an operator as string in the second element, and the value the field is to be checked against as the third element. This is what we did in the first action, and this is interpreted as: All those conditions have to apply to the records we're interested in. This actually is a shortcut, because the domains know the two prefix operators & and |, where & is the default. So, in formal form, the first domain would be written as `['&', '&', ('customer', '=', True), ('user_id', '=', uid), ('lang', '!=', 'fr_FR')]`.

While a bit hard to read for bigger expressions, the advantage of prefix operators is that their scope is rigidly defined, which saves you having to worry about operator precedence and brackets. It's always the following two expressions: The first & applies to `'&'`, `('customer', '=', True)`, `('user_id', '=', uid)` as the first operand and `('lang', '!=', 'fr_FR')` as the second. Then, the second & applies to `('customer', '=', True)` as the first operand and `('user_id', '=', uid)` as the second.

In the second action, we have to write out the full form because we need the | operator.

There is also a ! operator for negation, but, given logical equivalences and negated comparison operators such as != and not in, it is not really necessary. Note that this is a unary prefix operator, so it only applies to the following expression in the domain and not to everything that follows.

Note that the right operand doesn't need to be a fixed value when you write a domain for a window action or other client side domains. You can use the same minimal Python as described earlier for contexts, so you can write filters such as *changed last week*, *my partners*, and so on.

There's more...

The preceding domains work only on fields of the model itself, while we often need to filter based on the properties of linked records. To do this, you can use the notation also used in @api.depends definitions or related fields: create a dotted path from the current model to the model you want to filter for. To search partners which have a sales person that is a member of a group starting with the letter G, you would use the domain [('user_id.groups_id.name', '=like', 'G%')]. The path can be arbitrarily long, so you only have to take care that there are relation fields between the current model and the model you want to filter for.

Operators

The following table lists the available operators and their semantics:

Operator (equivalent)	Semantics
=, != (<>)	Exact match, not equal (deprecated notation of not equal)
in, not in	Checks if the value is one of the values named in a list in the right operand, given as a Python list: [('uid', 'in', [1, 2, 3])]
<, <=	Greater than, greater or equal
>, >=	Less than, less or equal
like, not like	Checks if the right operand is contained (substring) in the value
ilike, not ilike	The same as the preceding one but case insensitive
=like, =ilike	You can search for patterns here: % matches any string and _ matches one character. This is the equivalent of PostgreSQL's like.
child_of	For models with a parent_id field, this searches for children of the right operand, with the right operand included in the results.
=?	Evaluates to true if the right operand is false, otherwise it behaves like "= -" this is useful when you generate domains programmatically and want to filter for some value if it is set, but ignore it otherwise.

Pitfalls

This all works fine for traditional fields, but a notorious problem is searching for the value of a non-stored function field. It's a problem that people often omit the search function, while this is simple enough to fix by providing the search function in your own code as described in *Chapter 4, Application Models*.

Another issue that might baffle the developers is Odoo's behavior when searching through **one2many** or **many2many** fields with a negative operator. Imagine you have a partner with a tag A and you search for `[('category_id.name', '!=', 'B')]`. Your partner shows up in the result and this is what you expected. But if you add the tag B to this partner, it still shows up in your results, because for the search algorithm it is enough that there is one linked record (A in this case) that does not fulfill the criterion. Now if you remove the tag A so that B is the only tag, the partner will be filtered out. If you also remove the tag B so that the partner has no tags, it is still filtered out, because conditions on the linked records presuppose the existence of this record. In other situations though, this is the behavior you want, so it is not really an option to change the standard behavior. In case you need a different behavior here, provide a search function of your own that interprets the negation the way you need.

 A small gotcha is that people forget they are writing XML files when it is about domains. You need to escape the less-than operator. Searching for records that have been created before today would have to be `[('create_date', '&lt;', current_date)]` in XML.

See also

If you ever need to manipulate a domain you didn't create programmatically, use the utility functions provided in `openerp.osv.expression`. Especially `is_leaf`, `normalize_domain`, `AND`, and `OR` will allow you to combine domains exactly the way Odoo does it. Don't do this yourself, because there are many corner cases you have to take into account and it's very probable you'll overlook one.

For the standard application of domains, see the recipe *Search views*.

List views

After having spent quite some time on the form view, we'll now have a quick look at how to define list views. Internally, they are called tree views in some places and list views in others, but, given there is another construction within the Odoo view framework called tree, we'll stick to the wording **list** here.

How to do it...

1. Define your list view:

```
<record id="tree_all_customers" model="ir.ui.view">
    <field name="model">res.partner</field>
    <field name="arch" type="xml">
        <tree colors="blue: customer and supplier;
                      green:customer;
                      red: supplier">
            <field name="name" />
            <field name="customer" invisible="1" />
            <field name="supplier" invisible="1" />
        </tree>
    </field>
</record>
```

2. Tell the action from the first recipe to use it:

```
<record id="action_all_customers_tree" model="ir.actions.act_
window.view">
    <field name="act_window_id" ref="action_all_customers" />
    <field name="view_id" ref="tree_all_customers" />
    <field name="sequence">5</field>
</record>
```

How it works...

You already know most of what happens here. We define a view, this time of type `tree`, and attach it to our action with an `ir.actions.act_window.view` element. So the only thing left to discuss is the `tree` element and its semantics. With a list you don't have many design choices, so the only valid children of this element are the `field` and `button` elements. They follow the same semantics as earlier, save for the fact that there are a lot less choices for widgets – the only really interesting choices are `progressbar`, `many2onebutton`, and `handle`. The first two behave like their form namesakes. `handle` is specific to list views. It is meant for integer fields and renders a drag handle that the user can use to drag a row to a different position in the list, thereby updating the field's value. This is useful for sequence or priority fields.

What is new here is the `colors` attribute in the `tree` element. It contains rules which font color is chosen for the row, given in the form `color: Python code`, separated by semicolons. The first match wins, so what the previous view does is to render partners who are both supplier and customer in blue, customers in green, and suppliers in red. In your Python code, you can use the fields you named in the view definition, which is why we have to pull the `customer` and `supplier` fields too. We made them invisible because we only need the data and don't want to bother our users with those two extra columns. The possible colors are those that HTML defines, so you can either use names or a hex string.

There's more...

For numeric fields, you can add an attribute `sum` that causes this column to be summed up with the text you set in the attribute as a tooltip. Less common are the attributes `avg`, `min`, and `max`, that display the average, minimum, and maximum respectively. Note that these four only work on the records currently visible, so you might want to adjust the action's `limit` (see above) in order for the user to see all the records immediately.

Analogous to the `colors` attribute in the `tree` element is the `fonts` attribute. With it, you can choose to have a record be `bold`, `italic`, or `underline` (sic). On the right part of a font definition, you can run the same Python expressions as previously. There is a subtle difference though. Here, the last definition wins if multiple expressions apply to a row.

A very interesting attribute for the `tree` element is `editable`. If you set this to **top** or **bottom**, the list behaves entirely different than before. Without it, clicking a row opens a form view for the row. With it, clicking a row makes it editable inline, with the visible fields rendered as form fields. This is particularly useful in embedded list views, which are discussed later in this chapter. The choice is if new lines will be added on the top or bottom of the list.

By default, records are ordered according to the `_order` property of the displayed model. The user can change ordering by clicking a column header, but you can also set a different initial order by setting the `default_order` property in the tree element. The syntax is the same as in `_order`.

 Ordering is often a source of frustration for new developers. As Odoo lets PostgreSQL do the work here, you can only order by fields that PostgreSQL knows about and also only the fields that live in the same database table. So if you want to order by a function or a related field, be sure to set `store=True`. If you need to order by a field inherited from another model, declare a stored related field.

The `create`, `edit`, and `delete` attributes of the `tree` element work the same as for the `form` element described earlier. They also determine the available controls if the `editable` attribute is set.

Search views

When opening your list view, you'll notice the search field to the upper right. If you type something there, you get suggestions about what to search for and there is also a set of predefined filters to choose from. This recipe will walk you through how to define those suggestions and options.

How to do it...

1. Define your search view:

```
<record id="search_all_customers" model="ir.ui.view">
    <field name="model">res.partner</field>
    <field name="arch" type="xml">
        <search>
            <field name="name" />
            <field name="category_id"
                    filter_domain="[('category_id', 'child_of',
self)]" />
            <field name="bank_ids" widget="many2one" />
            <filter name="suppliers"
                    string="Suppliers"
                    domain="[('supplier', '=', True)]" />
        </search>
    </field>
</record>
```

2. Tell your action to use it:

```
<record id="action_all_customers" model="ir.actions.act_window">
    <field name="name">All customers</field>
    <field name="res_model">res.partner</field>
    <field name="domain">[('customer', '=', True)]</field>
    <field name="search_view_id" ref="search_all_customers" />
</record>
```

When you type something in the search bar now, you'll be offered to search for this term in the name, categories, and bank accounts fields. If your term happens to be a substring of a bank account number in your system, you'll even be offered to search exactly for this bank account.

How it works...

In the case of `name`, we simply listed the field as the one to be offered to the user to search for. We left the semantics at the defaults, which is a substring search for character fields.

For categories, we do something more interesting. By default, your search term applied to a many2many field triggers `name_search`, which would be a substring search in the categorie's names in this case. But depending on your category structure, it can be very convenient to search for partners who have the category you're interested in or a child of it. Think about a main category *Newsletter subscribers* with sub categories *Weekly newsletter, Monthly newsletter*, and a couple of other newsletter types. Searching for *newsletter subscribers* with the preceding search view definition will give you everyone who is subscribed to any of those newsletters in one go, which is a lot more convenient than searching for every single type and combining the results.

The `filter_domain` attribute can contain an arbitrary domain, so you're neither restricted to searching for the same field you named in the `name` attribute, nor to using only one term. The variable `self` is what the user filled in, and also the only variable you can use here. A more elaborate example from the default search view for partners is:

```
<field name="name" filter_domain="['|','|',
('display_name','ilike',self),('ref','=',self),('email','ilike',se
lf)]"/>
```

This allows the user to not even think a lot about what to search for; just type some letters, hit *Enter*, and, with a bit of luck, one of the fields mentioned contains the string we're looking for.

For the `bank_ids` field, we used another trick. The type of a field not only decides the default way of searching for the user's input, it also defines the way Odoo presents the suggestions. And given `many2one` fields are the only ones that offer auto completion, we force Odoo to do that, even though `bank_ids` is a `one2many` field by setting the `widget` attribute. Without this, the offer would be simply to search in this field, without completion suggestions. The same applies to `many2many` fields. Note that every field with a `many2one` widget set will trigger a search on its model for every one of the user's keystrokes – don't use too many of them.

You should also put the most used fields to the top, because the first field is what is searched if the user just types something and hits *Enter*. It also seems worth mentioning that the search bar is very well usable with the keyboard; select a suggestion by pressing the down arrow and open a `many2one`'s completion suggestion by pressing the right arrow. If you educate your users in this and pay attention to a sensible ordering of fields in the search view, they will be much more efficient than by typing something first, grabbing the mouse, and selecting some option.

The `filter` element creates a button that adds the content of the filter's `domain` attribute to the search domain. You should add a logical internal `name` and a `string` attribute to describe the filter to your users.

There's more...

You can group the filters with the `group` tag, which causes them to be rendered slightly closer together than the other filters, but this has semantic implications too. If you put multiple filters in the same group and activate more than one of them, their domains will be combined with the operator `|`, while filters and fields not in the same group are combined with the operator `&`. Cases where you want disjunction for your filters are when they filter for mutually exclusive sets, in which case selecting both of them always would lead to an empty result set. Within the same group, you can achieve the same effect with the `separator` element.

Note that if the user fills in multiple queries for the same field, they will be combined with `|` too, so you don't need to worry about that.

As well as the `field`, the `filter` element can have a `context` attribute whose content will be merged with the current context and eventual other context attributes in the search view. This is essential for views that support grouping (see recipes about kanban and graph views), because the resulting context determines the field(s) to be grouped by with the key `group_by`. We'll look into the details of grouping in the appropriate recipes, but the context has other uses too. For example, you can hide columns depending on a context value by setting the `field` element's `invisible` attribute in the list view to something like the following:

```
invisible="not context.get('show_col1')"
```

You can use a filter to switch this column on or off. Or you could write a function field that returns different values depending on the context, then you can change the values by activating a filter.

The search view itself also responds to context keys. In a very similar way to default values when creating records, you can pass defaults for a search view via the context. If we had set a context of `{'search_default_supplier': 1}` in our previous action, the suppliers filter would have been preselected in the search view. This works only if the filter has a name though, which is why you should always set it. To set defaults for fields in the search view, use `search_default_$fieldname`.

Further, the `field` and the `filter` elements can have a groups property with the same semantics as in the form views in order to make the element only visible for certain groups.

See also

For details about manipulating the context, see the recipe *Passing parameters to forms and actions: Context*.

Changing existing views: View inheritance

Up until now, we ignored the existing views and declared completely new ones. While this is didactically sensible, you'll rarely be in situations where you want to define a new view for an existing model. What you'll rather want to do is to slightly modify the existing views, be it to simply have it show a field you added to the model in your addon, or to customize it to your needs or your customer's.

In this recipe, we'll change the default partner form to show the record's last modification date and also allow searching for that. Then we'll also show this column in the partners' list view.

How to do it...

1. Inject the field in the default form view:

```xml
<record id="view_partner_form" model="ir.ui.view">
    <field name="model">res.partner</field>
    <field name="inherit_id" ref="base.view_partner_form" />
    <field name="arch" type="xml">
        <field name="website" position="after">
            <field name="write_date" />
        </field>
    </field>
</record>
```

2. Add the field to the default search view:

```xml
<record id="view_res_partner_filter" model="ir.ui.view">
    <field name="model">res.partner</field>
    <field name="inherit_id" ref="base.view_res_partner_filter" />
    <field name="arch" type="xml">
        <xpath expr="." position="inside">
            <field name="write_date" />
        </xpath>
    </field>
</record>
```

3. Add the field to the default list view:

```xml
<record id="view_partner_tree" model="ir.ui.view">
    <field name="model">res.partner</field>
    <field name="inherit_id" ref="base.view_partner_tree" />
    <field name="arch" type="xml">
        <field name="email" position="before">
            <field name="write_date" />
        </field>
    </field>
</record>
```

After updating your module, you should see the extra field **Last updated on** beneath the website field on the partner form. When you type in something that looks like a date (a digit or two) in the search box, it should propose to search for partners last modified on this date, and in the partner's list view, you should see the modification date left of the e-mail column.

How it works...

The crucial field here is, as you probably have guessed, `inherit_id`. You need to pass it the XML ID of the view you want to modify (inherit from), and the `arch` field then contains instructions on how to modify the existing XML nodes within the view you're inheriting from. You actually should think of the whole process as quite simple XML processing, because all the semantic parts come only a lot later.

The most canonic instruction within the `arch` field of an inherited view is the `field` element, which has the required attributes `name` and `position`. Because you can have every field only once on a form, the name already uniquely identifies a field, and with the `position` attribute, we can place whatever we put within the field element either `before` (1), `inside` (2), or `after` (3) the field we named. The default is **inside**, but for readability you should always name the position you mean. Remember that we're not talking semantics here; this is about the position in the XML tree relative to the field we have named. How this will be rendered afterwards is a completely different matter.

Example 2 above demonstrates a different approach. The `xpath` element selects the first element matching the XPath expression named in the attribute `expr`. Also, here the `position` attribute tells the processor where to put the `xpath` element's contents.

XPath might look somewhat scary, but is a very efficient means of selecting the node you need to work on. Take the time to look through some simple expressions, it's worth it. Probably in the tutorials you'll find, you'll stumble upon the term **context node** to which some expressions are relative. In Odoo's view inheritance, that's always the root element of the view you're inheriting from.

For all the other elements found in the `arch` field of an inheriting view, the processor looks for the first element with the same node name and matching attributes (with the attribute position excluded, as this is part of the instruction). Use this only in cases where it is very improbable that this combination is not unique, like a group element combined with a name attribute.

 Note that you can have as many instruction elements within the arch field as you need. We only used one per inherited view because there's no more we currently want to change.

There's more...

The position attribute has two other possible values: `replace` and `attributes`. Using `replace` causes the selected element to be replaced with the content of the instruction element. Consequently, if you don't have any content, the selected element is simply removed. In the list or form view above would cause the email field to be removed.

```
<field name="email" position="replace" />
```

Removing fields can cause other inheriting views to break and several similarly ugly side effects, so avoid that if possible. If you really need to remove fields, do so in a view which comes late in order of evaluation (see next).

Using `attributes` has a very different semantics from all of the above. The processor then expects the element to contain the `attribute` elements with a `name` attribute. Those elements will then be used to set attributes on the selected element. If you want to heed the warning from above, you'd better set the `invisible` attribute to 1 for the email field:

```
<field name="email" position="attributes">
    <attribute name="invisible">1</attribute>
</field>
```

Order of evaluation in view inheritance

Because we have only one parent view and one inheriting view, we don't run into any problems with conflicting view overrides. When you have installed a couple of modules, you'll find a lot of overrides for the partner form. This is all fine as long as they change different things in a view, but there are occasions where it is important to understand how the overriding works in order to avoid conflicts. Direct descendants of a view are evaluated in ascending order of their `priority` field, so views with a lower priority are applied first. Every step of inheritance is applied to the result of the first, so if a view with priority 3 changes a field and another one with priority 5 removes it, things are fine, but they break if the priorities are reversed.

Then you can also inherit from a view that is itself an inheriting view. In this case, the second level inheriting view is applied to the result of the view it inherits from. So, if you have four views A, B, C, and D, where A is a standalone form, B and C inherit from A, and D inherits from B, the order of evaluation is A, B, D, C. Use this to enforce an order without having to rely on priorities; that's safer in general. Especially if some inheriting view adds a field and you need to apply changes to this field, inherit from the inheriting view and not from the standalone one.

 This kind of inheritance always works on the complete XML tree from the original view, with modifications from the previous inheriting views applied.

See also

For inheriting views, a very useful and not very well known field is `groups_id`. This field causes the inheritance to take place only if the user requesting the parent view is member of one of the groups mentioned there. This can save you a lot of work when adapting the user interface for different levels of access, because with inheritance you can have more complex operations than just showing or not showing the elements based on group membership, as is possible with the `groups` attribute on form elements as discussed earlier. You can for example remove elements if the user is member of some group (which is the inverse of what the `groups` attribute does), but also some quite elaborate tricks like adding attributes based on group membership, think about simple things like making a field read only for certain groups, or more interesting ones like using different widgets for different groups.

What was described here is the case if the `mode` field of the original view is set to primary, while the inheriting views have mode extension, which is the default. We'll look into the case that `mode` of an inheriting view is set to **primary** later, where the rules are slightly different.

Document-style forms

In this recipe, we'll review some design guidelines in order to present a uniform user experience.

How to do it...

1. Start your form with a header element:

```
<header>
    <button name="do_something_with_the_record"
            string="Do something" type="object" class="oe_
highlight" />
    <button name="do_something_else" string="Second action" />
    <field name="state" widget="statusbar" />
</header>
```

2. Then add a sheet element for content:

```
<sheet>
```

3. Put some prominent field(s) first:

```
<div class="oe_left oe_title">
    <label for="name" />
    <h1>
        <field name="name" />
    </h1>
</div>
```

4. Put buttons that link to resources relevant for the object in its own box (if applicable):

```
<div class="oe_right oe_button_box" name="buttons">
    <button name="open_something_interesting"
        string="Open some linked record"
        type="object" class="oe_stat_button" />
```

5. Add your content, possibly within a notebook if there are a lot of fields:

```
<group name="some_fields">
    <field name="field1" />
    <field name="field2" />
</group>
```

6. After the sheet, add the chatter widget (if applicable):

```
</sheet>
<div class="oe_chatter">
    <field name="message_follower_ids" widget="mail_followers"/>
    <field name="message_ids" widget="mail_thread"/>
</div>
```

How it works...

The header should contain buttons that execute actions on the object the user currently sees. Use the oe_highlight class to make the buttons visually stand out (that's bright blue at the time of writing), which is a good way to guide the user regarding which would be the most logical action to execute at the moment. Try to have all the highlighted buttons to the left of the non-highlighted buttons and hide the buttons not relevant in the current state (if applicable). If the model has a state, show it in the header using the statusbar widget. This will be rendered right aligned in the header.

The sheet element is rendered as a stylized sheet and the most important fields should be the first thing the user sees when glancing at it. Use the oe_title and oe_left classes to have them rendered in a prominent place (floating left with slightly adjusted font sizes at the time of writing).

If there are other records of interest concerning the record the user currently sees (like the partner's invoices on a partner form), put them in an element with the oe_right and oe_button_box classes; this aligns the buttons in it to the right. On the buttons themselves, use the oe_stat_button class to enforce a uniform rendering of the buttons.

 Even in case you don't like this layout, stick to the element and class names described here, and adjust what you need with CSS and possibly JavaScript. This will make the user interface more compatible with the existing addons and allow you to integrate better with the core addons.

Dynamic form elements using attrs

So far, we have only looked into changing forms depending on the user's groups (the groups attribute on elements and the groups_id field on inherited views), but nothing more. This recipe will show you how to change forms based on the content of some fields in it.

How to do it...

1. Define an attribute attrs on some form element:

    ```
    <field name="parent_id"
           attrs="{'invisible': [('is_company', '=', True)],
           'required': [('is_company', '=', False)]}" />
    ```

2. Take care that all the fields you refer to are available on your form:

    ```
    <field name="is_company" invisible="True" />
    ```

This will make the field parent_id invisible if the partner is a company, and required if it's not a company.

How it works...

The attrs attribute contains a dictionary with the keys invisible, required, and readonly (all of them optional). The values are domains that may refer to the fields existing on the form (and really only those, so no dotted paths), and the whole dictionary is evaluated according to the rules for client side Python described earlier. So for example, you can access the context in the right hand operand.

There's more...

While this mechanism is quite straightforward for the scalar fields, it's less obvious how to handle the one2many and many2many fields. In fact, in standard Odoo you can't do much with those fields within an attrs attribute. But if you only need to check if such a field is empty or not, use [[6, False, []]] as your right hand operand.

Embedded views

When you show a one2many or a many2many field on a form, you don't have much control over how it is rendered up to now if you haven't used one of the specialized widgets. Also, in the case of many2one fields, it is desirable sometimes to be able to influence the way the linked record is opened. In this recipe, we'll look into how to define private views for those fields.

How to do it...

1. Define your field as usual, but don't close the tag:

```
<field name="child_ids">
```

2. Simply write the view definition(s) into the tag:

```
<tree>
    <field name="name" />
    <field name="email" />
    <field name="phone" />
</tree>
<form>
    <group>
        <field name="name" />
        <field name="function" />
    </group>
</form>
```

3. Close the tag:

```
</field>
```

How it works...

When Odoo loads a form, it first checks for reference fields if there are views embedded as outlined previously. Those embedded views can have the exact same elements as views we defined before. Only if Odoo doesn't find an embedded view of some type, does it use the model's default view of this type.

There's more...

While embedded views seem like a great feature in the first place, they complicate view inheritance a lot. For example, as soon as embedded views are involved, the field names are not guaranteed to be unique and you'll usually have to use some quite elaborate XPaths to select elements within an embedded view.

So, in general, you should better served defining the standalone views and use the keys `form_view_ref` and `tree_view_ref` described earlier.

Kanban views

Up until now, we have presented the user with a list of records that can be opened to show a form. While those lists are efficient when presenting a lot of information, they tend to be rather dull given the lack of design possibilities. In this recipe, we'll have a look at kanban views, which allow us to present lists of records in a more appealing way.

How to do it...

1. Define a view of type kanban:

```
<record id="kanban_all_customers" model="ir.ui.view">
    <field name="model">res.partner</field>
    <field name="arch" type="xml">
        <kanban>
```

2. List the fields you're going to use in your view:

```
<field name="name" />
<field name="supplier" />
<field name="customer" />
```

3. Do some design:

```
<templates>
    <t t-name="kanban-box">
        <div class="oe_kanban_card">
            <a type="open">
                <field name="name" />
            </a>
            <t t-if="record.supplier.raw_value or
                record.customer.raw_value">
                is
                <t t-if="record.customer.raw_value">
                    a customer
                    <t t-if="record.supplier.
                        raw_value"> and </t>
                </t>
                <t t-if="record.supplier.raw_value">
                    a supplier
                </t>
            </t>
        </div>
    </t>
</templates>
```

4. Close all the tags:

    ```
            </kanban>
          </field>
        </record>
    ```

5. Add this view to one of your actions. This is left as an exercise for the reader.

How it works...

We need to give a list of fields to load in (2) in order to be able to access them later. The content of the `templates` element must be a single `t` element with the attribute `t-name` set to the value `kanban-box`.

What you write inside this element will be repeated for each record, with special semantics for the `t` elements and the `t-*` attributes. For details about that, refer to *Chapter 15, Web Client Development*, and the recipe *Client side QWeb* because, technically, kanban views are a repetition of QWeb templates.

There are a few modifications which are peculiar to kanban views. You have access to the variables `instance`, `read_only_mode`, `record`, and `widget`. Fields can be accessed by using `record.fieldname`, which is an object with the properties `value` and `raw_value`, where `value` is the field's value formatted in a way presentable to the user and `raw_value` is the field's value as it comes from the database.

> Many2many fields make an exception here. You'll only get an id list via the `record` variable. For a user readable representation, you must use the `field` element.

Note the `type` attribute of the link at the top of the template. This attribute makes Odoo generate a link that opens the record in the view mode (open) or in the edit mode (edit), or it deletes the record (delete). The `type` attribute can also be **object** or **action**, which will render links that call a function of the model or an action. In both cases, you need to supplement the attributes for buttons in form views as outlined earlier. Instead of the a element, you can also use the `button` element; the `type` attribute has the same semantics there.

There's more...

There are a few more helper functions worth mentioning. If you need to generate a pseudo-random color for some element, use the function `kanban_color(some_variable)`, which will return a CSS class that sets the `background` and `color` properties. This is usually used in the `t-att-class` elements.

If you want to display an image stored in a binary field, use `kanban_image(modelname, fieldname, record.id.raw_value)`, which returns a data URI if you included the field in your fields list and the field is set, a placeholder if the field is not set, or a URL that makes Odoo stream the field's contents if you didn't include it in your fields list. Do not include the field in the fields list if you need to display a lot of records simultaneously or you expect very big images. Usually, you'd use this in a `t-att-src` attribute of an `img` element.

For arbitrary length text fields, consider using `kanban_text_ellipsis(yourstring, size)`, which crops the string to the given size and adds an ellipsis (. . .).

Show kanban cards in columns according to their state

This recipe shows you how to setup a kanban view where the user can drag and drop a record from one column to the other, thereby pushing the record in question into another state.

Getting ready

Now and in the rest of this chapter, we'll make use of the project module here as it defines models that lend themselves better to date and state based views than the ones defined in the base module. So before proceeding, add `project` to the dependencies list of your addon.

How to do it...

1. Define a kanban view for tasks:

```xml
<record id="kanban_tasks" model="ir.ui.view">
    <field name="model">project.task</field>
    <field name="arch" type="xml">
        <kanban default_group_by="stage_id">
            <field name="stage_id" />
            <field name="name" />
            <templates>
                <t t-name="kanban-box">
                    <div class="oe_kanban_card">
                        <field name="name" />
                    </div>
                </t>
            </templates>
        </kanban>
    </field>
</record>
```

2. Add a menu and an action using this view. This is left as an exercise for the reader.

How it works...

Kanban views support grouping, which allows you to display records that have the group field in common in the same column. This is commonly used for a `state` or `stage_id` field, because it allows the user to change this field's value for a record by simply dragging it into another column. Set the attribute `default_group_by` on the `kanban` element to the name of the field you want to group by in order to make use of this functionality.

There's more...

If not defined in the dedicated attribute, any search filter can add grouping by setting a context key named `group_by` to the field name(s) to group by.

Calendar views

This recipe walks you through how to display and edit information about dates and durations in your records in a visual way.

How to do it...

1. Define a calendar view:

```xml
<record id="calendar_project_task" model="ir.ui.view">
    <field name="model">project.task</field>
    <field name="arch" type="xml">
        <calendar date_start="date_start" date_stop="date_end"
                color="project_id">
            <field name="name" />
            <field name="user_id" />
        </calendar>
    </field>
</record>
```

2. Add menus and actions using this view. This is left as an exercise for the reader.

How it works...

The calendar view needs to be passed field names in the attributes `date_start` and `date_stop` to indicate which fields to look at when building the visual representation. Use fields of type `Datetime` as everything else will get you weird results. While `date_start` is required, you can leave out `date_stop` and set the attribute `date_delay` instead, which is expected to be a `Float` field representing the duration in hours.

The calendar view allows you to give records which have the same value in a field the same (arbitrarily assigned) color. To use this functionality, set the attribute `color` to the name of the field you need. In our example, we can see in one glance which tasks belong to the same project, because we assigned `project_id` as the field to determine the color groups.

The fields you name in the calendar element's body are shown within the block representing the time interval covered, separated by commas.

There's more...

The calendar view has some other helpful attributes. If you want to open calendar entries in a popup instead of the standard form view, set `event_open_popup` to 1. If you want to be able to create a new entry by just filling in some text, set `quick_add` to 1. Internally, this calls the model's `name_create` function to actually create the record.

If your model has a notion of covering a whole day, set `all_day` to a field's name that is true if the record covers the whole day, and false otherwise.

In case you need more fine grained control over the text displayed within the calendar items, set the attribute `display` to a format string using field names in brackets. In our case, we could say `display="[name] (assigned to [user_id])"` to have a more verbose representation of which task is assigned to whom.

Note that this recipe contained information about a legacy view type `gantt`, which has been obsoleted during writing and was removed from the text.

Graph and pivot views

In this recipe, we'll have a look at Odoo's business intelligence views. These are read only views meant to present data.

Getting ready

We're still making use of the project module here. First, we need some configuration. Activate the checkbox **Manage time estimation on tasks** in **Configuration | Settings** and also install the module **project_timesheet** in order to be able to record some time on different tasks.

Now create some projects meant to be umbrella projects for the customers. Then, create a couple of tasks for each customer project. They are meant to model different activities you have per customer. Assign different managers to these projects and activate the box **Use tasks**. Finally, create tasks in these projects, give a time estimation per task, and write some work hours on these tasks.

How to do it...

1. Define a graph view using bars:

```xml
<record id="graph_project_task_bar" model="ir.ui.view">
    <field name="model">project.task</field>
    <field name="arch" type="xml">
        <graph type="bar">
            <field name="project_id" type="row" />
            <field name="user_id" type="row" />
            <field name="effective_hours" type="measure" />
        </graph>
    </field>
</record>
```

2. Define a graph view using pivot tables:

```xml
<record id="graph_project_task_pivot" model="ir.ui.view">
    <field name="model">project.task</field>
    <field name="arch" type="xml">
        <graph type="pivot">
            <field name="parent_id" type="row" />
            <field name="user_id" type="row" />
            <field name="planned_hours" type="measure" />
            <field name="effective_hours" type="measure" />
        </graph>
    </field>
</record>
```

3. Add menus and actions using this view. This is left as an exercise for the reader.

If everything went well, you should see graphs that show you how many hours were worked per customer (the projects we defined) under the responsibility of the different project managers.

How it works...

The `type` attribute determines the initial mode of a graph view. Possible values are **pivot**, **bar**, **line**, and **chart**, while **bar** is the default. The graph view is highly interactive, so the user can switch between the different modes and also add and remove fields.

The `field` elements tell Odoo what to display on which axis. For all the graph modes, you need at least one field with type `row` and one with type **measure** to see anything useful. Fields of type row determine the grouping, while type measure stands for the value(s) to be shown. Line graphs only support one field of each type, while charts and bars handle two group fields with one measure nicely. The pivot table supports an arbitrary amount of group and measure fields. No worries, things don't break if you switch to a mode that doesn't support the amount of groups and measures you defined. It's just that they'll ignore some of the fields and won't always show a very interesting result.

There's more...

For all the graph types, the `Datetime` fields are tricky for grouping, because you'll rarely encounter the same field value here. So if you have a `Datetime` field of type row, also specify the `interval` attribute with one of the following values: **day**, **week**, **month**, **quarter**, or **year**. This will cause the grouping to take place in the given interval.

The pivot table also supports grouping in columns. Use type **col** for the fields you want to have there.

Grouping, like sorting, relies heavily on PostgreSQL. So here also the rule applies that a field must live in the database and in the current table in order to be usable.

It is common practice to define database views that collect all the data you need and define a model on top of this view in order to have all the necessary fields available.

Depending on the complexity of your view and the grouping, building the graph can be quite an expensive exercise. Consider setting the attribute `auto_search` to `False` in those cases, so that the user can first adjust all the parameters and only afterwards trigger a search.

QWeb reports

The last part of the presentation layer is printing out reports. In case you haven't till now, install `wkhtmltopdf` as described in *Chapter 1, Installing the Odoo Development Environment* otherwise you won't get shiny PDFs as result of your efforts.

Getting ready

The conversion mechanism to PDFs is implemented in the addon **report**, so you should add it as dependency of your addon. Also double check that the configuration parameter `web.base.url` (or alternatively, `report.url`) is a URL accessible from your Odoo instance, otherwise report generation takes ages and the result looks funny.

How to do it...

1. Define a view for your report:

```xml
<template id="qweb_res_partner_birthdays">
  <t t-call="report.html_container">
    <t t-call="report.internal_layout">
      <div class="page">
        <h2>Partner's birthdays</h2>
        <div t-foreach="docs" t-as="o" class="row mt4 mb4">
          <div class="col-md-6"><t t-esc="o.name" /></div>
          <div class="col-md-6">
            <t t-if="o.birthdate" t-esc="o.birthdate" />
            <t t-if="not o.birthdate">-</t>
          </div>
        </div>
      </div>
    </t>
  </t>
</template>
```

2. Use this view in a report tag:

```xml
<report id="report_res_partner_birthdays"
      name="ch08.qweb_res_partner_birthdays"
      model="res.partner"
      string="Birthdays"
      report_type="qweb-pdf" />
```

Now when opening a partner form or selecting partners in the list view, you should be offered to print the birthday list.

How it works...

Instead of using the `record` syntax as we did earlier, we use the `template` element here. This is entirely for convenience; QWeb views are just views as all the others. The reason to use this element is that the `arch` field of QWeb views has to follow quite strict rules and the `template` element takes care to generate an `arch` content which fulfills these rules.

Don't worry about the syntax within the `template` element now. This topic will be addressed extensively in the recipe *QWeb* in *Chapter 14, CMS Website Development*.

The `report` element is another shortcut for an action of type `ir.actions.report.xml` and a glue record of type `ir.value`. The crucial part here is that you set the `name` field to the complete XML ID of the view you defined, otherwise the report generation will fail. The `model` attribute determines on which type of record the report operates, and the `string` attribute is the name shown to the user in the print menu.

By setting `report_type` to `qweb-pdf`, we request that the HTML generated by our view is run through `wkhtmltopdf` in order to deliver a PDF to the user. There are a couple of other (mostly deprecated) choices, but in some cases, `qweb-html` can be convenient to just render the HTML within the browser.

There's more...

There are some marker classes in a report's HTML that are crucial for the layout. Be sure to wrap all your content in an element with the class `page` set. If you forget that, you'll see nothing at all. To add a header or footer to your record, use the class `header` or `footer`.

Also remember that this is HTML, so make use of CSS attributes such as `page-break-before`, `page-break-after`, and `page-break-inside`.

You'll have noticed that all of our template body is wrapped in two elements with the `t-call` attribute set. We'll examine the mechanics of this attribute later, but it is crucial that you do the same in your reports. These elements take care that the HTML generated links to all the necessary CSS files and contains some other data needed for the report generation. While `html_container` doesn't really have an alternative, the second `t-call` could also be `report.external_layout`. The difference is that the external layout already comes with a header and footer displaying the company logo, the company's name, and some other information you expect from a company's external communication, while the internal layout just gives you a header with pagination, the print date, and the company's name. For the sake of consistency, always use one of the two.

Note that `report.internal_layout`, `report.external_layout`, `report.external_layout_header`, and `report.external_layout_footer` (the last two are called by the external layout) are just views by themselves, and you already know how to change them by inheritance. To inherit with the template element, use the attribute `inherit_id`.

9
Module Data

In this chapter, we will cover the following topics:

- ▸ Using external IDs and namespaces
- ▸ Loading data using XML files
- ▸ Using the noupdate and forcecreate flags
- ▸ Loading data using CSV files
- ▸ Loading data using YAML files
- ▸ Addon updates and data migration

In order not to have to repeat a lot of code, we'll make use of the models defined in *Chapter 4, Application Models*. So in order to follow the examples, grab this chapter's code.

Introduction

In this chapter, we'll look at how addons can provide data at installation time. This is useful for providing default values and adding metadata such as view descriptions, menus, or actions. Another important usage is providing demonstration data, which is loaded when the database is created with the **Load demonstration data** checkbox activated.

Using external IDs and namespaces

There was a lot of talk about XML IDs already, without specifying what an XML ID is. This recipe will give a deeper understanding of this.

How to do it...

We write into already existing records to demonstrate how to use cross module references:

1. Add a data file to your module manifest:

```
'data': [
    'data/res_partner.xml',
],
```

2. Change the name of our main company:

```
<record id="base.main_company" model="res.company">
    <field name="name">Packt publishing</field>
</record>
```

3. Set our main company's partner as publisher:

```
<record id="book_cookbook" model="library.book">
    <field name="publisher_id" ref="base.main_partner" />
</record>
```

On installation of this module, the company will be renamed and the book from the next recipe will be assigned to our partner. On subsequent updates of our module, only the publisher will be assigned, but the company's name will be left untouched.

How it works...

An XML ID is a string referring to a record in the database. The IDs themselves are records of model `ir.model.data`. This table's rows contain the module-declaring ID, the identifier string, the referred model, and the referred ID. Every time an ID has to be looked up, Odoo checks whether the string is namespaced already (that is, it contains exactly one dot), and if not adds the current module name as namespace. Then it looks up if there is already a record in `ir.model.data` with the specified name. If so, an UPDATE statement for the listed fields is executed; if not, a CREATE statement is executed. This is why you can give partial data when a record already exists, as we did above.

> A widespread application for partial data, apart from changing records defined by other modules, is using a shortcut element to create a record in a convenient way and writing a `field` on this record which is not supported by the shortcut element:
>
> ```
> <act_window id="my_action" name="My action"
>             model="res.partner" />
> <record id="my_action" model="ir.actions.act_window">
>     <field name="auto_search" eval="False" />
> </record>
> ```

The `ref` function, as used below in the recipe *Loading data using XML files*, also adds the current module as namespace if appropriate, but raises an error if the resulting XML ID does not exist already. This also applies to the **id** attribute if it is not namespaced already.

There's more...

You probably need to access records with an XML ID from your code sooner or later. Use the function `self.env.ref()` in those cases, which returns a browse record of the referenced record. Note that here, you always have to pass the full XML ID.

See also

Consult the recipe *Using the noupdate and forcecreate flags* to find out why the company's name is changed only on installation of the module.

Loading data using XML files

Using *Chapter 4, Application Models* data model, we'll add a book and an author as demonstration data, while we add a well known publisher as normal data in our module.

How to do it...

Create two XML files and link them in your `__openerp__.py` manifest file:

1. Add in a file called `data/demo.xml` to your manifest, in the demo section:

   ```
   'demo': [
       'data/demo.xml',
   ],
   ```

2. Add content to this file:

   ```
   <odoo>
       <record id="author_af" model="res.partner">
           <field name="name">Alexandre Fayolle</field>
       </record>
       <record id="author_dr" model="res.partner">
           <field name="name">Daniel Reis</field>
       </record>
       <record id="author_hb" model="res.partner">
           <field name="name">Holger Brunn</field>
       </record>
       <record id="book_cookbook" model="library.book">
           <field name="name">Odoo Cookbook</field>
           <field name="short_name">cookbook</field>
   ```

```
                <field name="date_release">2016-03-01</field>
                <field name="author_ids" eval="[(6, 0, [ref('author_af'),
                    ref('author_dr'), ref('author_hb')])]" />
                <field name="publisher_id" ref="res_partner_packt" />
        </record>
    </odoo>
```

3. Add a file called `data/res_partner.xml` to your manifest, in the data section:

```
'data': [
    'data/res_partner.xml',
],
```

4. Add content to this file:

```
<odoo>
    <record id="res_partner_packt" model="res.partner">
        <field name="name">Packt Publishing</field>
        <field name="city">Birmingham</field>
        <field name="country_id" ref="base.uk" />
    </record>
</odoo>
```

When you update your module now, you'll see in any case the publisher we created, and, if your database has demo data enabled, as pointed out in *Chapter 1, Installing the the Odoo Development Environment*, you'll also find this book and its authors.

How it works...

As you've seen above, demo data is technically just the same as normal data. The only difference is that the first is pulled by the **demo** key in the manifest, the latter by the **data** key.

To create a record, use the record element, which has the mandatory attributes `id` and `model`. For the `id` attribute, consult the recipe *Using external IDs and namespaces*; the model attribute refers to a model's `_name` property.

Then you use the `field` element to fill columns in the database as defined by the model you named. The model also decides which are the mandatory fields to fill and also possibly defines default values, in which case you don't need to give those fields a value explicitly.

As shown above, the field element can contain its value as simple text in case of scalar values.

For setting up references, there are two possibilities. The simplest is using the **ref** attribute, which works for many2one fields and just contains the XML ID of the record to be referenced.

For one2many and many2many fields, we need to resort to the **eval** attribute. This is a general purpose attribute that can be used to evaluate Python code to use as the field's value - think of `strftime('%Y-01-01')` as an example - to populate a date field. X2many fields expect to be populated by a list of 3-tuples, where the first value of the tuple determines the operation to be carried out. Within an `eval` attribute, we have access to a function called `ref`, which returns the database ID of an XML ID given as a string. This allows us to refer to a record without knowing its concrete ID, which is probably different per database, as explained in the following:

- `(2, id, False)` deletes the linked record with `id` from the database, the third element of the tuple is ignored.

- `(3, id, False)` only cuts the link to a record with `id`, but leaves the existing record as it is. Here also, the last element of the tuple is ignored.

- `(4, id, False)` adds a link to the existing record `id`, the last element of the tuple is ignored too. This should be what you use most of the time, usually accompanied by using the `ref` function to get the database ID of a record known by its XML ID.

- `(5, False, False)` only works for many2many fields and cuts all links, but keeps the linked records intact.

- `(6, False, [id, ...])` only works for many2many fields and first clears out currently referenced records to replace them with the ones mentioned in the list of IDs. The second element of the tuple is ignored.

> Note that order matters in data files and that records within data files can only refer to records defined in data files earlier in the list. This is why you should always check if your module installs in an empty database, because during development, it often happens that you add records all over the place, which works because the records defined afterwards are already in the database from a previous update.
>
> Demo data is always loaded after the files from the data key, which is why the reference in the example works.

There's more...

While you can do basically anything with the record element, there are shortcut elements defined that make it more convenient for the developer to create certain kinds of records. Examples are **menuitem**, **template** or **act window**. Refer to *Chapter 8, Backend Views* and *Chapter 14, CMS Website Development* for information about those.

A `field` element can also contain the `function` element, which calls a function defined on a model to provide a field's value. See the recipe *Using the noupdate and forcecreate flags* for an application where we simply call a function to directly write to the database, circumventing the loading mechanism.

The above list misses out entries for 0 and 1, because they are not very useful when loading data. They are entered as follows for the sake of completeness:

- ▸ (0, False, {'key': value}) creates a new record of the referenced model, with its fields filled from the dictionary at position three. The second element of the tuple is ignored. As those records don't have an XML ID and are evaluated every time the module is updated, leading to double entries, it's better in general to avoid this, create the record in its own record element, and link it as will be explained later.

- ▸ (1, id, {'key': value}) can be used to write on an existing linked record. For the same reasons as above, you should avoid this syntax.

You will use both of them extensively in *Chapter 5, Basic Server Side Business Logic*.

Using the noupdate and forcecreate flags

Most addons have different types of data. Some data simply needs to exist for the module to work properly, other data shouldn't even be changed by the user, while most data is meant to be changed per the user's pleasure and is only provided as a convenience. This recipe will detail how to address the different types. First, we'll write a field in an already existing record, then, we'll create a record that is supposed to be recreated during a module update.

How to do it...

We can enforce different behaviors from Odoo when loading data by setting certain attributes on the enclosing odoo element or the record element itself.

1. Add a publisher only created at installation time, but not updated on subsequent updates. However, if the user deletes it, it will be recreated:

```xml
<odoo noupdate="1">
    <record id="res_partner_packt" model="res.partner">
        <field name="name">Packt publishing</field>
    </record>
</odoo>
```

2. Add a book category that is not changed during addon updates and not recreated if the user deletes it:

```xml
<odoo noupdate="1">
    <record id="book_category_all" model="library.book.category"
            forcecreate="false">
        <field name="name">All books</field>
    </record>
</odoo>
```

How it works...

The `odoo` element can have a `noupdate` attribute, which is propagated to the **ir.model.data** records created when reading the enclosed data records for the first time, ending up as a column in this table.

When Odoo installs an addon (called *init* mode), all noupdate records are written. When you update an addon (called *update* mode), existing XML IDs are checked to see if they have the `noupdate` flag set, and if so, elements trying to write to this XML ID are ignored. This is not the case if the record in question was deleted by the user, which is why you can force not recreating noupdate records also in *update* mode by setting the flag **forcecreate** on the record to `false`.

> In legacy addons (<= 8.0), you'll often find an **openerp** element enclosing a **data** element and only there **record** and other elements. This is still possible, but deprecated. By now, **odoo**, **openerp**, and **data** have exactly the same semantics, they are meant as a bracket to enclose XML data.

There's more...

You can force *init* mode by starting your Odoo server with the parameter `--init=your_addon`, this way overwriting all existing noupdate records. This will also cause deleted records to be recreated. Note that this can cause double records and related installation errors if a module circumvents the XML ID mechanism, for example, by creating records in Python code called by YAML files.

For modules you write from scratch, you don't need to worry too much about noupdate records in either your own addon or other ones, as long as you only install it after all development is done. But imagine you add a new feature to an existing module that is already out in the wild. Then you might need to set a specific value on, for example, the main partner, which is a noupdate record. For users with a previous version already installed, this data update will never be executed! You can work around this by using the `function` element to temporarily unset the record to noupdate, as follows:

```
<function name="write" model="ir.model.data">
    <function name="search" model="ir.model.data">
        <value eval="[('module', '=', 'base'), ('name', '=', 'main_
partner')]" />
    </function>
    <value eval="{'noupdate': False}" />
</function>
<record id="base.main_partner" model="res.partner">
    <field name="book_ids" eval="[(4, ref('book_cookbook'))]"
</record>
```

```xml
<function name="write" model="ir.model.data">
    <function name="search" model="ir.model.data">
        <value eval="[('module', '=', 'base'), ('name', '=', 'main_
partner')]" />
    </function>
    <value eval="{'noupdate': True}" />
</function>
```

With this code, you can circumvent any noupdate flag, but be sure this is really what you want. Another option for solving the scenario sketched here is to write a migration script, as outlined in the following recipe.

See also

Odoo also uses XML IDs to keep track of which data is to be deleted after an addon update. If a record had an XML ID from the module's namespace before the update, but the XML ID is not reinstated during the update, the record and its XML ID will be deleted from the database because they're considered obsolete. For a deeper discussion of this mechanism, see the following recipe: *Addon updates and data migration*.

Loading data using CSV files

While you can do everything you need with XML files, this format is not the most convenient when you need to provide larger amounts of data, especially given that many people are more comfortable preprocessing data in Calc, or some other spreadsheet software. Another advantage of this format is that it is what you get when you use the standard export function. In this recipe, we'll have a look at importing table-like data.

How to do it...

Traditionally, **access control lists** (**ACLs**), (refer to *Chapter 10*, *Access Security*) are a type of data that is loaded via CSV files:

1. Add `security/ir.model.access.csv` to your data files:

    ```
    'data': [
        ...
        'security/ir.model.access.csv',
    ],
    ```

2. Add an ACL for our books in this file:

    ```
    "id","name","model_id:id","group_id:id","perm_read",
        "perm_write","perm_create","perm_unlink"
    "access_library_book_user","ACL for books",
        "model_library_book","base.group_user",1,0,0,0
    ```

Now we have an ACL that permits normal users to read book records, but does not allow them to edit, create or delete them.

How it works...

You simply drop all your data files in your manifest's **data** list. Odoo will use the file extension to decide which type of file it is. A specialty of CSV files is that their file name must match the name of the model to be imported, in our case, **ir.model.access**. The first line needs to be a header with column names that match the model's field names exactly.

For scalar values, you can use a quoted (if necessary because the string contains quotes or commas itself) or an unquoted string.

When writing many2one fields with a CSV file, Odoo first tries to interpret the column value as an XML ID: If there's no dot, add the current module name as a namespace, lookup the result in **ir.model.data**. In case this fails, the model's `name_search` function is called with the column's value as a parameter and the first result returned wins. When this also fails, the line is considered invalid and Odoo raises an error.

 Note that data read from CSV files is always `noupdate=False` and there's no convenient way around this. This means subsequent updates of your addon will always overwrite possible changes made by the user.

There's more...

Importing one2many and many2many fields with CSV files is possible, but a bit tricky. In general, you're better off creating the records separately and setting up the relation with an XML file afterwards, or working with a second CSV file that sets up the relationship.

If you really need to create related records within the same file, order your columns so that all scalar fields are to the left and fields of the linked model are to the right, with a column header consisting of the linking field's name and the linked model's field, separated by a colon:

```
"id","name","model_id:id","perm_read","perm_read", "group_id:name",
"access_library_book_user","ACL for books","model_library_book",1,"my
group"
```

This would create a group called `my group`, you could write more fields in the group record by adding columns to the right. If you need to link multiple records, repeat the line and only change the right hand columns as appropriate. Given that Odoo fills empty columns with the previous line's value, you don't need to copy all data, but simply add a line with empty values saved for the fields of the linked model you want to fill.

Loading data using YAML files

A third format for data import is YAML, which gives you less overhead than XML, but still more control than CSV. Traditionally, it was used for tests rather than for data import, which is why you have more possibilities to call code here.

How to do it...

Take the following steps to translate the first recipe in this chapter to YAML:

1. Add in a file called `data/demo.yml` to your manifest, in the demo section:

    ```
    'demo': [
        'data/demo.yml',
    ],
    ```

2. Add content to this file:

    ```
    -
      !record {id: author_af, model: res.partner}
        name: Alexandre Fayolle

    -
      !record {id: author_dr, model: res.partner}
        name: Daniel Reis

    -
      !record {id: author_hb, model: res.partner}
        name: Holger Brunn

    -
      !record {id: book_cookbook, model: library.book}
        name: Odoo cookbook
        short_name: cookbook
        date_release: 2016-03-01
        author_ids: [(6, 0, [ref('author_af'), ref('author_dr'),
                             ref('author_hb')])]
        publisher_id: res_partner_packt
    ```

3. Add a file called `data/res_partner.yml` to your manifest, in the data section:

    ```
    'data': [
        'data/res_partner.yml',
    ],
    ```

4. Add content to this file:

    ```
    -
      !record {id: res_partner_packt, model: res.partner}
        name: Packt publishing
        city: Birmingham
        country_id: base.uk
    ```

We did the same as in the first recipe, but in YAML syntax. Note that YAML files need the extension `.yml` to be recognized correctly.

How it works...

Odoo introduces a YAML datatype `record`, which is where most of the Odoo-specific behavior is implemented. As with XML, a **record** needs an **ID** and a **model** set in order to do something useful.

For field values, you use YAML's standard notation, which means you don't need quoting for strings. When filling many2one fields, Odoo will simply presuppose that what you give here is a XML ID, so there is no need for extra marking here either.

There's more...

We've seen that linking one2many and many2many fields is a bit awkward with XML and CSV, and in the example above, we used the same syntax to do the linking. In YAML, you could have done it more elegantly by simply writing the following:

```
  -
    !record {id: book_cookbook, model: library.book}
        name: Odoo cookbook
        short_name: cookbook
        date_release: 2016-03-01
        author_ids:
        -   name: Alexandre Fayolle
        -   name: Daniel Reis
        -   name: Holger Brunn
```

This way, you created three records of type **res.partner**, linked in the field **author_ids**. Note that here also, creating records inline means they have no XML ID, which makes it difficult to refer to them from other places.

See also

This recipe focused on using YAML files to load data. If you're interested in testing using YAML files, refer to *Chapter 7, Debugging and Automated Testing*.

Addon updates and data migration

The data model you choose when writing an addon might turn out to have some weaknesses, so you may need to adjust it during the life cycle of your addon. In order to allow that without a lot of hacks, Odoo supports versioning in addons and running migrations if necessary.

How to do it...

We assume that in an earlier version of our module, the **date_release** field was a character field, where people wrote whatever they saw fit as the date. Now we realize we need this field for comparisons and aggregations, which is why we want to change its type to Date. Odoo does a great job at type conversions, but, in this case, we're on our own, which is why we need to provide instructions on how to transform a database with the previous version of our module installed to a database where the current version can run:

1. Bump the version in your __openerp__.py manifest:

   ```
   'version': '9.0.1.0.1',
   ```

2. Provide pre-migration code in migrations/9.0.1.0.1/pre-migrate.py:

   ```python
   def migrate(cr, version):
       cr.execute('ALTER TABLE library_book RENAME COLUMN
           date_release TO date_release_char')
   ```

3. Provide post migration code in migrations/9.0.1.0.1/post-migrate.py:

   ```python
   from openerp import fields
   from datetime import date


   def migrate(cr, version):
       cr.execute('SELECT id, date_release_char FROM library_book')
       for record_id, old_date in cr.fetchall():
           # check if the field happens to be set in Odoo's internal
           # format
           new_date = None
           try:
               new_date = fields.Date.from_string(old_date)
           except:
               if len(old_date) == 4 and old_date.isdigit():
                   # probably a year
                   new_date = date(int(old_date), 1, 1)
               else:
                   # try some separators, play with day/month/year
                   # order
                   # ...
           if new_date:
               cr.execute('UPDATE library_book SET date_release=%s',
                   (new_date,))
   ```

Without this code, Odoo would have renamed the old **date_release** column to **date_release_moved** and created a new one, because there's no automatic conversion from character fields to date fields. From the point of view of the user, the data in **date_release** would simply be gone.

How it works...

The first crucial point is that you increase the version number of your addon, as migrations run only between different versions. During every update, Odoo writes the version number from the manifest at the time of the update into the table `ir_module_module`. The version number is prefixed with Odoo's major and minor version, if the version number has three or fewer components. In the example above, we explicitly also named Odoo's major and minor version, which is good practice, but a value of `1.0.1` would have had the same effect, because, internally, Odoo prefixes short version numbers for addons with its own major and minor version number. Generally, using the long notation is a good thing because you can see with just a glance at the manifest file for which version of Odoo an addon is meant.

The two migration files are just code files that don't need to be registered anywhere. When updating an addon, Odoo compares the addon's version as noted in `ir_module_module` with the version in the addon's manifest. If the manifest's version is higher (after possibly adding Odoo's major and minor version), this addon's `migrations` folder will be searched if it contains folders with the version(s) in between, up to, and including the version that is currently updated.

Then, within the folders found, it searches for Python files whose names start with `pre-`, loads them, and expects them to define a function called `migrate,` which has two parameters. This function is called with a database cursor as the first argument and the currently installed version as the second argument. This happens before Odoo even looks at the rest of the code the addon defines, so you can assume nothing changed in your database layout compared to the previous version.

After all `pre-migrate` functions run successfully, Odoo loads the models and data declared in the addon, which can cause changes in the database layout. Given we renamed **date_release** in `pre-migrate.py`, Odoo will just create a new column with that name, but with the correct data type.

After that, with the same search algorithm, `post-migrate` files will be searched and executed if found. In our case, we need to look at every value and see if we can make something usable out of it, otherwise, we keep `NULL` as data. Don't write scripts iterating over a whole table yourself if not absolutely necessary; in this case, we should have written a very big unreadable SQL switch that does what we want.

 If you simply want to rename a column, you don't need a migration script. In this case, you can set the `oldname` parameter of the field in question to the field's old column name, Odoo then takes care of the renaming itself.

There's more...

In both the pre- and post-migration steps, you only have access to a cursor, which is not very convenient if you're used to Odoo environments. It can lead to unexpected results to use models at this stage, because in the `pre-` step, the addon's models are not yet loaded and also, in the post- step, models defined by addons depending on the current addon are not yet loaded too. But if this is not a problem for you, either because you want to use a model your addon doesn't touch or a model for which you know the aforementioned is not a problem, you can create the environment you're used to by writing the following:

```
from openerp import SUPERUSER_ID
from openerp.api import Environment

def migrate(cr, version):
    env = Environment(cr, SUPERUSER_ID, {})
    # env holds all currently loaded models
```

See also

When writing migration scripts, you'll often be confronted with repetitive tasks like checking if a column or table exists, renaming things, or mapping some old values to new values. It's frustrating and error-prone to reinvent the wheel here; consider using `https://github.com/OCA/openupgradelib` if you can afford the extra dependency.

10
Access Security

In this chapter, we will see how to:

- ▶ Create security groups and assign them to users
- ▶ Add security access to models
- ▶ Limit access to fields in models
- ▶ Limit record access using record rules
- ▶ Use security group to activate features

In order to concisely get the point across, the recipes in this chapter make small additions to an existing module. We chose to use the module created by the recipes in *Chapter 3*, *Creating Odoo Modules*. To better follow the examples here, you should have that module created and ready to use.

Create security groups and assign them to users

Security access in Odoo is configured through security groups: permissions are given to groups and then groups are assigned to users. Each functional area has base security groups provided by a central *application*.

When the addon modules extend an existing *application*, they should add permissions to the corresponding groups, as shown in the *Add security access to models* recipe later.

When the addon modules add a new functional area, not yet covered by an existing central *application*, they should add the corresponding security groups. Usually, we should have at least the user and manager roles.

Taking the Library example we introduced in *Chapter 3*, *Creating Odoo Modules*, it doesn't fit neatly in any of the Odoo core apps, so we add the security groups for it.

Getting ready

This recipe assumes you have an instance ready, with the `my_module` available, as described in *Chapter 3, Creating Odoo Modules*.

How to do it...

To add new access security groups to a module, perform the following steps:

1. Make sure that the addon module manifest `__openerp__.py` has the `category` key defined:

   ```
   'category': 'Library',
   ```

2. Add the new `security/library_security.xml` file to the manifest `data` key:

   ```
   'data': [
       'security/library_security.xml',
       'views/library_book.xml',
   ],
   ```

3. Add the new XML file for the data records at `security/library_security.xml`, starting with an empty structure:

   ```xml
   <?xml version="1.0" encoding="utf-8"?>
   <odoo>
     <data noupdate="0">
       <!-- Data records go here -->
     </data>
   </odoo>
   ```

4. Add inside the data XML element the `record` tags for the two new groups:

   ```xml
   <record id="group_library_user" model="res.groups">
     <field name="name">User</field>
     <field name="category_id"
             ref="base.module_category_library"/>
     <field name="implied_ids"
             eval="[(4, ref('base.group_user'))]"/>
   </record>

       <record id="group_library_manager" model="res.groups">
           <field name="name">Manager</field>
           <field name="category_id" ref="base.module_category_
   library"/>
           <field name="implied_ids" eval="[(4, ref('group_library_
   user'))]"/>
           <field name="users" eval="[(4, ref('base.user_root'))]"/>
       </record>
   ```

If we upgrade the addon module, these two records will be loaded and we will be able to see them at the menu option **Settings | Users | Groups**:

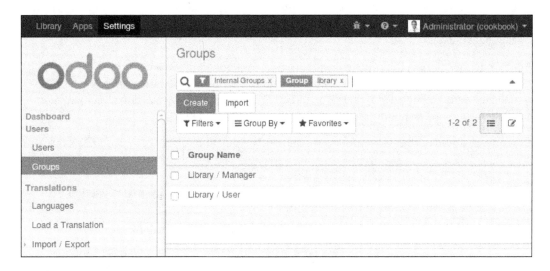

How it works...

Addon modules are organized in functional areas, or major *applications*, such as *Accounting & Finance*, *Sales*, or *Human Resources*. These are defined by the `category` key in the manifest file.

If a category name does not exist yet, it will be automatically created. For convenience, a `base.module_category_<category>` XML ID will also be generated for the new category name in lowercase letters, replacing spaces with underscores. This is useful to relate security groups with application categories.

In our example, we used the **Library** category name, and it generated a `base.module_category_library` XML identifier.

> Avoid using non-ASCII characters in the category name, but if you do, make sure to use a unicode string. For example: `u'Library'`.

By convention, the data files adding security related elements should be placed inside a `security` subdirectory.

The order in which the files are declared in the `data` attribute is important, since you can't use an identifier before it has been defined. We may want to use references in views for the security groups we had defined, so it's best to place the security data file at the top of the list before the ACL definition files and the other user interface data files.

Security groups should be added using an XML file. It can add records that we want to be customizable by the end users. To prevent those possible changes being lost on a module upgrade, we should add those records inside a `<data noupdate="1">` element. This is usually the case for security record rules, discussed in the *Limit record access using record rules* recipe later.

But for security groups, the practice used in Odoo core addon modules is to have them defined inside a `<data noupdate="0">` element. This means that they will be rewritten on a module upgrade, and so should not be directly customized. Customization should instead be done by creating new groups that inherit from the default ones.

Groups are stored in the `res.groups` model, and its most important columns are as follows:

▶ `name`: This is the group's display name.

▶ `category_id`: This is a reference to the application category, and is used to organize the groups in the users form.

▶ `implied_ids`: These are the other groups to inherit permissions from.

▶ `users`: This is the list of users belonging to this group. In the new addon modules, usually we want the admin user to conveniently belong to the application's manager group.

The first security group uses as `implied_ids` the `base.group_user`. This is the employee user, and is the basic security group all the backend users are expected to share.

The second security group sets a value on the `users` field to assign it to the administrator user, that has the `base.user_root` XML ID.

Users belonging to a security group will automatically belong to its implied groups. If **Library Manager** has implied the **Library User** group, assigning it to a user will also include him in the **Library User** group.

Also, the access permissions granted by security groups are cumulative. A user has some permission in any of the groups he belongs to (directly or implied) grants that permission.

Some security groups are shown in the user form as a selection box instead of individual checkboxes. This happens when the involved groups are in the same application category and are linearly interrelated through `implied_ids`. For example, Group A has implied Group B, and Group B has implied Group C.

Note that the relations defined in the preceding fields also have reverse relations that can be edited in the related models, such as security groups and users.

Setting values on reference fields, such as `category_id` and `implied_ids`, is done using the related records XML IDs and some special syntax.

For Many2one relations, the `ref` attribute is used to link with the record with the corresponding XML ID. For One2many fields, such as `implied_ids`, the `eval` attribute is used with a list of tuple *commands*. For example, the tuple 4 as the first element adds the references in the next element or elements. This syntax is explained in detail in *Chapter 9, Module Data*.

There's more...

Also noteworthy is the special `base.group_no_one` security group. In the previous Odoo versions, it was used for advanced features hidden by default, and only made visible when the **Technical Features** flag was activated. Since version 9.0 this has changed, and those features are made visible as long as the **Developer Mode** is activated.

The access permissions granted by security groups are cumulative only. There is no way to deny an access given by some group. This means a manually created group to customize permissions should inherit from the closest group with fewer permissions than those intended (if any), and then add all the remaining permissions needed.

Groups also have available these additional fields:

- Menus (the `menu_access` field): These are the menu items the group has access to
- Views (the `view_access` field): These are the UI views the group has access to
- Access rights (the `model_access` field): These are the access it has on models, detailed in the *Add security access to models* recipe
- Rules (the `rule_groups` field): These are the record level access rules that apply to the group, detailed in the *Limit record access using record rules* recipe
- Notes (the `comment` field): This is a description or comment text for the group

Add security access to models

It's common for the addon modules to add new models. For example, in the previous chapter we had examples adding a new Library Books model.

It is easy to miss the creation of security access for the new models defined in an addon module if you test it using the convenient `admin` user, because `admin` bypasses all the security checks.

However, models with no ACLs will trigger a warning log message on loading, informing about the missing ACL definitions: **The model library.book has no access rules, consider adding one**. To avoid that, you should watch for such messages during tests, and before publishing your code make sure you run the tests with the `demo` user rather than `admin`.

So, for new models to be usable by non-admin users, we need to define their security access control lists, so that Odoo knows how it should access them and what operations each user group should be allowed.

Getting ready

We will take the module created in *Chapter 3*, *Creating Odoo Modules* and add to it the missing ACLs.

How to do it...

`my_module` should already contain the `models/library_book.py` Python file creating the `library.book` model. We will now add a data file describing this model's security access control by performing the following steps:

1. Edit the `__openerp__.py` manifest file to declare a new data file:

    ```
    data: [
        # ...Security Groups
        'security/ir.model.access.csv',
        # ...Other data files
    ]
    ```

2. Add to the module a new file `security/ir.model.access.csv`, with the following lines:

    ```
    id,name,model_id:id,group_id:id,perm_read,perm_write,perm_
    create,perm_unlink
    access_library_book_user,library.book.user,model_library_
    book,base.group_user,1,0,0,0
    access_library_book_admin,library.book.admin,model_library_
    book,base.group_system,1,1,1,1
    ```

We should then upgrade the module to have these ACL records added to our Odoo database. More importantly, if we sign in to a demonstration database using the **demo** user, we should be able to access the **Library** menu option without any security errors.

How it works...

The security access control lists are stored in the core `ir.model.access` model. We just need to add to it the records describing the intended access rights for each user group.

Any type of data file would do, but the common practice is to use a CSV file. The file can be placed anywhere inside the addon module directory, but the convention is to have all the security related files inside a `security` subdirectory.

The first step in our recipe declares this new data file to the manifest and the second adds the file describing the security access control rules. The CSV file must be named after the model where the records will be loaded, so the name used is not just a convention and is mandatory.

If the module also creates new security groups, its data file should be declared before the ACLs' data file, since you may want to use them for the ACLs and so they must already be created when the ACL file is processed.

The columns in the CSV file are as follows:

- `id`: This is the XML ID internal identifier for this rule. Any unique name inside the module would do, but the convention is to use `access_<model>_<group>`.
- `name`: This is a title for the access rule and, by convention, the common practice is to use a `access.<model>.<group>` name.
- `model_id:id`: This is the XML ID for the model. Odoo automatically assigns such an ID to models with a format `model_<name>`, using the model's _name with underscores instead of dots. If the model was created in a different addon module, a fully qualified XML ID is needed, including the module name.
- `group_id:id`: This is the XML ID for the user group. If left empty, it applies to all the users. The base module provides some basic groups, such as `base.group_user`, for all the employees and `base.group_system` for the administration user. Other apps can add their own user groups.
- `perm_read`: This can read the model records (0 or 1).
- `perm_write`: This can update the model records (0 or 1).
- `perm_create`: This can add new model records (0 or 1).
- `perm_unlink`: This can delete model records (0 or 1).

The CSV file we used adds read only access to the **Human Resources | Employee** standard security group, and full write access to the **Administration | Settings** group.

The **Employee** user group, `base.group_user`, is particularly important because the user groups added by the Odoo standard apps inherit from it. This means that if we need a new model to be accessible by all the backend users, regardless of the specific apps they work with, we should add that permission to the **Employee** group.

The resulting ACLs can be viewed from the GUI in **Settings | Technical | Security | Access Controls List**, as shown in the following screenshot:

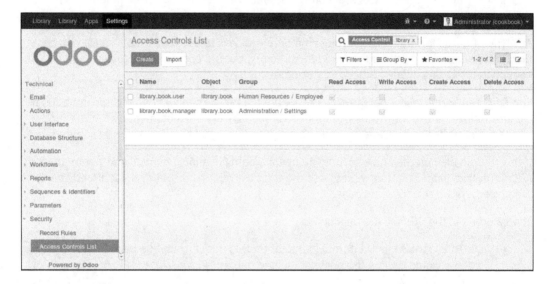

Some people find it easier to use this user interface to define ACLs and then use the export feature to produce a CSV file.

There's more...

It would make sense for us to give this permission to the Library user and Library manager groups defined in the *Create security Groups and assign them to Users* recipe. If you followed that recipe, it's a good exercise to then follow this one, adapting the group identifiers to the Library ones.

It's important to note that the access lists provided by the addon modules should not be directly customized, since they will be reloaded at the next module upgrade, destroying any customization that could have been done from the GUI.

To customize ACLs, two approaches can be used. One is to create new security groups that inherit from the one provided by the module and add additional permissions on it, but this allows only to add, not to remove. A more flexible approach can be to uncheck the **Active** flag to false on the particular ACL lines, to disable them. It is not visible by default, so we need to edit the tree view to add the `<field name="active" />` column. We can also add new ACL lines for additional or replacement permissions. On a module upgrade, the deactivated ACLs won't be reactivated and the added ACL lines won't be affected.

It's also worth noting that ACLs only apply to regular models and don't need to be defined for *Abstract* or *Transient* models. If defined, these will be disregarded and a warning message will be triggered into the server log.

Limit access to fields in models

In some cases we may need more fine grained access control and to limit the access to specific fields in a model.

It is possible for a field to be accessible only by specific security groups, using the `groups` attribute. We will show how to add to the Library Books model a field with limited access.

How to do it...

To add a field with access limited to specific security groups, perform the following steps:

1. Edit the model file to add the field:

```
private_notes = fields.Text(groups='base.group_system')
```

2. Edit the view in the XML file to add the field:

```
<field name="private_notes" />
```

That's it. Now upgrade the addon module for the changes in the model to take place. If you sign in with a user with no system configuration access, such as `demo` in a database with demonstration data, the Library books form won't display the field.

How it works...

Fields with the `groups` attribute are specially handled to check if the user belongs to any of the security groups indicated in the attribute, and if not removes it from UI views and ORM operations for the user.

Note that this security is not superficial. The field is not only hidden in the user interface, but is also made unavailable to the user in the other ORM operations, such as `read` and `write`. This is also true for the XML-RPC or JSON-RPC calls.

Be careful when using these fields in business logic, or *on change* UI events (`@api.onchange` methods); they can raise errors for users with no access to the field. One workaround for this is to use privilege elevation, such as the `sudo()` model method or the `compute_sudo` field attribute for computed fields.

The `groups` value is a string containing a comma separated list of valid XML IDs for security groups. The simplest way to find the XML ID for a particular group is to navigate to its form, at **Settings | Users | Groups**, and then access the **View Metadata** option from the debug menu, as shown in the following screenshot:

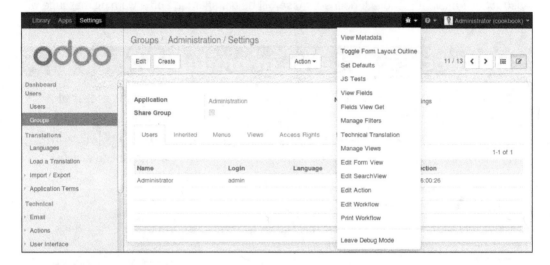

There's more...

In some cases, we need a field to be available or not depending on particular conditions, such as the values in a particular field, like `stage_id` or `state`. This is usually handled at the view level using attributes such as `states` or `attrs`, to dynamically display or hide the field according to certain conditions. You may refer to *Chapter 8*, *Backend Views* for a detailed description.

Note that these techniques work at the user interface level only and don't provide actual access security. For that you should add checks in the business logic layer. Either add model methods decorated with `@constrains`, implementing the specific validations intended, or extend the `create`, `write`, or `unlink` methods to add them validation logic. You can get more insight on how to do this in *Chapter 5*, *Basic Server Side Business Logic*.

Limit record access using record rules

A common need for an application is to be able to limit what records are available to each user on a specific model.

This is achieved using record rules. A record rule is a domain filter expression defined on a model that will then be added on every data query made by the affected users.

As an example, we will add a record rule on the Library books model so that the users in the employee group will only have access to books they created in the database.

Getting ready

This recipe assumes you have an instance ready, with `my_module` available, as described in *Chapter 3, Creating Odoo Modules*.

How to do it...

Record rules are added using a data XML file. To do so, perform the following steps:

1. Ensure that the `security/library_security.xml` file is referenced by manifest `data` key:

   ```
   'data': [
       'security/library_security.xml',
       # ...
   ],
   ```

2. We should have a `security/library_security.xml` data file, with a `<data>` section creating the security group. After it, add this second `<data>` section for the record rules:

   ```xml
   <data noupdate="1">
     <record model="ir.rule" id="library_book_user_rule">
         <field name="name">Library: see only own books</field>
         <field name="model_id" ref="model_library_book"/>
         <field name="groups" eval="[(4, ref('base.group_
   user'))]"/>
         <field name="domain_force">
         [('create_uid', '=', user.id)]</field>
     </record>
     <record model="ir.rule" id="library_book_all_rule">
         <field name="name">Library: see all books</field>
         <field name="model_id" ref="model_library_book"/>
   ```

```
            <field name="groups" eval="[(4, ref('base.group_
    system'))]"/>
            <field name="domain_force">[(1, '=', 1)]</field>
        </record>
    </data>
```

Upgrading the addon module will load the record rules into the Odoo instance.

To keep the recipe simple, we used the core employee and settings security groups. We could instead have used the Library user and manager groups as defined in the *Add security access to models* recipe. It's a good exercise to follow it and modify this module so that it uses those security groups instead.

How it works...

Record rules are just data records loaded into the `ir.rule` core model. While the file adding them could be anywhere in the module, the convention is for it to be in the `security` subdirectory. It is common to have a single XML file with both security groups and record rules.

Unlike groups, in the standard modules, the record rules are loaded in a `data` section with the `noupdate="1"` attribute. With this, those records will not be reloaded on a module upgrade, meaning that manual customizations on them are safe and will survive later upgrades.

To stay consistent with the official modules, we should also have our record rules inside a `<data noupdate="1">` section.

Record rules can be seen from the GUI at the menu option **Settings | Technical | Security | Record Rules**, as shown in the following screenshot:

Following are the most important record rule fields used in the example:

- ▸ Name (name) is a descriptive title for the rule.
- ▸ Object (model_id) is a reference to the model the rule applied to.
- ▸ Groups (groups) are the security groups that the rule applies to. If none, the rule is considered *global* and is applied in a different way (more details follow later).
- ▸ Rule definition (domain) is a domain expression with the record filter to apply.

The first record rule we created was for the Employee security group. It uses the domain expression [('create_uid', '=', user.id)] to select only those books where the creation user is the current user. Thus, they will only be able to see the books created by themselves.

The domain expressions used in the record rules run on the server side using ORM objects. Because of this, dot notation can be used on the fields on the left-hand side (the first tuple element). The right side (third tuple element) is a Python expression, evaluated in a context having available the user record object, for the current user, and the time Python library.

For the settings security group, we want it to be able to see all the books, independent of who created them in the database. Since it inherits the Employee group, unless we do something about it, it too will be able to see only the books created by itself.

The several (non global) record rules are joined together using the OR logical operator: each rule adds access and never removes the access. For the Library Manager to have access to all the books, we can add to it a record rule to add access to books created by other users, like this: [('create_uid', '!=', user.id)].

We chose to do differently and use the special rule [(1, '=', 1)] to unconditionally give access to all the book records. While this may seem redundant, remember that otherwise the Library user rule can be customized in a way that would keep some books out of reach to the Settings user. It is special because the first element of a domain tuple must be a field name; this exact case is the only case where that is not true.

 Record rules are ignored for the built-in admin user. When testing your record rules, make sure you use some other user for that.

There's more...

When a record rule is not assigned to any security group, it is marked as **Global** and is handled differently from the other rules.

Global record rules have a stronger effect than group level record rules, and set access restriction that those can't override. Technically, they are joined with an AND operator. In the standard modules, they are used to implement multi-company security access, so that each user can see only his company's data.

In summary, regular non global record rules are joined together with an OR operator: they are added together and a record is accessible if any of the rule grants that access. Global record rules then add restrictions to the access given by the regular record rules, using an AND operator. Restrictions added by global record rules can't be overridden by regular record rules.

Using security group to activate features

Security groups can restrict some features so that they are accessible only to users belonging to these groups. Security groups can also inherit other groups, so they also grant their permissions.

These two features combined are used to implement a usability feature in Odoo: feature toggling. Security groups can also be used as a way to enable or disable features for some or all of the users in an Odoo instance.

This recipe shows how to add options to configuration settings and showcases the two methods to enable the additional features, making them visible using security groups or adding them by installing an additional module.

For the first case, we will make the book release dates an optional additional feature and for the second, as an example, we will provide an option to install the Notes module.

Getting ready

This recipe uses `my_module` described in *Chapter 3, Creating Odoo Modules*. We will need security groups to work with, so you also need to have followed the *Add security access to models* recipe.

In this recipe, some identifiers need to refer to the addon module's technical name. We will assume that it is `my_module`. In case you are using a different name, replace `my_module` with the actual technical name of your addon module.

How to do it...

To add the configuration options, follow the given steps:

1. To add the needed dependency and the new XML data files, edit the `__openerp__.py` manifest like this:

```
# -*- coding: utf-8 -*-
{   'name': 'Cookbook code',
```

```
    'category': 'Library',
    'depends': ['base_setup'],
    'data': [
        'security/ir.model.access.csv',
        'security/library_security.xml',
        'views/library_book.xml',
        'views/res_config_settings.xml',
    ],
}
```

2. To add the new security group used for feature activation, edit the `security/library_book.xml` file and add the following record to it:

```
<record id="group_release_dates" model="res.groups">
    <field name="name">Library: release date feature</field>
    <field name="category_id"
    ref="base.module_category_hidden" />
</record>
```

3. To make the book release date visible only when this option is enabled, we edit the field definition in the `models/library_book.py` file:

```
# class LibraryBook(models.Model):
    # ...
    date_release = fields.Date(
        'Release Date',
        groups='my_module.group_release_dates')
```

4. Edit the `models/__init__.py` file to add a new Python file for the configuration settings model:

```
from . import library_book
from . import res_config_settings
```

5. To extend the core configuration wizard adding new options to it, add the `models/res_config_settings.py` file with this code:

```
# -*- coding: utf-8 -*-
from openerp import models, fields

class ConfigSettings(models.TransientModel):
    _inherit = 'base.config.settings'
    group_release_dates = fields.Boolean(
            "Manage book release dates",
            group='base.group_user',
            implied_group='my_module.group_release_dates')
    module_note = fields.Boolean("Install Notes app")
```

6. To make the options available in the UI, add `views/res_config_settings.xml` extending the form view:

```xml
<?xml version="1.0" encoding="utf-8"?>
<odoo>
    <record id="view_general_config_library" model="ir.ui.view">
      <field name="name">
          Configuration: add Library options</field>
      <field name="model">base.config.settings</field>
      <field name="inherit_id"
            ref="base_setup.view_general_configuration" />
      <field name="arch" type="xml">
        <group name="google" position="before">
          <group name="library_release_date" string="Library">
            <!-- Release Dates option -->
            <label for="id" string="Releases" />
            <div>
              <field name="group_release_dates"
                     class="oe_inline"/>
              <label for="group_release_dates" />
            </div>
            <!-- Notes option -->
            <label for="id" string="Notes" />
            <div>
              <field name="module_note" class="oe_inline"/>
              <label for="module_note" />
            </div>
          </group>
        </group>
      </field>
    </record>
</odoo>
```

After upgrading the addon module, the two new configuration options should be available at **Settings | General Settings**. The screen should look like this:

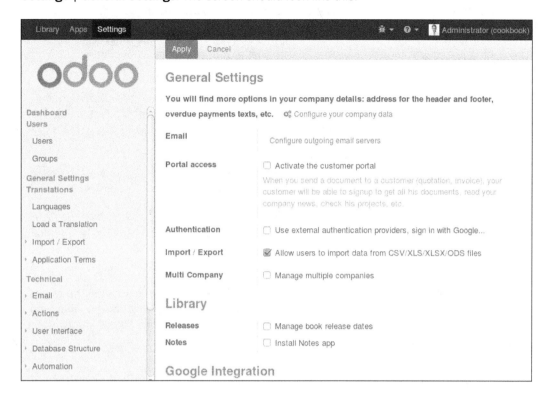

How it works...

The core `base` module provides a `res.config.settings` model providing the business logic behind option activation. The `base_setup addon` module uses it to provide the several basic configuration options to make available in a new database. It also makes available the **Settings | General Settings** menu.

The `base_setup` derived configuration model is `base.config.settings`, so we need to extend it to add our own configuration settings.

If we were to decide to create a specific settings form for the Library app, we could inherit directly from the `res.config.settings` model instead, and then provide the menu option and form view for those settings.

We used two different ways to activate the features: one by enabling a security group, making the feature visible to the user, and the other by installing a module addon providing the feature. The logic to handle both these cases is provided by the base `res.config. settings` model.

The first recipe step adds the `base_setup addon` module to the dependencies, since it provides the `base.config.settings` model we want to use. It also adds an additional XML data file we will need to add the new options to the **General Settings** form.

In the second step, we create a new security group **Library: release date feature**. The feature to activate should be visible only for that group, so that it will be hidden until the group is enabled.

In our example, we want the book release date to be available only when the corresponding configuration option is enabled. To achieve this, we use the `groups` attribute on the field so that it is made available only for this security group. We did it at model level, so that it is automatically applied to all the UI views where the field is used.

Finally, we extend the `base.config.settings` model to add the new options. Each option is a Boolean field, and its name must begin either by `group_` or `module_`, according to what we want it to do.

The `group_` option field should have an `implied_group` attribute and be a string containing a comma separated list of XML IDs for the security groups to activate when it is enabled. The XML IDs must be in the complete form with module name dot identifier name.

We can also provide a `group` attribute to specify for which security groups the feature will be enabled. It will be for all the employee based groups, if no groups are defined. Thus they won't apply to portal security groups, since these don't inherit on the employee base security group, like the other regular security groups.

The mechanism behind the activation is quite simple: it adds the security group in the `group` attribute to the `implied_group`, thus making the related feature visible to the corresponding users.

The `module_` option field does not require any additional attributes. The remaining part of the field name identifies the module to be installed when activating the option. In our example, `module_note` will install the note module.

Caution:

Unchecking the box will uninstall the module without warning, which can cause data loss (models or fields removed and module data removed as a consequence). To avoid unchecking the box by accident, the `secure_uninstall` community module (from `https://github.com/OCA/server-tools`) prompts for a password before uninstalling the addon module.

The last step of the recipe adds the options to the **General Settings** form view, just before the **Google Integration** group, having `name="google"`.

There's more...

Configuration setting can also have fields named with the `default_` prefix. These when having a value will set it as a global default. The settings field should have a `default_model` attribute to identify the model affected, and the field name after the `default_` prefix identifies the model's field that will have set the default value.

Additionally, fields with none of the three prefixes mentioned can be used for other settings, but you will need to implement the logic to populate their values, using `get_default_` name prefixed methods, and to act when their values are edited, using `set_` name prefixed methods.

For those who would like to go deeper into configuration settings details, the best documentation available is in Odoo's `./openerp/addons/base/res/res_config.py` file.

11
Internationalization

In this chapter, we will cover the following topics:

- ▶ Installing a language and configure user preferences
- ▶ Configuring language-related settings
- ▶ Translating texts through the web client user interface
- ▶ Exporting translation strings to a file
- ▶ Using gettext tools to ease translations
- ▶ Importing translation files into Odoo

Many of these actions can be done either from the web client user interface or from the command line. Whenever possible, we will show how to use either option.

Installing a language and configure user preferences

Odoo is localization ready, meaning that it supports several languages and locale settings, such as date and number formats.

When first installed, only the default English language is available. To have other languages and locales available to the users, we need to install them.

Getting ready

We will need to have the **Developer Mode** activated. If it's not, activate it in the Odoo **About** dialog.

How to do it...

To install a new language in an Odoo instance, follow these steps:

1. Select the menu option **Settings | Translations | Load a Translation**. On the resulting dialog, select the language to install from the list of available languages. If the website is installed, you will also be given the option to pick the websites where the language will be available.

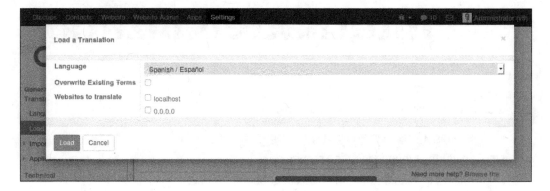

2. Now click on the **Load** button and the language will be installed.

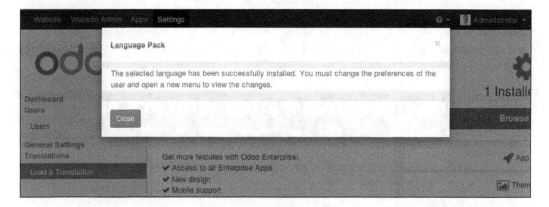

3. New languages can also be installed from the command line. The equivalent command for the preceding steps is:

```
$ ./odoo.py -d mydb --load-language=es_ES
```

4. To set the language used by a user, go to **Settings | Users | Users** and, in the **Preferences** tab of the user form, set the **Language** field value. While you are at it, you can use the opportunity to set the user's **Timezone**.

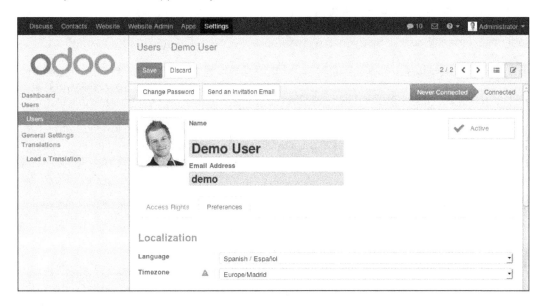

The users can also set these configurations themselves through the **Preferences** menu option, available when they click on the user name at the top right of the web client window.

How it works...

The users can have their own language and timezone preferences. The former is used to translate the user interface text into the chosen language and apply local conventions for the float and monetary fields. The latter is used to display the **datetime** fields in the correct timezone.

Before a language is made available for the users to select, it must be installed with the **Load a Translation** feature. The list of installed languages can be seen with the **Settings | Translations | Languages** menu option.

Each Odoo addon module is responsible for providing its own translation resources that should be placed inside an i18n subdirectory. Each language's data should be in a .po file. Following our example, for the Spanish language, the translation data is loaded from the es_ES.po data file.

Odoo also supports the notion of **base language**. For example, if we have an `es.po` file for Spanish and an `es_MX.po` file for Mexican Spanish, then `es.po` is detected as the base language for `es_MX.po`. When the Mexican Spanish language is installed, both data files are loaded; first the one for the base language and then the specific language is installed. Thus, the specific language translation file only needs to contain the strings that are specific to the language variant, Mexican Spanish in our example.

The `i18n` subdirectory is also expected to have a `<module_name>.pot` file, providing a template for translations and containing all the translatable strings. The *Export translation strings* to a file recipe explains how to export the translatable strings to generate this file.

When an additional language is installed, the corresponding resources are loaded from all installed addon modules and stored in the **Translated Terms** model. Its data can be viewed (and edited) with the **Settings | Translations | Application Terms | Translated Terms** menu option.

Translation files for the installed languages are also loaded when a new addon module is installed or an existing addon module is upgraded.

There's more...

Translation files can be reloaded without upgrading the addon modules by repeating the **Load a Translation** action. This can be used in case you have updated translation files and don't want to go through the trouble of upgrading the modules (and all their dependencies).

If the **Overwrite Existing Terms** checkbox is left empty, only new translated string is loaded. Thus, the changed translated string won't be loaded. Check the box if you want the already existing translations to also be loaded and overwrite the currently loaded translations.

The previous checkbox exists because we can do our specific translations editing **Settings | Translations | Application Terms | Translated Terms**, or using the **Technical Translation** shortcut option in the **Debug** menu. Translations added or modified this way won't be overwritten unless the language is reloaded with the **Overwrite Existing Terms** checkbox enabled.

It can be useful to know that the addon modules can also have an `i18n_extra` subdirectory with extra translations. The loading sequence for the translation files is: the `.po` files in the `i18n` subdirectory, first for the base language and then for the language; then the `.po` files in the `i18n_extra` subdirectory, first for the base language and then for the language. The last string translation loaded is the one that prevails.

See also

The list of language codes can be seen in the source code; in the `odoo/openerp/tools/misc.py` file, look for the `ALL_LANGUAGES` variable. The GitHub link for the file is `https://github.com/odoo/odoo/blob/9.0/openerp/tools/misc.py`.

Configure language-related settings

Languages and their variations (such as `es_MX` for Mexican Spanish) also provide locale settings such as date and number formats.

They come with appropriate defaults, so as long as the user is using the correct language, the locale settings should be the appropriate ones.

But you still might want to modify a language's settings. For example, you might prefer to have the user interface in the default English, but want to change the American default date and number formats to your needs.

Getting ready

We will need to have the **Developer Mode** activated. If it's not, activate it in the Odoo **About** dialog.

How to do it...

To modify a language's locale settings, follow these steps:

1. To check the installed languages and their configurations, select the **Settings | Translations | Languages** menu option. Clicking on one of the installed languages will open a form with the corresponding settings:

2. Edit the language settings. To change the date to the ISO format, change **Date Format** to **%Y-%m-%d**, and to change the number format to use a comma as a decimal separator, modify the **Decimal Separator** and **Thousands Separator** fields accordingly.

How it works...

When signing in and creating a new Odoo user session, the user language is checked in the user preferences and set in the `lang` context key. This is then used to format the outputs appropriately: the source texts are translated to the user language, and the dates and numbers are formatted according to the language's current locale settings.

There's more...

Server side processes are able to modify the context in which actions are run. For example, to get a record set where the dates are formatted according to the English format independent of the current user's language preference, you could do the following:

```
en_records = self.with_context(lang='en_EN').search([])
```

For more details, refer to *Chapter 6, Advanced Server Side Development Techniques* recipe *Calling a method with a modified context*.

Translate texts through the web client user interface

The simplest way to translate is to use the translation feature provided by the web client. These translation strings are stored in the database and can later be exported to a `.po` file, either to be included in an addon module or just to later be imported back manually.

Text fields can have translatable content, meaning that their value will depend on the current user's language. We will also see how to set the language-dependent values on these fields.

Getting ready

We need to have the **Developer Mode** activated. If it's not, activate it in the Odoo **About** dialog.

How to do it...

We will demonstrate how to use translate terms through the web client using the **User Groups** feature as an example:

1. Navigate to the screen to translate. Select the **Settings** top menu and then open **Users | Groups** to open the corresponding view.

2. On the top menu bar, click on the **Debug** menu icon and select the **Technical Translation** option:

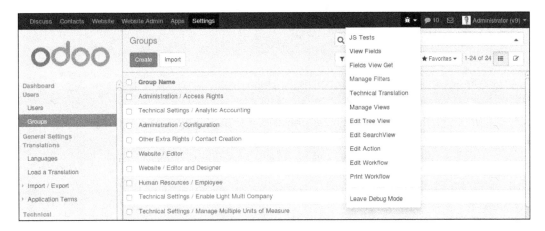

3. A list of the available translation terms for that view will be shown. Edit **Translation Value** in a line to change (or add) its translation text. If looking for a particular source string, use the list filters to narrow down the displayed texts:

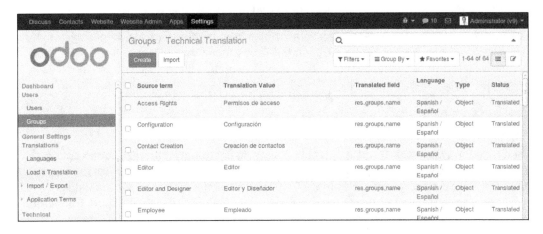

The Group name is a translatable field. Let's translate a record's value to the several languages installed:

4. Navigate again to the **User Groups** menu option, open one of the group records in the form view, and click on **Edit**:

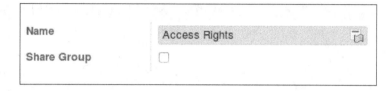

5. Note that the **Name** field has a special icon at the far right. This indicates that it is a translatable field. Clicking on the icon opens a **Translate** list with the different installed languages, allowing us to set the translation for each of those languages.

How it works...

Translated terms are stored in the database table for the model `ir.translation`. The **Technical Translation** option in the **Debug** menu provides a quick access to those terms, in context with the currently selected view.

Similarly, the model fields with translatable content feature an icon to access the list of the installed languages and to set the appropriate value for each language.

Alternatively, the translation terms can be accessed from the **Settings** top menu, using the **Translations | Application Terms | Translated Terms** menu option. Here we can see all the terms available for our instance, but should need to use data filters to locate the terms we might be interested in.

There's more...

Alongside the **Translated Terms** menu option, we also find the **Synchronize Terms** option. Selecting it will display a dialog window to provide the desired language, and will then launch the process to extract translatable strings from the installed addon modules and add any new ones to the **Translated Terms** table. It is equivalent to performing the **Export Translation** followed by the **Import Translation** steps described earlier.

This can be useful after changing some models or views, to have the new strings added so that we can translate them.

It can also be used to populate the strings from the `en_US` default language. We can then make use of the translation terms to replace the original English texts with new ones, better for the end user's specific business vocabulary.

Exporting translation strings to a file

Translation strings can be exported with or without the translated texts for a selected language. This can be either to include in a module `i18n` data, or to later perform the translations with a text editor or perhaps with a specialized tool.

We will demonstrate how to do it using the standard `mail` module, so feel free to replace `mail` with your own module.

Getting ready

We need to have the **Developer Mode** activated. If it's not, activate it in the Odoo **About** dialog.

How to do it...

To export the translation terms for the mail `addon` module, follow these steps:

1. In the web client user interface, from the **Settings** top menu select the **Translations | Import/Export | Export Translation** menu option.

2. At the **Export Translations** dialog, choose the language translation to export, the file format, and the modules to export. To export a translation template file, select **New Language (Empty translation template)** from the **Language** selection list. It's recommended to use the `.po` format and to export only one `addon` module at a time—the **Discuss** (`mail` technical name) module in our example:

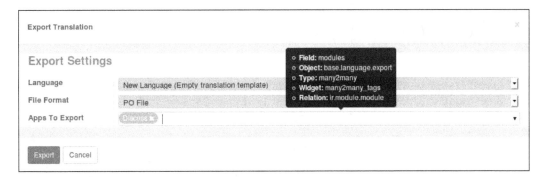

3. Once the export process is complete, a new window will be displayed, with a link to download the file and some additional advice:

Odoo ✕

Export Complete

Here is the exported translation file: Download mail.pot

This file was generated using the universal **Unicode/UTF-8** file encoding, please be sure to view and edit using the same encoding.

The next step depends on the file format:

- CSV format: you may edit it directly with your favorite spreadsheet software, the rightmost column (value) contains the translations
- PO(T) format: you should edit it with a PO editor such as POEdit, or your preferred text editor
- TGZ format: this is a compressed archive containing a PO file, directly suitable for uploading to Odoo's translation platform, Launchpad

For more details about translating Odoo in your language, please refer to the documentation.

`Close`

---

4. To export from the Odoo command line interface a translation template file for the mail addon module:

```
$ ./odoo.py -d mydb --i18n-export=mail.po --modules=mail
$ mv mail.po ./addons/mail/i18n/mail.pot
```

5. To export from the Odoo command line interface the translation template file for a language, `es_ES` for Spanish, for example:

```
$ ./odoo.py -d mydb --i18n-export=es_ES.po --modules=mail
--language=es_ES
$ mv es_ES.po ./addons/mail/i18n
```

How it works...

The **Export Translation** feature does two things: it first extracts the translatable strings from the target modules, adding the new ones in the `ir.translation` model, and then creates a file with the translation terms. This can be done both from the web client and the command line interface.

When exporting from the web client, we can choose to either export an empty translation template – a file with the strings to translate along with empty translations, or export a language, resulting in a file with the strings to translate along with translation already done for the selected language.

The file formats available are CSV, PO, and TGZ. The TGZ file format exports a compressed file containing a directory structure `<name>/i18n/` with the PO or POT file.

The CSV format can be useful to perform translations using a spreadsheet, but the format to use in the addon modules is the PO files. These are expected to be placed inside the `i18n` subdirectory, and if so are automatically loaded once the corresponding language is installed. When exporting these PO files, we should export only one module at a time. The PO file is also a popular format supported by translation tools, such as Poedit.

Translations can also be exported directly from the command line, using the `--i18n-export` option. The recipe shows how to extract both the template files and the translated language files.

In Step 4 of the previous section, we exported a template file. The `--i18n-export` option expects the path and the file name to export. Mind that the file extension is required to be either CSV, PO, or TGZ. This option requires the `-d` option, specifying the database to use. The `--modules` option is also needed to indicate the addon modules to export. Note that the `--stop-after-init` option is not needed, since the export command automatically returns to the command line when finished.

This exports a template file, that in a module is expected to have the POT extension. When working on a module, after the export operation we usually want to move the exported PO file to the module's `i18n` directory with a `<module>.pot` name.

In Step 5, the `--language` option was also used. With it, instead of an empty translation file, the translated terms for the selected language were also exported. One use case for this is to perform some translations through the web client user interface using the **Technical Translation** feature, and then exporting and including them in the module.

There's more...

Text strings in view and model definitions are automatically extracted for translation. For models, the `_description` attribute, the field names (the `string` attribute), help text, and selection field options are extracted, as well as the user texts for model constraints (`_constraints` and `_sql_constraints`).

Text strings to translate inside Python or JavaScript code can't be automatically detected, so the code should identify those strings, wrapping them inside the underscore function.

In a module Python file, we should make sure it is imported with the following:

```
from openerp import _
```

It can then be used wherever a translatable text is used with something like this:

```
_('Hello World')
```

For strings that use additional context information, we should use Python string interpolation, like this:

```
_('Hello %s') % 'World'
```

Note that the interpolation should go outside the translation function. For example, _("Hello %s" % 'World') is wrong. String interpolations should also be preferred to string concatenation, so that each interface text is just one translation string.

 Caution with the Selection fields! If you pass an explicit list of values to the field definition, then the displayed strings are automatically flagged for translation. On the other hand, if you pass a method returning the list of values, then the display strings must be explicitly marked for translation.

Regarding the manual translation work, any text file editor can do, but using a file supporting the PO file syntax makes the work easier by reducing the risk of formatting errors. Such editors include:

- poedit (https://poedit.net/)
- emacs (po-mode) (https://www.gnu.org/software/gettext/manual/html_node/PO-Mode.html)
- Lokalize (http://i18n.kde.org/tools)
- Gtranslator (https://wiki.gnome.org/Apps/Gtranslator)

Use gettext tools to ease translations

The PO file format is part of the gettext internationalization and localization system commonly used in Unix-like systems. This system includes tools to ease the translation work.

This recipe demonstrates how to use these tools to help translate our addon modules. We want to use it on a custom module, so my_module created in *Chapter 3, Creating Odoo Modules* is a good candidate. But feel free to replace it with some other custom module you have at hand, replacing the recipe's my_module references as appropriate.

How to do it...

To manage the translation from the command line, assuming that your Odoo installation is at ~/odoo-work/odoo, follow these steps:

1. Create a compendium of translation terms for the target language, for example, Spanish. If we name our compendium file odoo_es.po we should write the following code:

```
$ cd ~/odoo-work/odoo  # Use the path to your Odoo installation
$ find ./ -name es_ES.po | xargs msgcat --use-first | msgattrib \
--translated  --no-fuzzy -o ./odoo_es.po
```

2. Export from the Odoo command line interface the translation template file for the addon module and place it in the module's expected location:

```
$ ./odoo.py -d mydb --i18n-export=my_module.po --modules=my_module
$ mv my_module.po ./addons/my_module/i18n/my_module.pot
```

3. If no translation file is available yet for the target language, create the PO translation file, reusing the terms already found translated in the compendium:

```
$ msgmerge --compendium ./odoo_es.po \
  -o ./addons/my_module/i18n/es_ES.po \
  /dev/null ./addons/my_module/i18n/my_module.pot
```

4. If a translation file exists, add the translations that can be found in the compendium:

```
$ mv ./addons/my_module/i18n/es_ES.po /tmp/my_module_es_old.po
$ msgmerge --compendium ./odoo_es.po \
  -o./addons/my_module/i18n/es_ES.po \
  /tmp/my_module_es_old.po ./addons/my_module/i18n/my_module.pot
$ rm /tmp/my_module_es_old.po
```

5. To have a peek at the untranslated terms in a PO file:

```
$ msgattrib --untranslated ./addons/my_module/i18n/es_ES.po
```

6. Use your favorite editor to complete the translation.

How it works...

Step 1 of the preceding section calls `odoo.py` with the `--i18n-export` option. You need to specify a database on the command line, even if one is specified in the configuration file and the `--modules` option, with a comma separated list of modules to export the translation for.

Step 2 uses commands from the gettext toolbox to create a translation compendium for the chosen language, Spanish in our case. It works by finding all the `es_ES.po` files in the Odoo code base, and passing them to the `msgcat` command. We use the `--use-first` flag to avoid conflicting translations (there are a few in the Odoo code base). The result is passed to the `msgattrib` filter. We use the `--translated` option to filter out the untranslated entries and the `--no-fuzzy` option to remove the fuzzy translations. We then save the result in `odoo_es.po`.

 In the gettext world, *fuzzy* translations are those created automatically by the `msgmerge` command (or other tools) by using a proximity match on the source string. We want to avoid these in the compendium.

Step 3 creates a translation file using the translated values for texts already found in the compendium. The `msgmerge` command is used with the `--compendium` option to find in the compendium files the `msgid` lines matching those in the translation template file generated in Step 1. The result is saved in the `es_ES.po` file.

If you have a pre-existing `.po` file for your addon with translations you would like to preserve, then you should rename it and replace the `/dev/null` argument with this file. The rename is required to avoid using the same file both for input and output.

There's more...

This recipe only skims the rich tools of the GNU gettext toolbox. Full coverage is well beyond the scope of this book. If you are interested, the GNU gettext documentation contains a wealth of precious information about PO file manipulation, and is available at `http://www.gnu.org/software/gettext/manual/gettext.html`.

Import translation files

The usual practice to load translations is by placing the PO files inside the module's `i18n` subdirectory. Whenever the addon module is installed or upgraded, the translation files are loaded and the new translated strings are added.

But there may be cases where we want to directly import a translation file. In this recipe, we will see how to load a translation file, either from the web client or from the command line.

Getting ready

We need to have the **Developer Mode** activated. If it's not, activate it in the Odoo **About** dialog. We are also expected to have a translation file to be imported; `myfile.po`, for example.

How to do it...

To import the translation terms, follow these steps:

1. In the web client user interface, from the **Settings** top menu select the **Translations | Import/Export | Import Translation** menu option.
2. On the **Import Translations** dialog, fill out the language name and the language code, and select the file to import. Finally, click on the **Import** button to perform the action.

3. To import from the Odoo command line interface a translation file, we must place it inside the server addons path and then perform the import:

```
$ mv myfile.po ./addons/
$ ./odoo.py -d mydb --i18n-import="myfile.po" --lang=es_ES
```

How it works...

Import Translation takes a PO or CSV file and loads the translation strings into the `ir.translation` table.

The web client feature asks for the language name, but this is not used in the import process. It also has an overwrite option. If selected, it forces all the translations strings to be imported, even the ones that already exist, overwriting them in the process.

On the command line, the import can be done using the `--i18n-import` option. It must be provided with the path to the file, relative to an addon's path directory. `-d` and `--language` (or `-l`) are mandatory. Overwriting can also be achieved by adding the `--i18n-overwrite` option to the command. Note that we didn't use the `--stop-after-init` option. It is not needed, since the import action stops the server when it finishes.

12

Automation and Workflows

In this chapter, we will show cover the following topics:

- ▶ Using Kanban stages and features
- ▶ Creating server actions
- ▶ Adding messaging and tracking features
- ▶ Using Python code server actions
- ▶ Using automated actions on time conditions
- ▶ Using automated actions on event conditions
- ▶ Inspecting built-in workflows

Introduction

Business applications are expected not only to store records, but also to manage business workflows. Odoo includes a workflow engine, but it is increasingly used less in later versions of the product. Instead, automation rules and Kanban boards are used whenever possible.

The automation rules are most relevant for customization than for new addon modules development, but developers should still be familiar with them. Doing so can avoid over-engineered business rules that could be implemented through functional customizations. Some of these techniques can also be used by power users or functional consultants to add some simpler process automation without the need to create custom addons.

Using Kanban stages and features

The Kanban board is a simple method to manage workflows. It is organized in columns, each corresponding to stages, and the work items progress from left to right until they are finished.

There are a few features used across several Kanban boards, providing a common pattern that can also be used in our own custom modules. Let's visit those features.

Getting ready

To follow this recipe, you will need to have the Project Management app already installed.

How to do it...

To get started with a Project Tasks Kanban board:

1. Select the **Project** top menu option and then **Create** a new Project.
2. Give a name to the new Project and hit the **Save** button. Next, press on the **Tasks** smart button at the top right of the form. This will open the Kanban view for the Project Tasks.
3. Click on the **Add New Column** vertical bar at the right, type Now in the small dialog box, and click on **Add**. Repeat to also add the **Later** and **Done** stages.
4. Hover the mouse pointer over the **Done** stage and a cog wheel icon will be shown. Click on it and pick **Edit** from the option menu.
5. In the **Edit Columns** window, check the **Folded in Tasks Pipeline** box and save, as shown in the following screenshot:

How it works...

Kanban is one of the available view types, and it is able to organize items grouped in columns. If we use stages to group the work items, we get a **Kanban board**. The stage list can be configured to fit the user's specific needs.

Stages should have a folded attribute, meaning that the corresponding column in the Kanban view should be shown folded. Work in progress items are expected to be in an unfolded stage, and terminated items, usually **Done** and **Cancelled**, should be in **Folded** stages.

Each work item has a reference for the stage it is in. It may also have a Kanban State, represented by a traffic signal-like light, and a Priority, represented by a star. The Kanban cards can also have a color attribute, used for their background color.

While the stage represents the current status in the process for the work item, **Kanban State** provides information about its readiness to advance to the next stage. It is a **Selection** field, usually named `kanban_state`, in the form, and Kanban views is used with the `kanban_state_selection` widget and expects three possible options:

 ▸ A grey neutral value, the default (the `normal` database value)

 ▸ A red "Blocked" value (the `blocked` database value), meaning that there is some reason to retain the work item in the current stage

 ▸ A green "Ready for the next stage" value (the `done` database value), meaning that the work item is ready to be pulled for the next stage

The **Priority** is also a **Selection** field, and is displayed with the special `priority` widget in the form and Kanban views. The selection options are expected to be either a string with a number, starting at `0`, for normal value (not starred), and other values for starred options.

There's more...

Stages are added to models through a `Many2one` field referencing a stage model defining the possible stages. On form views, they can be represented with the help of the `statusbar` pipeline widget. For more details on views, widgets, and designing Kanban views, you can refer to *Chapter 8, Backend Views*.

The complementary Kanban state is supported by a **Selection** field and its typical definition is:

```
kanban_state = fields.Selection(
    [('normal', 'Normal'),('blocked', 'Blocked'),('done', 'Ready for
next stage')],
    'Kanban State',
    default='normal')
```

On form views, it should use the specific `kanban_state_selection` widget:

```
<field name="kanban_state" widget="kanban_state_selection" />
```

Regarding the **Priority** field, it is also a **Selection** field, and the number of options usually ranges between 2 and 4 selection items:

```
priority = fields.selection(
    [('0', 'Normal'), ('1', 'Low'), ('2', 'High'),
     ('3', 'Very High')],
    'Priority', default='0')
```

In form views, it can make use of the specific `priority` widget:

```
<field name="priority" widget="priority"/>
```

Creating server actions

Server actions underpin the Odoo automation tools. They allow us to describe the actions to perform. These actions are then available to be called by event triggers, or to be triggered automatically when certain time conditions are met.

The simplest case is to let the end user perform some action on a document by selecting it from the **More** button menu. We will create such an action for project tasks, to **Set as Priority** by starring the currently selected task and setting a deadline on it to three days from now.

Getting ready

We will need an Odoo instance with the Project app installed. We will also need the **Developer Mode** activated. If it's not, activate it in the Odoo **About** dialog.

How to do it...

To create a server action and use it from the **More** menu, follow these steps:

1. On the **Settings** top menu, select the **Technical | Actions | Server Actions** menu item, and click on the **Create** button at the top of the record list.

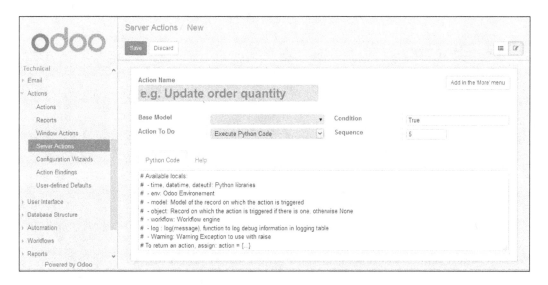

2. Fill out the server action form with these values:

   ❏ **Action Name: Set as Priority**

   ❏ **Base Model: Task**

   ❏ **Action To Do: Write On a Record**

   ❏ **Update Policy: Update the Current Record**

3. In the server action, under the **Value Mapping** field, add the following lines:

   ❏ As the first value, we will enter the following parameters:

      ❏ **Field**: Deadline

      ❏ **Evaluation Type**: Python expression

      ❏ **Value**: datetime.date.today() + datetime.
      timedelta(days=3)

   ❏ As the second value, we will enter the following parameters:

      ❏ **Field**: Priority

      ❏ **Evaluation Type**: Value

      ❏ **Value**: 1

The following screenshot shows the entered values:

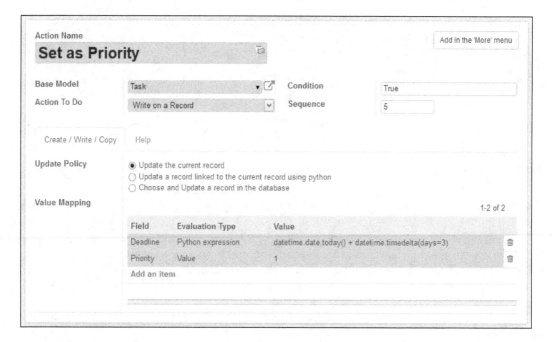

4. Save the server action and click on the **Add in the 'More' Button** at the top right, to make it available in the Project task's **More** button.

5. To try it out, go to the Project top menu, select the **Search | Tasks** menu item, and open a random task. By clicking on the **More** button, we should see the **Set as Priority** option. Selecting it will star the task and change the deadline date to three days from now.

How it works...

Server actions work on a Model, so one of the first things to do is to pick the **Base Model** we want to work with. In our example, we used Project Tasks.

Next, we should select the type of action to perform. There are a few options available:

▸ **Send Email** allows choosing an e-mail template, and will use it to send out an e-mail when the action is triggered.

▸ **Trigger a Workflow Signal** does just that. In Odoo Workflows, **Signals** can be triggered and used to fire workflow transitions.

▸ **Run a Client Action** triggers a client or window action, just like when a menu item is clicked.

▸ **Create or Copy a new Record** allows you to create a new record, on the current or on another Model.

▸ **Write on a Record** allows you to set values on the current or on another record.

▸ **Execute Python Code** allows you to write arbitrary code to execute, when none of the other options is flexible enough for what we need.

For our example, we used **Write on a Record** to set some values on the current record. We set **Priority** to 1, to star the task, and set a value on the **Deadline** field. This one is more interesting, since the value to use is evaluated from a Python expression. Our example makes use of the `datetime` Python module (see `https://docs.python.org/2/library/datetime.html`) to compute the date three days from today.

Arbitrary Python expression can be used there, as well as in several of the other action types available. For security reasons, the code is checked by the `safe_eval` function, implemented in `odoo/openerp/tools/safe_eval.py`. This means that some Python operations may not be allowed, but this rarely proves to be a problem.

There's more...

The Python code is evaluated in a restricted context, where the following objects are available to use:

- env: This is a reference for the Environment object, just like self.env in a class method.
- model: This is a reference to the model class the server action acts upon. In our example, it is equivalent to self.env['project.task].
- workflow: This is a reference to the Odoo workflow engine server object.
- Warning: This is a reference to openerp.exceptions.Warning, allowing for validations that block unintended actions. It can be used as: raise Warning('Message!').
- object or obj: This provides references to the current record, allowing you to access its field values and methods.
- log: This is a function to log messages in the ir.logging model, allowing for database side logging on actions.
- datetime, dateutil, and time: These provide access to the Python libraries.

Adding messaging and tracking features

Odoo social features are used in many of the standard apps. They provide an easy way for the user to be updated and to collaborate around business documents. It is, therefore, important for the custom addon modules to also support them.

These features are provided by the **Discuss** app (the mail technical name) and their most visible aspect is the message wall at the bottom of the form for a business document, along with the follower box on its right-hand side.

Getting ready

We will use `my_module` introduced in *Chapter 3, Creating Odoo Modules*, defining the `Library Book` model. You can get that code or quickly create an addon around this model:

```
# -*- coding: utf-8 -*-
from openerp import models, fields
class LibraryBook(models.Model):
    _name = 'library.book'
    name = fields.Char('Title', required=True)
    date_release = fields.Date('Release Date')
    author_ids = fields.Many2many('res.partner', string='Authors')
```

We will also need an XML file with the corresponding form view:

```
<form>
    <group>
        <field name="name"/>
        <field name="author_ids" widget="many2many_tags"/>
    </group>
    <group>
        <field name="date_release"/>
    </group>
</form>
```

How to do it...

To enable the social network and tracking features on the `Library Book` model, follow these steps:

1. Add the `mail` dependency to the addon module's `__openerp__.py` manifest file:

    ```
    'depends': ['mail'],
    ```

2. Edit the `library.book` model to add the code highlighted next:

    ```python
    class LibraryBook(models.Model):
        _name = 'library.book'
        _description = 'Library Book'
        _inherit = ['mail.thread']
        name = fields.Char('Title', required=True,
                            track_visibility=True)
        date_release = fields.Date('Release Date',
                            track_visibility=True)
        author_ids = fields.Many2many('res.partner', string='Authors')
    ```

3. Add to the `library.book` model the following method:

    ```python
    def _track_subtype(self, init_values):
        if 'date_release' in init_values:
            return 'mail.mt_comment'
        return False
    ```

4. Add the message wall widgets into the form view, just before the `</form>` closing tag:

    ```xml
    <div class="oe_chatter">
        <field name="message_follower_ids"
                widget="mail_followers" groups="base.group_user" />
        <field name="message_ids"
                widget="mail_thread" />
    </div>
    ```

After installing these changes, we should see the message wall at the bottom of the `Library Book` form, and changes to the **Title** and **Release Date** fields should be logged on it.

How it works...

The **Discuss** addon (the `mail` technical name) provides the `mail.thread` model to use on other business models as a mixin class. Our first steps are to add the module dependency and to have the `library.book` module to inherit features from it.

Among other things, the `message_follower_ids` and `message_ids` fields are added to store the follower list and related messages. These should be added to the form view, using the `mail_followers` and `mail_thread` special widgets.

We also added the optional `_description` attribute to the model's class. It is used by some of the tracking messages, such as **Library Book created**, and will inappropriately display messages such as **Email Thread is created** if not explicitly defined. After addon installation, the display name that'll be used can also be set at **Settings | Technical | Database Structure | Models**, in the **Model Description** field.

The `mail.thread` model can keep track of changes made to a document, posting them as messages on the message wall. For this, we just need to add `track_visibility=True` (or any true value) on the fields to track. By default, these are posted as internal notes, meaning that no e-mail messages are triggered.

 Unlike version 8.0, in version 9.0 the changed values are stored in the database, in the `mail.tracking.value` model. This is accessible in the web client at **Settings | Technical | Email | Tracking Values**. This can be useful for reporting or auditing.

The message types are called **Subtypes**. The mail module comes with two subtypes: discussion messages and internal notes. The first can trigger e-mail notifications and is visible to all the followers. The second one does not trigger notifications and can only be seen by users in the Employee security group. We can set the subtype when posting messages using their XML IDs. For these two, the corresponding XML IDs are `mail.mt_comment` and `mail.mt_note`.

The subtype for the tracking messages can be changed by the `_track_subtype()` method. It receives a dictionary with the tracked field names with changes, and their values before the changes were made. It is expected to return a string with the XML ID of the subtype to use. Subtypes provided by the `mail` addon do not need the module suffix, so we can use just `mt_comment` for discussion messages. If no specific subtype is returned, messages will use the default `mt_note` subtype.

Followers can subscribe to different subtypes, so they are able to choose when to be notified. For example, the Project addon adds subtypes such as **Task change stage** or **Task is blocked**. With `_track_subtype()`, we can detect such events and report them through messages with the proper subtype. Inside that method, `self` makes available the recordsets involved in the write operation, so that distinct message subtypes can be selected based on arbitrary record values.

There's more...

Posting messages can be done using the following method:

```
obj.message_post(body="Body text", subject="Subject", subtype="mt_
note")
```

The subject and subtype are optional.

Followers can be either partners or message channels. To add followers, use the following:

```
obj.message_subscribe(partner_ids=..., channel_ids=..., subtype_
ids=[])
```

The `subtype_ids` argument is optional, and allows you to subscribe specific subtypes. If not provided, the defaults defined in the subtypes will be used.

Sometimes we want to add a user as a follower. A user is also a partner, so `user.partner_id` should be used for this. However, the following specific method is also provided for this:

```
obj.message_subscribe_users(user_ids, subtype_ids=[])
```

It is reasonable to expect to be able to post messages or follow documents even if the connected user has no write access to them. Special security logic is implemented to allow this, and these particular operations are performed with the Administrator user, through the `sudo()` ORM method.

Message subtypes can be managed in the **Settings** top menu, by navigating to the **Technical | Email | Subtypes** menu item. There we can inspect the existing subtypes and customize them. **Description** is the text displayed in the message, and the **Default** field indicates if the subtype is subscribed by default for the new followers.

Subtypes support an inheritance mechanism. It is, for example, used by projects to allow the followers to automatically subscribe events on tasks and issues, such as **Task Opened**. This is done using the fields in the **Auto Subscription** area of the subtype:

- ▶ **Parent** is the related subtype to be automatically subscribed. For the `project.project` Task Opened, this would be the `project.task` Task Opened.

- ▶ **Relation Field** is the field in the related model to use. For a `project.task` subtype, this is `project_id`, for the Project to inherit subscription from.

Odoo also supports a **Need Action** indicator, shown on the menu item, to signal that action is required on a number of items. For example, it is used by the `mail` addon to display the number of unread messages.

To use it, our model should also inherit `ir.needaction_mixin`, and the `_needaction_domain_get()` method should be extended. It is an `@api.model` static method, meaning that it does not act upon a recordset. It is expected to return a domain expression to be used to identify the items needing action.

As an example, to signal that items with a **Blocked** Kanban state need action, we would use the following:

```
def _needaction_domain_get(self):
    return [('kanban_state', '=', 'blocked')]
```

Using Python code server actions

Server actions have several types available, but executing arbitrary Python code is surely the most flexible one. Used wisely, it can provide power users with the capability to implement advanced business rules from the user interface, without the need to create specific addon modules to install that code.

We will demonstrate using this type of server actions by implementing one that sends reminder notifications to the followers of a Project task.

Getting ready

We will need an Odoo instance with the Project app installed.

How to do it...

To create and try a Python code server action, follow these steps:

1. Create a new server action: On the **Settings** top menu, select the **Technical | Actions | Server Actions** menu item, and click on the **Create** button at the top of the record list.

2. Fill out the **Server Action** form with the following values:

   - **Action Name**: **Send Reminder**
   - **Base Model**: **Task**
   - **Action To Do**: **Execute Python Code**

3. In the **Python code** text area, remove the default text and replace it with the following:

```python
if not obj.date_deadline:
    raise Warning('Task has no deadline!')
deadline_dt = datetime.datetime.strptime(
    obj.date_deadline, '%Y-%m-%d')
delta = deadline_dt.date() - datetime.date.today()
days = delta.days
if days==0:
    msg =  'Task is due today.'
elif days < 0:
    msg = 'Task is %d day(s) late.' % abs(days)
else:
    msg = 'Task will be due in %d day(s).' % days
obj.message_post(msg, subject='Reminder', subtype='mt_comment')
```

4. Save the **Server Action** and click on **Add in the 'More' Button**, at the top right, to make it available in the Project task's **More** button.

5. Now click on the **Project** top menu and select the **Search | Tasks** menu item. Pick a random task, set a deadline date on it, and then try the **Send Reminder** option in the **More** button.

How it works...

The *Create server actions* recipe provides a detailed explanation on how to create a server action in general. For this particular type of action, we need to pick the **Execute Python Code** option and then write the code to run the text area.

The code can have multiple lines, as is the case in our recipe, and it runs in a context that has available references to objects such as the current record object or the session user. The references available are described in the *Create server actions* recipe.

The used code computes the number of days from the current date until the deadline date, and uses that to prepare an appropriate notification message. The last line does the actual posting of the message in the task's message wall. The `subtype='mt_comment'` argument is needed for e-mail notifications to be sent to the followers, just like when we use the **New Message** button. If no subtype is given, `mt_note` is used as a default, posting an internal note without notification, as if we used the **Log an internal note** button.

There's more...

Python code server actions are a powerful and flexible resource, but do have some limitations compared to the custom addon modules.

Since the Python code is evaluated at run time, in case of an error the stack trace is not so informative and it can be harder to debug. It is also not possible to insert a breakpoint in the code of a server action using the techniques shown in *Chapter 7, Debugging and Automated Testing*, so debugging needs to be done by using logging statements. Another concern is, when trying to track down the cause from a behavior in module code, you may miss that; it's probably caused by a server sction.

When carrying out a more intensive use of server actions, we can get complex interactions, so it is advised to plan properly and keep them organized.

Using automated actions on time conditions

Automated actions can be used to automatically trigger actions based on time conditions. We can use them to automatically perform some operation on records that meet certain criteria and reach time condition.

As an example, we can trigger a reminder notification for Project tasks one day before their deadline, if they have any. Let's see how this can be done.

Getting ready

To follow this recipe, we will need to have both the **Project Management** app and the **Automated Action Rules** addon already installed, and have the **Developer Mode** activated. We will also need the server action created in the *Using Python code server actions* recipe.

How to do it...

To create an automated action with a timed condition on tasks, follow these steps:

1. In the **Settings** top menu, select the **Technical | Automation | Automated Actions** menu item, and press on the **Create** button.

2. Fill out the basic information on the **Automated Actions** form:
   - **Rule Name: Deadline Near Notification**
   - **Related Document Model: Task**
   - Under the **Conditions tab**, for **When to Run**, select **Based on Time Condition**

3. To set the record criteria, on the **Filter** field text box, just after the **Select Records** link, set a valid domain expression: `[('date_deadline', '!=', False), ('stage_id.fold', '=', False)]`. When changing to another field, information on the number of records meeting the criteria is updated, and the **Select Records** link changes to **Change Selection**. By clicking on it we can check the records list of the records meeting the domain expression.

4. To set the time condition, on **Trigger Date** select the field to use, **Deadline**, and set the **Delay After Trigger Date** to **-1 Days**.

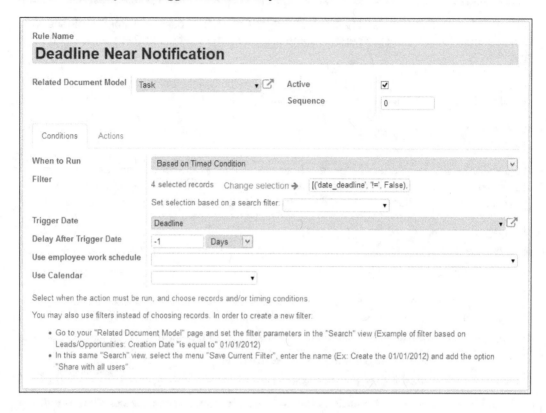

Rule Name

Deadline Near Notification

| Related Document Model | Task | Active | ✔ |
| | | Sequence | 0 |

Conditions   Actions

When to Run	Based on Timed Condition
Filter	4 selected records Change selection → [('date_deadline', '!=', False),
	Set selection based on a search filter:
Trigger Date	Deadline
Delay After Trigger Date	-1 Days
Use employee work schedule	
Use Calendar	

Select when the action must be run, and choose records and/or timing conditions.

You may also use filters instead of choosing records. In order to create a new filter:

- Go to your "Related Document Model" page and set the filter parameters in the "Search" view (Example of filter based on Leads/Opportunities: Creation Date "is equal to" 01/01/2012)
- In this same "Search" view, select the menu "Save Current Filter", enter the name (Ex: Create the 01/01/2012) and add the option "Share with all users"

5. On the **Actions** tab, under **Server actions to run**, click on **Add an item** and pick **Send Reminder** from the list that should have been created previously. If not, we could now also create the server action to run using the **Create** button.

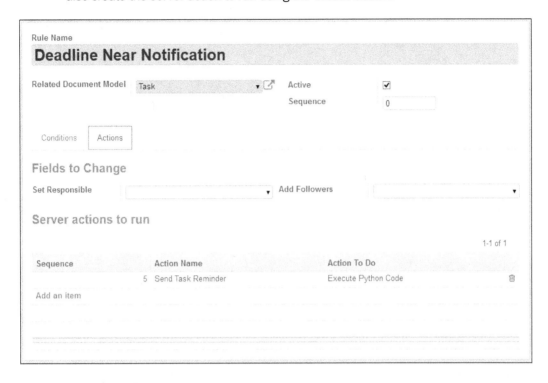

Rule Name

Deadline Near Notification

Related Document Model — Task — Active ✔

Sequence — 0

Conditions | Actions

Fields to Change

Set Responsible — Add Followers —

Server actions to run

1-1 of 1

Sequence	Action Name	Action To Do	
5	Send Task Reminder	Execute Python Code	🗑

Add an item

6. Click on **Save** to save the automated action. Perform the following steps to try it out:

    1. Go to the **Project** top menu, **Search | Tasks**, and set a deadline on some task with a date in the past.

2. Go to the **Settings** top menu, to the **Technical | Automation | Scheduled Actions** menu item, find the **Check Action Rules** action in the list, open its form view, and press on the **Run Manually** button, at the top left. This forces timed automated actions to be checked now. Note that this should work on a newly created demo database, but might not work like this in an existing database.

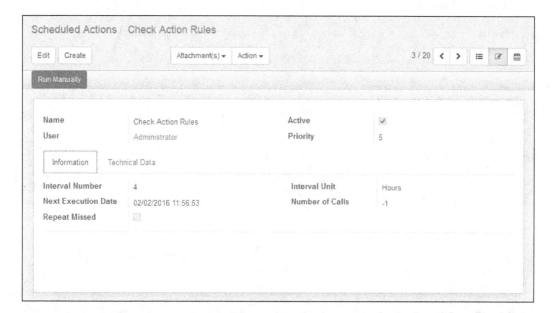

3. Again go to the **Project** top menu and open the same task you previously set a deadline date to. Check the message board below; you should see the notification generated by the server action triggered by our automated action.

How it works...

Automated actions act on a Model, and can be triggered either by events or by time conditions. The first steps are to set the **Model** and **When to Run** values.

Both methods can use a filter to narrow down the records eligible to perform the action on. We can use a domain expression for this. You can find details on writing domain expressions in *Chapter 8, Backend Views*. Alternatively, you can create and save a filter on project tasks, using the user interface features, and then copy here the automatically generated domain expression, selecting it from the **Set selection based on a search filter** list.

The domain expression we used selects all the records with a non-empty **Deadline** date, in a stage where the **Fold** flag is not checked. Stages without the **Fold** flag are considered to be working in progress. This way, we avoid triggering notifications on tasks that are in the **Done**, **Canceled**, or **Closed** stages.

Then we should define the time condition: the date field to use and when in time the action should be triggered. The time period can be in minutes, hours, days, or months, and number of periods can be positive, for time after the date, or negative, for time before the date. When using a time period in days, we can provide a **Resource Calendar** defining the working days, and the day count will use it.

These actions are checked by the **Check Action Rules** scheduled job. Note that by default it is run every four hours. This is appropriate for actions that work on the days or months scale, but if you need actions that work in the hour or minute timescales, you need to change the running interval to a smaller value.

Actions will be triggered for records that meet all the criteria and whose triggering date condition (field date plus the interval) is after the last action execution. This is so as to avoid repeatedly triggering the same action. And this is why manually running the preceding action will work in a database where the scheduled action was not yet triggered, but might not work immediately in a database where it was already run by the scheduler.

Once an automated action is triggered, the **Actions** tab tells you what should happen. This can be a list of server actions, doing things such as changing values on the record, posting notifications, sending out e-mails, and so on.

Additionally, two special operations are available. **Set Responsible** expects the target Model to have a `user_id` field and sets its value when the action is triggered. **Add Followers** gives a list of partners to be added to the record followers.

There's more...

These types of automated actions are triggered once a certain time condition is reached. This is not the same as regularly repeating some action while some condition is still true. For example, an automated action would not be capable of posting a reminder every day after the deadline has exceeded.

This type of action can instead be performed by **Scheduled Actions**, stored in the `ir.cron` model. However, scheduled actions do not support server actions; they can only call an existing method of a model object. So, to implement a custom action, we need to write an addon module adding the underlying Python method.

For reference, the technical name for the **Automated Actions** Model is `base.action.rule`.

Using automated actions on event conditions

Business applications provide systems with records for business operations, but are also expected to support dynamic business rules that are specific to the organization use cases.

Carving these rules into custom addon modules can be inflexible and out of the reach of functional users. Automated actions triggered by event conditions can bridge this gap and provide a powerful tool to automate or enforce the organization procedures.

As an example, we will enforce a validation on Project tasks such that only the Project Manager can change **Tasks** to the **Done** stage.

Getting ready

To follow this recipe, you will need to have the Project Management app already installed. We also need to have the **Developer Mode** activated. If it's not, activate it in the Odoo **About** dialog.

How to do it...

To create an automated action with an event condition on tasks, follow these steps:

1. In the **Settings** top menu, select the **Technical | Automation | Automated Actions** menu item, and press on the **Create** button.

2. Fill out the basic information on the **Automated Actions** form:

   - **Rule Name**: Validate Closing Tasks
   - **Related Document Model**: Task
   - **Conditions tab |When to Run**: On Update

3. The `on update` rules allow you to set two record filters, before and after the update operation. On the **Before Update Filter** field text box, after the **Select Records** link, set a valid domain expression: `[('stage_id.name', '!=', 'Done')]`. On the **Filter** field text box, set the following domain: `[('stage_id.name', '=', 'Done')]`, as shown in the following screenshot.

4. On the **Actions** tab, under **Server Actions to Run**, click on **Add an item**, and on the list dialog, press on the **Create** button to create a new server action.

5. Fill out the server action form with the following values and afterwards press on the **Save** button:

   - **Action Name**: Validate Closing Tasks
   - **Base Model**: Task
   - **Action To Do**: Execute Python Code
   - **Python Code**: Enter the following:

   ```
   if user != obj.project_id.user_id:
       raise Warning('Only the Project Manager can close
   Tasks')
   ```

The following screenshot shows the entered values:

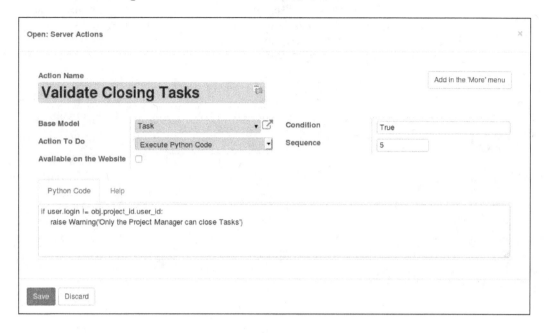

6. Click on **Save**, to save the automated action and try it out:

    1. On a database with demo data and logged in as Administrator, go to the **Project** top menu and click on the **E-Learning Integration** project to open its task Kanban.

    2. Then try dragging one of the tasks into the **Done** stage column. Since this Project's Manager is user Demo and we are working with the user Administrator, our automated action should be triggered, and our warning message is blocking the change.

How it works...

We start by giving a name to our automated actions and setting the Model it works with. For the type of action, we choose **On Update**, but the **On Creation**, **On Creation & Update**, **On Deletion**, and **Based On Form Modification** options are also possible.

Next, we should define the filters to determine when our action should be triggered. The **On Update** actions allow us to define two filters: one to check before and the other after the changes are made to the record. This can be used to express transitions: detect when a record changes from state A to state B. In our example, we want to trigger the action when a not-done task changes to the Done stage. The **On Update** action is the only one that allows for these two filters; the other actions types only allow for one filter.

It is important to note that our example condition will only work correctly for English language users. This is so because the **Stage Name** is a translatable field that can have different values for different languages. So, filters on the translatable fields should be avoided or used with care.

Finally, we create and add one (or more) server actions with whatever we want to be done when the automated action is triggered. In this case, we chose to demonstrate how to implement custom validation, making use of a Python code server action that uses the `Warning` exception to block the user changes.

There's more...

In *Chapter 5, Basic Server Side Development*, we saw how to redefine the `write()` methods of a model to perform actions on record update. Automated actions on record update provide another way to achieve the same, with some benefits and drawbacks.

Among the benefits, it is easy to define an action which is triggered by the update of a stored computed field, which is tricky to do in pure code. It is also possible to define filters on records and have different rules for different records, or for records matching different conditions which can be expressed with search domains.

But automated actions can have disadvantages when compared to Python business logic code inside modules. As a concern, with poor planning this flexibility can rapidly grow into complex interactions, hard to maintain and debug. Also, the before and after write filter operations bring some overhead, so for performing sensitive actions this could be an issue.

Inspecting built-in workflows

Odoo includes a built in workflow engine used to manage business document flows and interaction. However, this engine has been gradually replaced by Python business logic and automated actions. As an example of this, one of the most important workflows used to be the one linking sales orders, invoices, and deliveries, but since version 9.0, it has been removed.

But, there are a few workflows still used by some apps, so there may be cases where a developer will need to work with them. So it's still relevant to have some basic understanding of how they work.

The Marketing Campaigns app still uses a simple workflow, and we will use it to provide this brief overview on them.

Getting ready

We will need an Odoo instance with demo data and the Marketing Campaign's addon module installed (not that it's not an app). We also need to have the **Developer Mode** activated. If it's not, activate it in the Odoo **About** dialog.

How to do it...

To inspect the workflow defined on a model, follow these steps:

1. Open the **Lead Automation** top menu. Depending on the apps you have installed, it could instead be named **Marketing**. Click on a record on the **Campaigns** list to open its form view.

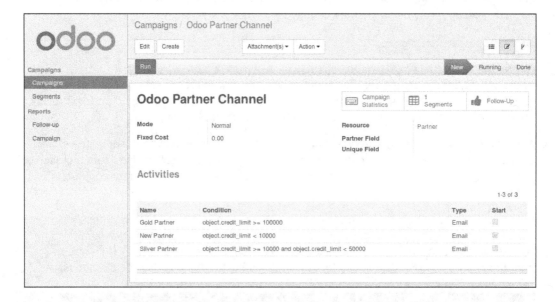

2. Open the **Debug** menu (the Bug icon at the right-hand side of the top bar) and choose the **Print Workflow** option. This will generate a PDF document with a graph of the campaign's workflow, displaying on a red background the workflow node the current document is at.

3. Again in the **Debug** menu, select the **Edit Workflow** option. This will navigate to the Workflow list view filtered by the current workflow. Click on the workflow line in the list to open and inspect its definition.

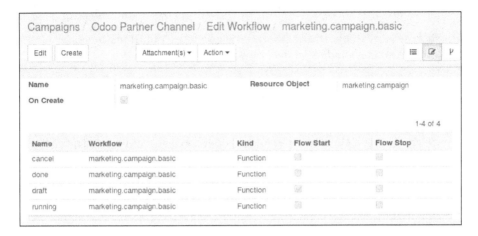

4. Workflows have a Third View mode, the diagram. Clicking on the Third View type icon, at the top right after the form view, we can see the workflow definition in a diagram. The diagram also allows editing: double click on the nodes to edit **Activities** and on the lines to edit **Transitions**.

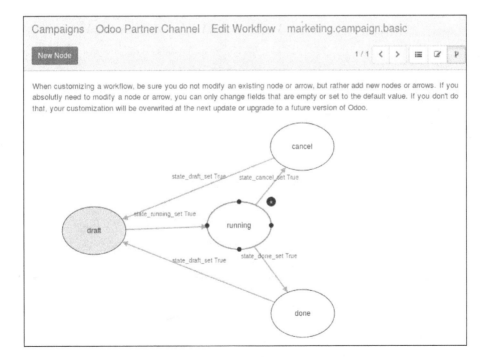

How it works...

The workflow definitions are stored in the `workflow` model, and are also reachable through the **Settings** top menu, and navigate to **Technical | Workflows** menu item.

Their definition has **Activities**. The nodes or workflow states, and **Transitions**, defining when a workflow's current state should move to another node.

Transitions often depend on a workflow **Signal** to be triggered. A common way to trigger a workflow signal is through form buttons. Buttons support a `type="workflow"` attribute for this.

Existing workflows are customizable: we can edit or add activities, and we can change the Transitions connecting them. Simple customizations usually involve editing a transition. In the workflow diagram, double clicking a transition arrow brings up its form view. There we rewire the workflow by modifying **Destination Activity**, adding **Condition** with a Python expression to evaluate, or using **Group Required** to limit the transition to be triggered only by users in a certain security group.

See also

- ▶ The official documentation provides more details about workflow definitions: https://www.odoo.com/documentation/9.0/reference/workflows.html.

13

Web Server Development

In this chapter, we'll cover the following topics:

- ▶ Making a path accessible from the network
- ▶ Restricting access to web accessible paths
- ▶ Consuming parameters passed to your handlers
- ▶ Modifying an existing handler
- ▶ Using the RPC API

Introduction

We'll introduce the basics of the web server part of Odoo in this chapter. Note that this covers the fundamental pieces. For high-level functionality, you should refer to *Chapter 14, CMS Website Development*.

All of Odoo's web request handling is driven by the Python library **werkzeug** (http:// werkzeug.pocoo.org). While the complexity of werkzeug is mostly hidden by Odoo's convenient wrappers, it is an interesting read to see how things work under the hood.

Make a path accessible from the network

In this recipe, we'll see how to make a URL of the form http://yourserver/path1/path2 accessible to users. This can either be a web page or a path returning arbitrary data to be consumed by other programs. In the latter case, you would usually use the JSON format to consume parameters and to offer your data.

Getting ready

We'll make use of the `library.book` model of *Chapter 4, Application Models*, so in case you haven't done so yet, grab its code to be able to follow the examples.

We want to allow any user to query the full list of books. Furthermore, we want to provide the same information to programs via a JSON request.

How to do it...

We'll need to add controllers, which go into a folder called `controllers` by convention:

1. Add a `controllers/main.py` file with the HTML version of our page:

```python
from openerp import http
from openerp.http import request

class Main(http.Controller):
    @http.route('/my_module/books', type='http', auth='none')
    def books(self):
        records = request.env['library.book'].sudo().search([])
        result = '<html><body><table><tr><td>'
        result += '</td></tr><tr><td>'.join(
                    records.mapped('name'))
        result += '</td></tr></table></body></html>'
        return result
```

2. Add a function to serve the same information in the JSON format:

```python
    @http.route('/my_module/books/json', type='json',
        auth='none')
    def books_json(self):
        records = request.env['library.book']\
                        .sudo().search([])
        return records.read(['name'])
```

3. Add the file `controllers/__init__.py`:

```python
from . import main
```

4. Add controllers to your `__init__.py` addon:

```python
from . import controllers
```

After restarting your server, you can visit /my_module/books in your browser and get presented with a flat list of book names. To test the JSON-RPC part, you'll have to craft a JSON request. A simple way to do that would be using the following command line to receive the output on the command line:

```
curl -i -X POST -H "Content-Type: application/json" -d "{}" \
localhost:8069/my_module/books/json
```

If you get **404** errors at this point, you probably have more than one database available on your instance. In this case, it's impossible for Odoo to determine which database is meant to serve the request. Use the --db-filter='^yourdatabasename$' parameter to force using the exact database you installed the module in. Now the path should be accessible.

How it works...

The two crucial parts here are that our controller is derived from openerp.http. Controller and that the methods we use to serve content are decorated with openerp. http.route. Inheriting from openerp.http.Controller registers the controller with Odoo's routing system in a similar way as models are registered, by inheriting from openerp. models.Model; also, Controller has a meta class that takes care of this.

In general, paths handled by your addon should start with your addon's name to avoid name clashes. Of course, if you extend some addon's functionality, you'll use this addon's name.

openerp.http.route

The route decorator allows us to tell Odoo that a method is to be web accessible in the first place, and the first parameter determines on which path it is accessible. Instead of a string, you can also pass a list of strings in case you use the same function to serve multiple paths.

The type argument defaults to http and determines what type of request is to be served. While strictly speaking JSON is HTTP, declaring the second function as type='json' makes life a lot easier, because Odoo then handles type conversions itself.

Don't worry about the auth parameter for now, it will be addressed in the recipe *Restrict access to web accessible paths* in this chapter.

Return values

Odoo's treatment of the functions' return values is determined by the type argument of the route decorator. For type='http', we usually want to deliver some HTML, so the first function simply returns a string containing it. An alternative is to use request.make_ response(), which gives you control over the headers to send in the response. So, to indicate when our page was updated last, we might change the last line in books() to:

```
    return request.make_response(
      result, [
```

```
('Last-modified', email.utils.formatdate(
  (
    fields.Datetime.from_string(
    request.env['library.book'].sudo()
    .search([], order='write_date desc', limit=1)
    .write_date) -
    datetime.datetime(1970, 1, 1)
  ).total_seconds(),
  usegmt=True)),
])
```

This code sends a `Last-modified` header along with the HTML we generated, telling the browser when the list was modified for the last time. We extract this information from the `write_date` field of the `library.book` model.

In order for the preceding snippet to work, you'll have to add some imports on the top of the file:

```
import email
import datetime
from openerp import fields
```

You can also create a `Response` object of `werkzeug` manually and return that, but there's little gain for the effort.

> Generating HTML manually is nice for demonstration purposes, but you should never do this in production code. Always use templates, as demonstrated in *Chapter 14, CMS Web Site Development*, recipe *QWeb*, and return them by calling `request.render()`.
>
> This will give you localization for free and makes your code better by separating business logic from the presentation layer. Also, templates provide you with functions to escape data before outputting HTML. The preceding code is vulnerable to cross-site-scripting attacks if a user manages to slip a `script` tag into the book name, for example.

For a JSON request, simply return the data structure you want to hand over to the client; Odoo takes care of serialization. For this to work, you should restrict yourself to data types that are JSON serializable, which are roughly dictionaries, lists, strings, floats and integers.

openerp.http.request

The `request` object is a static object referring to the currently handled request, which contains everything you need to take useful action. Most important is the property `request.env`, which contains an `Environment` object which is just the same as in `self.env` for models. This environment is bound to the current user, which is none in the preceding example because we used `auth='none'`. Lack of a user is also why we have to `sudo()` all our calls to model methods in the example code.

If you're used to web development, you'll expect session handling, which is perfectly correct. Use `request.session` for an `OpenERPSession` object (which is quite a thin wrapper around the `Session` object of `werkzeug`), and `request.session.sid` to access the session ID. To store session values, just treat `request.session` as a dictionary:

```
request.session['hello'] = 'world'
request.session.get('hello')
```

 Note that storing data in the session is no different from using global variables. Use it only if you must — that is usually the case for multi request actions like a checkout in the `website_sale` module. And also in this case, handle all functionality concerning sessions in your controllers, never in your modules.

There's more...

The `route` decorator can have some extra parameters to customize its behavior further. By default, all HTTP methods are allowed, and Odoo intermingles the parameters passed. Using the parameter `methods`, you can pass a list of methods to accept, which would usually be one of either `['GET']` or `['POST']`.

To allow cross origin requests (browsers block AJAX and some other types of requests to domains other than where the script was loaded from for security and privacy reasons), set the `cors` parameter to `*` to allow requests from all origins, or some URI to restrict requests to ones originating from this URI. If this parameter is unset, which is the default, the `Access-Control-Allow-Origin` header is not set, leaving you with the browser's standard behavior. In our example, we might want to set it on `/my_module/books/json` in order to allow scripts pulled from other websites accessing the list of books.

By default, Odoo protects certain types of requests from an attack known as cross-site request forgery by passing a token along on every request. If you want to turn that off, set the parameter `csrf` to `False`, but note that this is a bad idea in general.

See also

If you host multiple Odoo databases on the same instance and each database has different web accessible paths on possibly multiple domain names per database, the standard regular expressions in the `--db-filter` parameter might not be enough to force the right database for every domain. In that case, use the community module `dbfilter_from_header` from `https://github.com/OCA/server-tools` in order to configure the database filters on the proxy level.

To see how using templates makes modularity possible, see the recipe *Modify an existing handler* later in the chapter.

Restrict access to web accessible paths

We'll explore the three authentication mechanisms Odoo provides for routes in this recipe. We'll define routes with different authentication mechanisms in order to show their differences.

Getting ready

As we extend code from the previous recipe, we'll also depend on the `library.book` model of *Chapter 4, Application Models*, so you should get its code in order to proceed.

How to do it...

Define handlers in `controllers/main.py`:

1. Add a path that shows all books:

```
@http.route('/my_module/all-books', type='http', auth='none')
def all_books(self):
    records = request.env['library.book'].sudo().search([])
    result = '<html><body><table><tr><td>'
    result += '</td></tr><tr><td>'.join(
            records.mapped('name'))
    result += '</td></tr></table></body></html>'
    return result
```

2. Add a path that shows all books and indicates which was written by the current user, if any:

```
@http.route('/my_module/all-books/mark-mine',
    type='http', auth='public')
def all_books_mark_mine(self):
    records = request.env['library.book'].sudo().search([])
```

```
        result = '<html><body><table>'
        for record in records:
            result += '<tr>'
            if record.author_ids & request.env.user.partner_id:
                result += '<th>'
            else:
                result += '<td>'
            result += record.name
            if record.author_ids & request.env.user.partner_id:
                result += '</th>'
            else:
                result += '</td>'
            result += '</tr>'
        result += '</table></body></html>'
        return result
```

3. Add a path that shows the current user's books:

```
@http.route('/my_module/all-books/mine', type='http',
    auth='user')
def all_books_mine(self):
    records = request.env['library.book'].search([
        ('author_ids', 'in',
        request.env.user.partner_id.ids),
    ])
    result = '<html><body><table><tr><td>'
    result += '</td></tr><tr><td>'.join(
            records.mapped('name'))
    result += '</td></tr></table></body></html>'
    return result
```

With this code, the paths `/my_module/all_books` and `/my_module/all_books/`
`mark_mine` look the same for unauthenticated users, while a logged in user sees her books
in a bold font on the latter path. The path `/my_module/all-books/mine` is not accessible
at all for unauthenticated users. If you try to access it without being authenticated, you'll be
redirected to the login screen in order to do so.

How it works...

The difference between authentication methods is basically what you can expect from the
content of `request.env.user`.

For `auth='none'`, the user record is always empty, even if an authenticated user is
accessing the path. Use this if you want to serve content that has no dependencies on
users, or if you want to provide database agnostic functionality in a server wide module.

The value `auth='public'` sets the user record to a special user with XML ID `base.public_user`, for unauthenticated users, and to the user's record for authenticated ones. This is the right choice if you want to offer functionality to both unauthenticated and authenticated users, while the authenticated ones get some extras, as demonstrated in the preceding code.

Use `auth='user'` to be sure that only authenticated users have access to what you've got to offer. With this method, you can be sure `request.env.user` points to some existing user.

There's more...

The magic for authentication methods happens in the `ir.http` model from the base addon. For whatever value you pass to the `auth` parameter in your route, Odoo searches for a function called `_auth_method_<yourvalue>` on this model, so you can easily customize this by inheriting this model and declaring a method that takes care of your authentication method of choice.

As an example, we provide an authentication method `base_group_user` which enforces a currently logged in user who is a member of the group with XML ID `base.group_user`:

```
from openerp import exceptions, http, models
from openerp.http import request

class IrHttp(models.Model):
  _inherit = 'ir.http'

  def _auth_method_base_group_user(self):
    self._auth_method_user()
    if not request.env.user.has_group('base.group_user'):
      raise exceptions.AccessDenied()
```

Now you can say `auth='base_group_user'` in your decorator and be sure that users running this route's handler are members of this group. With a little trickery you can extend this to `auth='groups(xmlid1,...)'`, the implementation of this is left as an exercise to the reader, but is included in the example code.

Consume parameters passed to your handlers

It's nice to be able to show content, but it's better to show content as a result of some user input. This recipe will demonstrate the different ways to receive this input and react to it. As in the previous recipes, we'll make use of the `library.book` model.

How to do it...

First, we'll add a route that expects a traditional parameter with a book's ID to show some details about it. Then, we'll do the same, but we'll incorporate our parameter into the path itself:

1. Add a path that expects a book's ID as parameter:

    ```
    @http.route('/my_module/book_details', type='http',
        auth='none')
    def book_details(self, book_id):
        record = request.env['library.book']
                        .sudo().browse(int(book_id))
        return u'<html><body><h1>%s</h1>Authors: %s' % (
            record.name,   u', '.join(
            record.author_ids.mapped('name')) or 'none',
        )
    ```

2. Add a path where we can pass the book's ID in the path:

    ```
    @http.route("/my_module/book_details/<model(\
                'library.book'):book>",
                type='http', auth='none')
    def book_details_in_path(self, book):
        return self.book_details(book.id)
    ```

If you point your browser to /my_module/book_details?book_id=1, you should see a detail page of the book with ID 1. If this doesn't exist, you'll receive an error page.

The second handler allows you to go to /my_module/book_details/1 and view the same page.

How it works...

By default, Odoo (actually werkzeug) intermingles with GET and POST parameters and passes them as keyword argument to your handler. So by simply declaring your function as expecting a parameter called book_id, you introduce this parameter as either GET (the parameter in the URL) or POST (usually passed by forms with your handler as action) parameter. Given that we didn't add a default value for this parameter, the runtime will raise an error if you try to access this path without setting the parameter.

The second example makes use of the fact that in a werkzeug environment, most paths are virtual anyway. So we can simply define our path as containing some input. In this case, we say we expect the ID of a library.book as the last component of the path. The name after the colon is the name of a keyword argument. Our function will be called, with this parameter passed as keyword argument. Here, Odoo takes care of looking up this ID and delivering a browse record, which of course only works if the user accessing this path has appropriate permissions. Given that book is a browse record, we can simply recycle the first example's function by passing book.id as parameter book_id to give out the same content.

There's more...

Defining parameters within the path is a functionality delivered by `werkzeug`, which is called *converters*. The `model` converter is added by Odoo, which also defines the converter `models`, that accepts a comma separated list of IDs and passes a record set containing those IDs to your handler.

The beauty of converters is that the runtime coerces the parameters to the expected type, while you're on your own with normal keyword parameters. These are delivered as strings, and you have to take care of the necessary type conversions yourself, as seen in the first example.

Built-in `werkzeug` converters include `int`, `float`, and `string`, but also more intricate ones such as `path`, `any`, or `uuid`. You can look up their semantics at `http://werkzeug.pocoo.org/docs/0.11/routing/#builtin-converters`.

See also

Odoo's custom converters are defined in `ir_http.py` in the base module and registered in the `_get_converters` method of `ir.http`. As an exercise, you can create your own converter that allows you to visit the `/my_module/book_details/Odoo+cookbook` page to receive the details of this book (if you added it to your library before). This converter's implementation is included in the example code for this recipe.

Modify an existing handler

When you install the website module, the path `/website/info` displays some information about your Odoo instance. In this recipe, we override this in order to change this information page's layout, but also to change what is displayed.

Getting ready

Install the `website` module and inspect the path `/website/info`. Now craft a new module that depends on `website` and uses the following code.

How to do it...

We'll have to adapt the existing template and override the existing handler:

1. Override the `qweb` template in a file called `views/templates.xml`:

    ```xml
    <?xml version="1.0" encoding="UTF-8"?>
    <odoo>
      <template id="show_website_info"
        inherit_id="website.show_website_info">
    ```

```
<xpath expr="//dl[@t-foreach='apps']"
    position="replace">
    <table class="table">
        <tr t-foreach="apps" t-as="app">
            <th>
                <a t-att-href="app.website">
                <t t-esc="app.name" /></a>
            </th>
            <td><t t-esc="app.summary" /></td>
        </tr>
    </table>
</xpath>
</template>
</odoo>
```

2. Override the handler in a file called `controllers/main.py`:

```
from openerp import http
from openerp.addons.website.controllers.main import Website

class Website(Website):
    @http.route()
    def website_info(self):
        result = super(Website, self).website_info()
        result.qcontext['apps'] = \
        result.qcontext['apps'].filtered(
            lambda x: x.name != 'website')
        return result
```

Now, when visiting the info page, we'll only see a filtered list of installed applications, and in a table as opposed to the original definition list.

How it works

In the first step, we override an existing QWeb template. In order to find out which that is, you'll have to consult the code of the original handler. Usually, it will end with the following command line, which tells you that you need to override `template.name`:

```
return request.render('template.name', values)
```

In our case, the handler uses a template called `website.info`, but this one is immediately extended by another template called `website.show_website_info`, so it's more convenient to override this one. Here, we replace the definition list showing installed apps with a table. For details about how QWeb inheritance works, consult *Chapter 14, CMS Website Development*.

In order to override the handler method, we must identify the class that defines the handler, which is `openerp.addons.website.controllers.main.Website`, in this case. We import the class to be able to inherit from it. Now we override the method and change the data passed to the response. Note that what the overridden handler returns is a `Response` object and not a string of HTML, as the previous recipes did for the sake of brevity. This object contains a reference to the template to be used and the values accessible to the template, but is only evaluated at the very end of the request.

In general, there are three ways to change an existing handler:

▶ If it uses a QWeb template, the simplest way to change it is to override the template. This is the right choice for layout changes and small logic changes.

▶ QWeb templates get a context passed, which is available in the response as the field `qcontext`. This is usually a dictionary where you can add or remove values to suit your needs. In the preceding example, we filter the list of apps to only contain apps which have a website set.

▶ If the handler receives parameters, you could also preprocess those in order to have the overridden handler behave the way you want.

There's more...

As seen in the preceding section, inheritance with controllers works slightly differently than model inheritance: you actually need a reference to the base class and to use Python inheritance on it.

Don't forget to decorate your new handler with the `@http.route` decorator; Odoo uses it as a marker for which methods are exposed to the network layer. If you omit the decorator, you actually make the handler's path inaccessible.

The `@http.route` decorator itself behaves similarly to field declarations: every value you don't set will be derived from the decorator of the function you're overriding, so we don't have to repeat values we don't want to change.

After receiving a `response` object from the function you override, you can do a lot more than just changing the QWeb context:

▶ You can add or remove HTTP headers by manipulating `response.headers`.

▶ If you want to render an entirely different template, you can set `response.template`.

▶ To detect if a response is based on QWeb in the first place, query `response.is_qweb`.

▶ The resulting HTML code is available by calling `response.render()`.

See also

> ▸ Details of QWeb templates will be explained in *Chapter 14, CMS Website development*.

Using the RPC API

One of Odoo's strengths is its interoperability, which is helped by the fact that basically any functionality is available via JSON-RPC 2.0 and XMLRPC. In this recipe, we'll explore how to use both of them from client code. This interface also enables you to integrate Odoo with any other application. Making functionality available via any of the two protocols on the server side is explained in the *There's more* section of this recipe.

We'll query a list of installed modules from the Odoo instance, so that we could show a list like the one displayed in the previous recipe in our own application or website.

How to do it...

The following code is not meant to run within Odoo, but as simple scripts:

1. First, we query the list of installed modules via XMLRPC:

```python
#!/usr/bin/env python2
import xmlrpclib

db = 'odoo9'
user = 'admin'
password = 'admin'
uid = xmlrpclib.ServerProxy(
    'http://localhost:8069/xmlrpc/2/common')\
        .authenticate(db, user, password, {})
odoo = xmlrpclib.ServerProxy(
    'http://localhost:8069/xmlrpc/2/object')
installed_modules = odoo.execute_kw(
    db, uid, password, 'ir.module.module', 'search_read',
    [[('state', '=', 'installed')], ['name']], {'context':
        {'lang': 'fr_FR'}})
for module in installed_modules:
    print module['name']
```

2. Then we do the same with JSONRPC:

```python
import json
import urllib2

db = 'odoo9'
user = 'admin'
```

```
            password = 'admin'

    request = urllib2.Request(
      'http://localhost:8069/web/session/authenticate',
        json.dumps({
           'jsonrpc': '2.0',
             'params': {
               'db': db,
               'login': user,
               'password': password,
             },
        }),
        {'Content-type': 'application/json'})
    result = urllib2.urlopen(request).read()
    result = json.loads(result)
    session_id = result['result']['session_id']
    request = urllib2.Request(
            'http://localhost:8069/web/dataset/call_kw',
            json.dumps({
               'jsonrpc': '2.0',
               'params': {
                 'model': 'ir.module.module',
                 'method': 'search_read',
                 'args': [
                   [('state', '=', 'installed')],
                   ['name'],
                 ],
                 'kwargs': {'context': {'lang': 'fr_FR'}},
               },
            }),
            {
                'X-Openerp-Session-Id': session_id,
                'Content-type': 'application/json',
            })
    result = urllib2.urlopen(request).read()
    result = json.loads(result)
    for module in result['result']:
      print module['name']
```

Both code snippets will print a list of installed modules, and because they pass a context that sets the language to French, the list will be in French if there are translations available.

How it works...

Both snippets call the function `search_read`, which is very convenient because you can specify a search domain on the model you call, pass a list of fields you want to be returned, and receive the result in one request. In older versions of Odoo, you had to call `search` first to receive a list of IDs and then call `read` to actually read the data.

`search_read` returns a list of dictionaries, with the keys being the names of the fields requested and the values the record's data. The ID field will always be transmitted, no matter if you requested it or not.

Now we need to look at the specifics of the two protocols.

XMLRPC

The XMLRPC API expects a user ID and a password for every call, which is why we need to fetch this ID via the method `authenticate` on the path `/xmlrpc/2/common`. If you already know the user's ID, you can skip this step.

As soon as you know the user's ID, you can call any model's method by calling `execute_kw` on the path `/xmlrpc/2/object`. This method expects the database you want to execute the function on, the user's ID and password for authentication, then the model you want to call your function on, and then the function's name. The next two mandatory parameters are a list of positional arguments to your function, and a dictionary of keyword arguments.

JSONRPC

Don't be distracted by the size of the code example; that's because Python doesn't have built in support for JSONRPC. As soon as you've wrapped the `urllib` calls in some helper functions, the example will be as concise as the XMLRPC one.

As JSONRPC is stateful, the first thing we have to do is to request a session at `/web/session/authenticate`. This function takes the database, the user's name, and their password.

The crucial part here is that we record the session ID Odoo created, which we pass in the header `X-Openerp-Session-Id` to `/web/dataset/call_kw`. Then the function behaves the same as `execute_kw` from; we need to pass a model name and a function to call on it, then positional and keyword arguments.

There's more...

Both protocols allow you to call basically any function of your models. In case you don't want a function to be available via either interface, prepend its name with an underscore – Odoo won't expose those functions as RPC calls.

Furthermore, you need to take care that your parameters, as well as the return values, are serializable for the protocol. To be sure, restrict yourself to scalar values, dictionaries, and lists.

As you can do roughly the same with both protocols, it's up to you which one to use. This decision should be mainly driven by what your platform supports best. In a web context, you're generally better off with JSON, because Odoo allows JSON handlers to pass a CORS header conveniently (see the *Make a path accessible from the network* recipe of this chapter for details). This is rather difficult with XMLRPC.

See also

The most interesting business methods to call on models are explained in *Chapter 5, Basic Server Side Business Logic*.

14

CMS Website Development

In this chapter, we will cover the following topics:

- ▶ Extending CSS and JavaScript for the website
- ▶ Creating or modifying templates: QWeb
- ▶ Offering snippets to the user

Introduction

Odoo comes with a fully featured CMS system implemented by the **website** addon. Some low level functionality is provided by the **web** addon, so if you need to look up code, keep both modules in mind.

Extending CSS and JavaScript for the website

In this recipe, we'll see how to add custom style sheets and JavaScript to the website.

Getting ready

Create an empty module named `ch13_r01` and install it in your test database. Make sure this module depends on the `website` module, as we use some of its functionality.

a

How to do it...

Override the main website template to inject your code:

1. Add a file called `views/templates.xml` and add an empty view override:

```
<odoo>
    <template id="assets_frontend"
              inherit_id="website.assets_frontend">
        <xpath expr="." position="inside">
            <!-- points 2 & 3 go here /-->
        </xpath>
    </template>
</odoo>
```

2. Add a reference to your CSS file:

```
<link href="/ch13_r01/static/src/css/ch13_r01.css"
      rel="stylesheet" type="text/css"/>
```

3. Add a reference to your JavaScript file:

```
<script src="/ch13_r01/static/src/js/ch13_r01.js"
        type="text/javascript" />
```

4. Add some CSS code to `static/src/css/ch13_r01.css`.

```
body
{
    background: yellow;
}
```

5. Add some JavaScript code to `static/src/js/ch13_r01.js`.

```
odoo.define('ch13_r01', function(require)
{
    var core = require('web.core');
    alert(core._t('Hello world'));
    return {
        // if you created functionality to export, add it here
    }
});
```

After updating your module, you should see that Odoo websites have a yellow background and a somewhat annoying **Hello world** popup on each page load.

How it works...

At the base of Odoo's CMS lies an XML templating engine called QWeb, which is discussed in detail in the following recipe. For now, it's enough to know that we can use it to inject nodes into existing documents. In the example, we change the view `website.assets_frontend` to link to our CSS and JavaScript files. This view will be pulled to construct all the HTML for the website, so you can be sure your code is available on all pages.

As we can be sure the view `website.assets_frontend` is pulled within a HTML **head** node, we can simply add the files we need and possibly adjust or add other nodes in the **head** element too.

For CSS files, order matters. So if you need to override a style defined in another addon, you'll have to take care that your file is loaded after the original file you want to modify. This can be done by either adjusting your view's **priority** field or directly inheriting from the addon's view that injects the reference to the CSS. For details, consult the *Chapter 8, Backend Views*, recipe *Changing existing views: View inheritance*.

To avoid ordering issues with JavaScript, Odoo uses a mechanism very similar to RequireJS (`http://requirejs.org`): In your JavaScript file, you call `odoo.define()`, which receives the namespace you want to define as the first argument, and a function that contains the actual implementation as the second argument.

The name to be defined should be your addon's name. In case you export a lot of logically different parts of functionality, define them in different functions, with your addon's name prepended and separated by dots to avoid naming conflicts in the future. This is what the `web` module does, which defines, among others, `web.core` and `web.data`. The definition function receives only one parameter, `require`, which is a function you can use to obtain references to JavaScript namespaces defined in other modules or in the core. Use this for all interactions with Odoo and never rely on the global `odoo` object.

Your own function can then return an object pointing to the references you want to make available for other addons, or nothing if there are no such references. Be lavish with exporting your own objects; few things are more frustrating than having to jump through hoops in order to use some existing functionality just because its developer didn't bother to export it properly. The object you return here is what other code gets when it calls `require('yourmodule')`.

Per convention, your files should be called as your module with the appropriate extension added and live in `static/src/css` or `static/src/js` respectively. Only if your files become large enough to be a maintenance issue should you split them up into smaller chunks.

The `require` mechanism discussed here is new for Odoo 9.0. In older versions, addons dealing with JavaScript need to define a function with the same name as the addon in the `openerp` namespace. This function receives a reference to the currently-loaded instance as a parameter, from which API functions are to be accessed. So, in order to upgrade existing code, change this to a `odoo.define` clause and import the necessary objects via `require`.

There's more...

Instead of passing plain CSS to Odoo, you can also make use of **less** (http://lesscss.org), which is a higher level notation for CSS that helps you write more efficient CSS code. Certainly for big code bases, it will improve maintainability a lot. Given Odoo uses this internally anyway, you can rely on it being available. So, to use less instead of plain CSS, just point to the less file in your link element and use type="text/less" - this will make Odoo run lessc on your file in order to generate CSS on the fly without you having to do anything for it.

Creating or modifying templates - QWeb

We'll add website capabilities to the library addon developed in *Chapter 4, Application models*, and following. What we're interested in is allowing users to browse through the library and, if they are logged in with the appropriate permissions, enable them to edit book content right from the website interface.

Getting ready

As we make use of the library.book model, get chapter 4's code for my_module. For convenience, this recipe's code contains a copy of it.

How to do it...

We'll need to define a couple of controllers and views:

1. Add a template that displays a list of books in views/library_book_templates.xml.

```
<odoo>
  <template id="books">
    <t t-call="website.layout">
      <section>
          This is an editable text before the list of books.
      </section>
      <t t-foreach="books" t-as="book">
          <article itemscope="itemscope"
                  itemtype="http://schema.org/Book"
                  t-attf-class="row book-#{book_parity}">
            <h2 t-field="book.name" class="col-md-12" />
            <t t-if="book.date_release">
                <div class="col-md-2"
                    t-att-dateCreated="book.date_release"
                    t-field="book.date_release" />
            </t>
```

```
            <ul  class="col-md-10">
                <li t-foreach="book.author_ids" t-as="author"
                    itemprop="author">
                    <t t-esc="author.name" />
                </li>
            </ul>
        </article>
    </t>
    <section contenteditable="False">
        This is a non-editable text after the list of books.
    </section>
    </t>
    </template>
</odoo>
```

2. Add a controller that serves the list of books in `controllers/main.py`:

```
@http.route('/books', type='http', auth="user", website=True)
def route(self):
    return request.render(
        'ch13_r02.books',
        {
            'books': request.env['library.book'].search([]),
        })
```

With this code in place, users can query existing books and see their details. Given appropriate permissions, users will also be offered to change book details and a couple of other texts.

How it works...

First, we create a template called `books` that is used to generate the HTML necessary to display a list of books. All of the code is wrapped in a `t` element with the **t-call** attribute set, which makes Odoo render the **website.layout** template and insert our content at the place the called template has designated for it. This way, we get a full Odoo web page with the menu, footer, and so on, without having to repeat any code. If you leave out this call, you'll have to generate this or similar code yourself.

Loops

For working on record sets, you need a construct to loop through lists. Have a look at the inside of the `t-call` element, where the actual content generation happens. The template expects to be rendered with a context that has a variable called `books` set and iterates through it in the **t-foreach** element. Iteration can happen in a **t** element, in which case its contents are repeated for every member of the iterable that was passed in the `t-foreach` attribute. You can also place a `t-foreach` and **t-as** attribute in some arbitrary element; then this element and its contents will be repeated for every item in the iterable. The `t-as` attribute is mandatory and will be used as the name of the iterator variable to use for accessing the iterated data. While the most common use for this construction is to iterate over record sets, you can use it on any Python object that is iterable.

Attributes

We use as many of the semantic HTML5 elements as possible, which is why the actual data is wrapped in an `article` tag. For machine readability, some `item*` properties are attached. You can read more about this in this recipe's *See also* section.

Now focus on the **t-attf-class** attribute here. This will be evaluated by QWeb to be the attribute `class` with the contents evaluated as a format string. That is, the string `row book-` is passed as it is and the contents of the `#{...}` snippet is evaluated as Python code. This is different from **t-att-dateCreated** (note the missing 'f', the first is an attribute format string, the latter an evaluation) used below, where the whole content is evaluated as Python code. Both forms just pass the part of their name after the second dash as the name of the attribute to be constructed.

It is pretty much up to you when to choose a **t-attf-*** construction and when to use **t-att-***, the rule of thumb is to use a format string if the result contains a lot of string literals anyway and an evaluation otherwise.

Fields

The `h2` and `div` tags that follow use the **t-field** attribute. This attribute needs to be passed a field within a record set with length one and transparently allows the user to change the content displayed when the website's edit mode is activated. Of course, this is subject to a permission check and only allowed if the current user has write permissions on the displayed record. With an optional **t-field-options** attribute, you can give a dictionary of options to be passed to the field renderer, including the widget to be used. Currently, there's no vast amount of widgets for the backend, so the choices are a bit limited here.

Conditionals

Note that the division showing the publication date is wrapped by a `t` element with the `t-if` attribute set. This attribute is evaluated as Python code and the element only rendered if the result is truthy . In the example, we only show the `div` class if there is actually a publication date set.

Note that t-if doesn't coexist well with other templating attributes like t-esc or t-field on the same element. Put each of them in its own element, because, otherwise, the t-if usually wins and the other attributes are not evaluated any more.

Inline editing

Changes made by a user will either be propagated to the connected database record if the change happened within a t-field node, or to the view in question if it is some other node marked as editable. Content nodes like section elements don't need to be marked as editable, they are editable by default. To turn an editable element read-only, use the attribute contenteditable=False.

 Note that editing a view via the website editor sets the **noupdate** flag on this view. This means that subsequent code changes will never make it into your customer's database. In order to also get the ease of use of inline editing and the possibility of updating your HTML code in subsequent releases, create one view that contains the semantic HTML elements and a second one that injects editable elements. Then only the latter view will be **noupdate** and you can still change the former.

For the CSS classes used here, consult bootstrap's documentation, as linked in this recipe's *See also* section.

The controller in step 2 just renders the template, please refer to the *Chapter 13, Web Server Development*, recipe *Modify an existing handler* for details.

There's more...

Given the way t-call elements are evaluated, you can use t-set elements to pass information to the template you call. This can be very useful if you have some generalized templates like **website.layout** or **report.external_layout,** which display data you want to see almost always. Adapt them not to print certain elements if some variable is set and set it via a t-set element on the page or report where you want to suppress the element in question. This helps to avoid a lot of code duplication.

Within `t-foreach` loops, you've got access to a couple of variables whose names are derived from the accompanying `t-as` attribute. As it is `book` in the example above, we have access to the variable `book_parity` which contains the value **even** for even indices while iterating and **odd** for odd ones. In this example, we use this to be able to have alternating background colors in our list. Other interesting variables in this case would be `book_index`, which returns the current (zero-based) index in the iteration, `book_first` and `book_last`, which are `True` if this is the first or last iteration respectively, and `book_value`, which would contain the item's value if the book variable we iterate over were a dictionary; in this case, `book` would iterate through the dictionary's keys.

The **template** element is a shorthand for a **record** element that sets some properties on the record for you. While there's never a reason not to use the convenience of the template element, you should know what happens under the hood: the element creates a record of the model **ir.ui.view** with type `qweb`. Then, depending on the `template` element's **name** and `inherit_id` attributes, the `inherit_id` field on the view record will be set. In case the template has the attribute `primary` set to `True`, the view record's `mode` field will be set to `primary`. Finally, an `arch` field is crafted with the correct root element (**t** for non-inheriting views, `data` for inheriting views) and a `t-name` attribute is set for primary views.

Keep in mind that QWeb is a perfectly generic templating engine, so whenever you need to generate content in an Odoo context, use a Qweb view that you render by calling `env['ir.ui.view'].render('xmlid', parameters)`. Especially for generating XML documents, this is convenient, but you can generate every other kind of text too.

See also

For a more in-depth discussion of controllers, see the *Chapter 13, Web Server Development,* recipes *Make a path accessible from the network* and *Restrict access to web accessible paths.*

For details on view inheritance, see the *Chapter 8, Backend Views,* recipe *Changing existing views: View inheritance.*

The code generated here makes use of microdata (`https://html.spec.whatwg.org/multipage/microdata.html`) using definitions from `http://schema.org` – it is advised you do the same for your publicly accessible websites in order to simplify reading your pages for machines. This also makes your content more accessible for search engines.

Odoo as a whole makes extensive use of bootstrap (`http://getbootstrap.com`), which you should use to get adaptive designs without much effort.

Offering snippets to the user

The website designer offers building blocks in website edit mode which can be dragged on the page. This recipe discusses how to offer your own blocks, called snippets, internally.

Getting ready

As we make use of the **library.book** model, get chapter 4's code for `my_module`. For convenience, this recipe's code contains a copy of it.

How to do it...

A snippet is actually just a QWeb view that gets injected in the **Insert blocks** bar, which is defined by a QWeb view itself:

1. Add a file called `views/snippets.xml`:

```xml
<?xml version="1.0" encoding="UTF-8"?>
<odoo>
    <template id="book_snippet" inherit_id="website.snippets">
        <!-- points 2, 3 go here /-->
    </template>
</odoo>
```

2. Add a view for your snippet:

```xml
<xpath expr="//div[@id='snippet_feature']/div[@class='o_panel_
body']" position="inside">
    <div>
        <div class="oe_snippet_thumbnail">
            <div style="background: white;box-shadow:none"
                class="oe_snippet_thumbnail_img" >
                <i class="fa fa-book fa-5x text-muted" />
            </div>
            <span class="oe_snippet_thumbnail_title">Latest
books</span>
        </div>
        <div class="oe_snippet_body book_snippet">
            <section class="container">
                <h2>Latest books</h2>
                <table class="table">
                    <tr>
                        <th>Name</th>
                        <th>Release date</th>
                    </tr>
                </table>
            </section>
        </div>
    </div>
</xpath>
```

3. Add options:

```
<xpath expr="//div[@id='snippet_options']" position="inside">
    <div data-selector=".book_snippet"
        data-drop-near="p, h1, h2, h3, blockquote, .well, .panel"
        data-drop-in=".content">
        <li class="dropdown-submenu">
            <a href="#">Show books</a>
            <ul class="dropdown-menu">
                <li data-select_class="book_snippet-show3">
                    <a>3</a>
                </li>
                <li data-select_class="book_snippet-show5">
                    <a>5</a>
                </li>
                <li data-select_class="book_snippetshow10">
                    <a>10</a>
                </li>
                <li data-select_class="book_snippetshow15">
                    <a>15</a>
                </li>
            </ul>
        </li>
    </div>
    <div data-selector=".book_snippet table">
        <li class="dropdown-submenu">
            <a href="#">Table style</a>
            <ul class="dropdown-menu">
                <li data-toggle_class="table-striped">
                    <a>Striped</a></li>
                <li data-toggle_class="tablebordered">
                    <a>Bordered</a></li>
                <li data-toggle_class="tablecondensed">
                    <a>Condensed</a>
                </li>
            </ul>
        </li>
    </div>
</xpath>
```

4. Add JavaScript code to populate our snippet:

```
odoo.define('ch13_r03.snippets_animation', function(require)
{
    "use strict";
    var animation = require('web_editor.snippets.animation'),
        Model = require('web.Model');

    animation.registry.book_snippet = animation.Class.extend({
        selector: ".book_snippet",
        start: function()
        {
            var self = this,
                number = 3;
            _.each(this.$el.attr('class').split(/\s+/),
            function(cls)
            {
                if(cls.indexOf('book_snippet-show') == 0)
                {
                    number = parseInt(
                        cls.substring('book_snippet-show'.length));
                }
            });
            this.$el.find('td').parents('tr').remove();
            new Model('library.book')
            .call(
                'search_read', [],
                {
                    domain: [],
                    fields: ['name', 'date_release'],
                    order: 'date_release desc',
                    limit: number,
                })
            .then(function(data)
            {
                var $table = self.$el.find('table');
                _.each(data, function(book)
                {
                    $table.append(
                        jQuery('<tr />')
                        .append(
                            jQuery('<td />').text(book.name),
                            jQuery('<td />').text(
                                            book.date_release)
                        )
```

```
                        );
                  })
              });
          },
      });
  });
```

After updating your module, you're offered a snippet called **Latest books,** which shows a configurable amount of books in a list, ordered by their publication date.

How it works...

You inject your snippet directly into the snippet bar's view. What is crucial is that you attach the right classes and insert your code at the right place.

A snippet needs to have one root element (in our case, the outermost **div**) that contains an element with the class `oe_snippet_thumbnail` and another with class `oe_snippet_body`. The first is used to display the snippet in the bar, the second contains the actual definition of the snippet. For the thumbnail, it makes sense to use a `fontawesome` icon and add some classes for the layout. For the snippet body, you can add whatever HTML you need for your goals. In general, it's a good idea to use **section** elements and the bootstrap classes, because, for them, Odoo's editor offers edit and resize controls out of the box.

The position to insert the snippet determines in which section of the bar it shows up. Our choice was `//div[@id='snippet_feature']/div[@class='o_panel_body']`, which places it in the features section. With the IDs **snippet_structure**, **snippet_content**, and **snippet_effect**, you can place your snippet in the respective other sections.

The **div** we injected in `//div[@id='snippet_options']` offers the user choices in the customize menu. Note the attribute **data-selector** that contains a JQuery selector determining for which element the option is to be shown. In the example, the first option list is shown when the whole container is selected, while the second one, about the table style, is shown when the table is selected.

The attributes **data-drop-near** and **data-drop-in** determine where the snippet can be placed when dragging it out of the snippet bar. Those are also JQuery selectors and, in the example, we allow putting the snippet basically anywhere that content can go.

For the options themselves, the attributes **data-select_class** and **data-toggle_class** allow the user to set either one (select) or multiple (toggle) classes on the element selected by the **data-selector** attribute. Our first set of options sets classes later used by the JavaScript code. The second set of options sets classes directly in the table, which will change its layout accordingly.

The JavaScript code uses the snippet animation framework to execute some code every time the snippet is loaded. We use it to query the current list of books to be presented to the user.

There's more...

After completing this recipe, you know enough to create Odoo themes. An addon is considered a theme if it contains only data files, CSS and JavaScript code. Use QWeb views and snippets to adapt the website's HTML code as necessary and CSS for styling. For the addon to be recognized as such in the app store, the addon's manifest must set the **application** key to `True` and use a subcategory of theme, as found on `https://www.odoo.com/apps/themes`.

15
Web Client Development

In this chapter, we will cover the following topics:

- ▶ Creating custom widgets
- ▶ Using client side QWeb templates
- ▶ Making RPC calls to the server
- ▶ Writing tests for client side code
- ▶ Debugging your client side code

Introduction

Odoo's web client, or backend, is the place where employees spend most of their time. In *Chapter 8, Backend Views*, you have seen how to use the existing possibilities the backend offers. Here, we'll have a look at how to extend and customize those possibilities. All of the following code will depend on the web module. Note that at the time of writing, there exist two versions of the web module for Odoo 9.0: the community version and the enterprise version, which are quite different from each other, even though they share the same name. We'll only talk about the community version here.

Creating custom widgets

As you've seen in *Chapter 8, Backend Views*, there's a plethora of widgets that display your data in a certain way. To demonstrate how to create your own widget, we'll write one that lets the user choose a `many2one` reference from a predefined selection of values in the form of a list of buttons. The result looks somewhat similar to the `many2many_checkboxes` widget, but with buttons instead of checkboxes.

Getting ready

You'll need to create an empty addon that depends on the `web` module; we call it `ch15_r01` here.

How to do it...

We'll add a JavaScript file that contains our widget's logic, and a CSS file to do some styling. Then, we also choose one field on the partner form to use our new widget. Follow the given steps:

1. Add a `static/src/js/ch15_r01.js` file. For the syntax used here, refer to *Chapter 14, CMS Website Development*, recipe *Extending CSS and JavaScript for the website*:

```
odoo.define('ch15_r01', function(require)
{
    var core = require('web.core'),
        form_common = require('web.form_common');
```

2. Create your widget by subclassing `AbstractField`:

```
var FieldMany2OneButtons = form_common.AbstractField.extend({
```

3. Set the CSS class for the widget's root `div` element:

```
className: 'oe_form_field_many2one_buttons',
```

4. Override `init` to do some initialization:

```
init: function()
{
    var result = this._super.apply(this, arguments);
    this.user_list = {
        1: {
            name: 'Administrator',
        },
        4: {
            name: 'Demo user',
        },
    };
    this.on(
        'change:effective_readonly', this,
        this.effective_readonly_changed)
    return result;
},
```

5. Capture some JavaScript events:

```
events: {
    'click .btn': 'button_clicked',
},
```

6. Override `start` to set up DOM elements:

```
start: function()
{
    var self = this;
    _.each(this.user_list, function(description, id)
    {
        self.$el.append(
            jQuery('<button>').attr({
                'data-id': id,
                'class': 'btn btn-default btn-sm',
            })
            .text(description.name)
        );
    });
    this.effective_readonly_changed();
    return this._super.apply(this, arguments);
},
```

7. Override `set_value` to actually display the value of the field:

```
set_value: function(_value)
{
    this.$el.find('button').removeClass('btn-primary');
    this.$el.find(
        _.str.sprintf('button[data-id="%s"]',
        _.isArray(_value) ? _value[0] : _value)
    ).addClass('btn-primary');
    return this._super.apply(this, arguments);
},
```

8. Define the handlers we referred to above:

```
button_clicked: function(e)
{
    this.set_value(
        parseInt(jQuqery(arguments[0].target)
                    .attr('data-id'))
    );
},
effective_readonly_changed()
{
```

```
            this.$el.find('button').
                prop('disabled', this.get('effective_readonly')));
        },
    });
```

9. Don't forget to register your widget:

```
core.form_widget_registry.add(
        'many2one_buttons', FieldMany2OneButtons);
```

10. Make it available for other addons:

```
return {
    FieldMany2OneButtons: FieldMany2OneButtons,
}
});
```

11. Add some CSS in `static/src/css/ch15_r01.css`:

```
.oe_form_field_many2one_buttons button
{
    margin: 0em .2em .2em 0em;
}
```

12. Register both files in the backend assets in `views/templates.xml`:

```
<?xml version="1.0" encoding="UTF-8"?>
<odoo>
    <template id="assets_backend" inherit_id="web.assets_backend">
        <xpath expr="." position="inside">
            <link href="/ch15_r01/static/src/css/ch15_r01.css"
                rel="stylesheet" type="text/css"/>
            <script src="/ch15_r01/static/src/js/ch15_r01.js"
                type="text/javascript" />
        </xpath>
    </template>
</odoo>
```

13. Finally, make the partner form use our widget for choosing the sales person:

```
<?xml version="1.0" encoding="UTF-8"?>
<openerp>
    <data>
        <record id="view_partner_form" model="ir.ui.view">
            <field name="model">res.partner</field>
            <field name="inherit_id" ref="base.view_partner_form"
    />
            <field name="arch" type="xml">
                <field name="user_id" position="attributes">
```

```
        <attribute name="widget">
            many2one_buttons</attribute>
        </field>
    </field>
</record>
</data>
</openerp>
```

When you open a partner form after installing the module, you'll see two buttons on the sales person field that allow you to select a user. The currently selected user's button is highlighted.

How it works...

The first choice when developing a widget is to choose the correct base class. The fundamental base class for widgets is `Widget` (defined by `web.widget`), but we didn't choose it because it's too basic. It only takes care of handling events and rendering, but we want more functionality for free. Still, this is an interesting class to study if you want to dig into Odoo's JavaScript internals.

We chose `AbstractField` (defined by `web.form_common`) because it brings all the functionality we need for our widget to behave as a form field. It does this by inheriting from `FormWidget` and implementing `FieldInterface`, which includes things like communicating with the parent form, saving the current field's value, and so on. You should study both classes, but the most important functions are overridden in the code example to make this widget do anything in the first place.

The `init` function should be used to do synchronous initialization tasks. Then, for asynchronous initialization, either use `willStart` (runs before rendering) or `start` (runs after rendering). Both those functions are supposed to return a deferred object, which we simply obtain from `super`. Then `set_value` needs to deal with the field's value that the widget is supposed to display. As the parent class handles the storage aspects, we only have to take care that it's displayed properly.

We use `init` to set up a list of users (this is only to keep it simple for now, generally, hard-coded data is a horrible idea of course. We'll fix this in the recipe *Making RPC calls to the server*) and to bind an event. Another possibility for binding events is using the mapping `events`, where you map an event name, possibly followed by a jQuery selector, to a function name. We use this to have the click events for the buttons we create later set up automatically.

The actual UI is created in `start`, where we simply create one button per user, and have `set_value` mark the appropriate button with the `btn_primary` class. The two event handlers `button_clicked` and `effective_readonly_changed` then are then necessary to implement our widget's behavior, that is, select the user a button displays, but don't allow selections in read only mode.

Note that there is also a property **readonly** and one called **effective_readonly**. The first is set when the field is marked as read only, either in the field definition or the form's. The latter is the conjunction of the first and eventual restrictions by permissions on model or record level, so be sure to use **effective_readonly** when you have to deal with widgets.

After we've defined our new widget, it's crucial to register it with the form widget registry, which lives in `web.core`. If you want to create widgets for other view types, you'll have to register them in an appropriate registry, like `web.core.list_widget_registry` or `web.core.search_widget_registry`.

Finally, we export our widget class so that other addons can extend it or inherit from it.

The rest of the code is some quite unspectacular styling for our buttons, registering our JavaScript and CSS files with the system, and using our widget on the partner form.

There's more...

The namespace `web.form_common` defines a couple of very helpful mixin classes you should not miss out on when developing form widgets. `ReinitializeFieldMixin` offers a simple interface for widgets that have to remove all DOM elements and rebuild them when switching between display (read only) mode and edit mode. `CompletionFieldMixin` is the base for fields that offer completion, like the `many2one` or `many2many_tags` widgets.

 When doing your overrides, always study the base class to see what the function is supposed to return. A very common cause of bugs is forgetting to return `super`'s **Deferred** object, which causes trouble with asynchronous operations.

As field widgets are responsible for managing values, they are also responsible for validation. Use the functions `is_valid` and `is_syntax_valid` to implement your customizations of this aspect. The latter is meant to be a very basic check, like the fact that a number field should only contain digits, while the former should also look at the broader picture, like the fact that a ratio should be less than or equal to 1 and greater than or equal to 0.

See also

In case you want to use something very similar to this in real life, have a look at the `radio` widget provided by the **web** addon, it supports `selection` and `many2one` fields.

A very good source for more widgets is the community repository `https://github.com/OCA/web`, where developers share their general purpose widgets (and other addons related to the web client).

Using client-side QWeb templates

Just as it's a bad pattern to programmatically create HTML code in controllers, you should create only the minimum amount of DOM elements in your client side JavaScript code. Fortunately, there's a templating engine available for the client side too and, even more fortunately, it's just the same as for server side code.

We'll use Qweb to make the module from the previous recipe, *Create custom widgets,* more modular by moving the DOM element creation to QWeb.

Getting ready

This recipe is just a modified version of the previous recipe, *Create custom widgets,* code, so grab a copy of it and use it to create the module `ch15_r02`.

How to do it...

We add the QWeb definition in the manifest and change the JavaScript code to use it:

1. Remove the entire function start from your JavaScript code in `static/src/js/ch15_r02.js`, but add a member called `template`:

    ```
    var FieldMany2OneButtons = form_common.AbstractField.extend({
        template: 'FieldMany2OneButtons',
    ```

2. Add the template file in `static/src/xml/ch15_r02.xml`:

    ```
    <templates>
        <t t-name="FieldMany2OneButtons">
            <div class="oe_form_field_many2one_buttons">
                <t t-foreach="widget.user_list" t-as="user_id">
                    <button
                        t-att-disabled="widget.get
                        ('effective_readonly') ? 'disabled' : False"
                        t-att-data-id="user_id"
                        class="btn btn-default btn-sm"
                    >
                        <t t-esc="widget.user_list[user_id].name" />
                    </button>
                </t>
            </div>
        </t>
    </templates>
    ```

3. Register the QWeb file in your manifest:

```
"qweb": [
    'static/src/xml/ch15_r02.xml',
],
```

Now other addons have a much easier time changing the HTML code our widget uses, because they can simply override it with the usual QWeb patterns.

How it works...

As there is already a comprehensive discussion of the basics of QWeb in the *Chapter 14, CMS Website Development*, recipe *Creating or modifying templates: QWeb*, we'll focus on what is different here. First of all, you need to realize that we're dealing with the JavaScript **QWeb** implementation here as opposed to the Python implementation on the server side. This means that you don't have access to browse records or the environment; you only have access to the current widget via variable `widget` and some helper objects like `datetime` with a subset of Python as described in the *Chapter 8, Backend Views*, recipe *Passing parameters to forms and actions: Context*.

This means that you should have all the intelligence in the widget's JavaScript code and have your template only access properties, or possibly functions, on the widget. Fortunately, the original version of our widget does this already, so the only thing we have to do is to iterate through the object we prepared in `init` and create buttons accordingly. Given that we can also call all functions available on the widget, we can simply ask it if it should behave as read-only by calling the `get` function, which returns properties saved before via `PropertiesMixin`'s (defined in `web.mixins`) `set` function.

As client side QWeb has nothing to do with QWeb views, there's a different mechanism to make those templates known to the web client; add them via the key `qweb` to your addon's manifest in a list of file names relative to the addon's root.

There's more...

The reason for making the effort to use QWeb here was extensibility and this is the second big difference between client side and server side Qweb. On the client side, you can't use Xpath expressions, but you need to use jQuery selectors and operations. If we, for example, want to change our widget in yet another module, we'd use the following code to have each of our buttons show a user icon before the user's name:

```
<t t-extend="FieldMany2OneButtons">
    <t t-jquery="button" t-operation="prepend">
        <i class="fa fa-user" />
    </t>
</t>
```

If we also gave a `t-name` attribute here, we'd have made a copy of the original template and left that one untouched. Other possible values for the `t-operation` attribute are **append**, **before**, **after**, **inner** and **replace**, which cause the content of the `t` element to be either appended to the content of the matched element, put before or after the matched element, replace the content of the matched element (`inner`), or replace the complete element (`replace`). There's also **t-operation='attributes'**, which allows you to set an attribute on the matches element, following the same rules as server-side QWeb.

Another tacit difference is that names in client side QWeb are not namespaced by the module name, so you have to choose names for your templates which are probably unique over all addons you install, which is why developers tend to choose rather long names.

See also

The client side QWeb engine has less convenient error messages and handling than other parts of Odoo. A small error often means that simply nothing happens and it's hard for beginners to continue from there. Fortunately, there are some debug statements for client side QWeb templates described later in the chapter, in the recipe *Debugging your client side code*.

Making RPC calls to the server

Sooner or later, your widget will need to look up some data from the server. This recipe shows you how to do that. We'll replace the hard coded list of users in the `many2one_buttons` widget with a list queried from the server, depending on the field's domain.

Getting ready

This recipe is just a modified version of the previous recipe, *Using client side templates: QWeb code*, so grab a copy of it and use it to create addon `ch15_r03`.

How to do it...

We just have to adapt some JavaScript code at the right places:

1. Require the `data` and `model` packages in `static/src/js/ch15_r03.js`:

```
odoo.define('ch15_r01', function(require)
{
    var core = require('web.core'),
        data = require('web.data'),
        model = require('web.Model'),
        form_common = require('web.form_common');
```

2. Delete the hard-coded list in `init` to have it only set up the event listener:

```
init: function()
{
    var result = this._super.apply(this, arguments);
    this.on(
        'change:effective_readonly', this,
        this.effective_readonly_changed)
    return result;
},
```

3. Query the server for the list we want in `willStart`:

```
willStart: function()
{
    var deferred = new jQuery.Deferred(),
        self = this;
    self.user_list = {};
    new data.Query(new model(this.field.relation),
    ['display_name'])
    .filter(this.field.domain)
    .all()
    .then(function(records)
    {
        _.each(records, function(record)
        {
            self.user_list[record.id] = record;
            self.user_list[record.id].name = record.
                                              display_name;
        });
        deferred.resolve();
    });
    return jQuery.when(
        this._super.apply(this, arguments),
        deferred
    );
},
```

Now you should see all users of your system, not just the two hard-coded ones as you did before. Also, the widget can be used for any `many2one` fields now, because it just queries what is available and doesn't need any knowledge about this beforehand. If you set a domain on the field, the buttons will be restricted to records matching this domain. In this specific case, you might want to restrict the selection to users of the group **Sale | User**.

How it works...

The `willStart` function is called before rendering, and, more importantly, returns a deferred object that must be resolved before rendering starts. So in a case like ours, where we need to run an asynchronous action before rending can occur, this is the right function to do it.

The `data` and `model` packages we required in the new code provide access to classes dealing with data access. The `model` class provides low-level access to model functions like `search` or `read`, or in this case, `search_read`. We could have just used them, but they are less convenient than the `Query` class, which behaves more like you'd expect from JavaScript objects: you can chain calls and set things like the domain in a persistent way on the object as opposed to passing it as a parameter, as you'd have to do with the `model` class. In the end, you'll be executing basically the same RPC functions, so this is up to your personal preference.

In any case, we'll have to collect the results asynchronously in our success handler. This will set up the internal data structure `user_list` the same way we did before in the hard-coded version, which is great, because this way, we don't have to change anything else.

Note that we request the field `display_name` here instead of `name`, because we can be sure that every model has a field `display_name`, whereas that's not guaranteed with the field `name`. Then we just assign the `name` property the same value as `display_name`, this, again, is in order not to have to change existing code more than necessary. Do this too instead of a lot of overrides if you just need to divert display to another field or something similar. For details about the `display_name` field, refer to the *Chapter 4, Application Models*, recipe *Define the Model representation and order*.

The end of the handler contains the crucial part, resolving the deferred object we created before. This, in combination with returning the deferred object wrapped together with **super**'s result in a new deferred object created by the `jQuery.when` call, causes rendering to only happen after the values are fetched and whatever asynchronous action super was busy with finished too. This way, you can be sure in the template code that `widget.user_list` is accessible and contains the values we need.

There's more...

The `AbstractField` class comes with a couple of interesting properties, one of which we used above. The `field` property contains the output of the model's `fields_get` function for the field the widget is displaying. Apart from the `relation` key that gives you the comodel for x2x fields or the `domain`, you can also use it to query the field's string, size or whatever other property you can set on the field during model definition.

Another helpful property is `options`, which contains data passed via the **options** attribute in the form definition. This is already JSON parsed, so you can access it like any object.

Odoo's RPC heavily relies on jQuery's deferred objects, so it can't be repeated often enough that you should dive into jQuery's documentation about this: `https://api.jquery.com/jQuery.Deferred`

Writing tests for client side code

The more code you have on the client side, the more it becomes a liability. For server side code, there's the well-entrenched unit tests, and for JavaScript, we have **QUnit** (`https://qunitjs.com`), which Odoo uses.

Getting ready

We'll add our tests to the addon developed in the previous recipes, so grab the code from the recipe *Making RPC calls to the server* and put it in a new module called `ch15_r04`.

How to do it...

We have to add our test file and make it known to the test mechanism in the appropriate template.

1. Add the `static/test/ch15_r04.js` file:

```
odoo.define_section('ch15_r04', ['ch15_r04'], function (test,
mock) {
    test('FieldMany2OneButtons', function(assert, ch15_r04)
    {
```

2. Create a minimal implementation of `FieldManager`:

```
        var fake_field_manager = {
            get_field_desc: function()
            {
                return {
                    'relation': 'res.users',
                    'domain': [],
                };
            },
            on: function() {},
            off: function() {},
            get: function() {},
            $el: jQuery(),
        },
```

3. Instantiate our widget:

```
widget = new ch15_r04.FieldMany2OneButtons(
    fake_field_manager,
    {
        attrs: {
            modifiers: '{}',
            name: 'field_name',
            widget: 'many2one_buttons',
        },
    }
),
```

4. Create a container to add our widget to:

```
$container = jQuery('<div/>'),
```

5. Tell the test framework we're testing an asynchronous action:

```
async_result = assert.async();
```

6. Add data to simulate our RPC call:

```
mock.add(
    '/web/dataset/search_read', function()
    {
        return {
            records: [
                {
                    id: 1,
                    display_name: 'Administrator',
                },
                {
                    id: 4,
                    display_name: 'Demo user',
                },
            ],
            length: 2,
        }
    }
);
```

7. Do the actual testing:

```
widget.attachTo($container)
.then(function()
{
    widget.renderElement();
    assert.deepEqual(
```

```
                    widget.$el.find('button').map(function()
                    {
                         return jQuery.trim(jQuery(this).text())
                    }).get(),
                    ['Administrator', 'Demo user'],
                    'Check if the widget shows the users we expect'
                );
                async_result();
            });
        })
    });
```

8. Make the test file known to the test mechanism in `views/templates.xml`:

```
<template id="qunit_suite" inherit_id="web.qunit_suite">
    <xpath expr="//head" position="inside">
        <script src="/ch15_r04/static/test/ch15_r04.js"
                type="text/javascript" />
    </xpath>
</template>
```

When you navigate to `/web/tests` now, the web client will run all tests available. You should find our test in this list too, hopefully with a positive result. Given a lot of tests will run there, it can be simpler to also pass the module you want to test. In our case, the path would be `/web/tests?module=ch15_r04`.

> Note that what you pass as the module parameter in the test URL is not necessarily the name of your addon, but whatever section name you define in your `define_section` call above.

How it works...

You define your JavaScript tests in a very similar manner to how you would make normal JavaScript code known to Odoo: You call a function that gets your code as a parameter. In the case of tests, this function is called `define_section` and expects a logical name for the tests to be run, the JavaScript packages the test requires (in our case, we just need the code our module provides, so we pass `['ch15_r04']` here), and a function that sets up the tests themselves.

This function is provided with a function called `test` and an object called `mock`. The `test` function is what we call to actually declare tests; it receives a name for the single test and the function that contains the test code. This function will be provided with an `assert` object and all the packages we required in the call to `define_section` as parameters.

Within this last function, the actual testing happens. We need to set up a couple of helper objects because a widget expects to live on a form, which in turn implements an interface called `FieldManager`. For simplicity, we provide a minimal implementation of that in order not to have to pull a whole form as dependency for our test. With this, we can instantiate our widget and also pass it an idealized version of a parsed XML node that would be the field's definition in the form view.

At the end of the function, we can attach our widget to the container element we created, call the `renderElement` function, and check if rendering caused the DOM elements to show up as we expected.

For doing those checks, the `assert` object has a few functions like `equal`, `deepEqual`, `notEqual` and `notDeepEqual`, which all deal with equality, but the deep* variants recurse into compound types like arrays and objects. Then there's `ok` and `notOk` which can be used to assert true or false value and `throws`, to assert a function, throws a certain exception or error message.

There's more...

The example code contains two peculiarities which makes this test more complicated than others; it needs to request data from the server, and as a consequence of that, run asynchronously. Both pose challenges to the test framework.

For fetching data, Odoo offers an object called `mock`, which we can fill with data that will be returned when code requests data from the server. So what we do here is assign a JavaScript function per server URL our test code is expected to query and have the function return what we consider the expected result. Then the test is if the client side code reacts to this data appropriately. If your test code makes calls to different models or functions, or to the same but with different parameters, this function would have to react to those parameters. But as we only read data once, it suffices to add a handler for `/web/dataset/search_read`, and we can just can return a fixed result. If your own code involves more interactions with the server, you'll probably need a smarter handler that actually looks at its parameters and returns different results for different requests.

Then, because of the asynchronous call, we need to tell the test framework that our function exiting is not yet the end of the test by calling `assert.async()`. This returns a function we are supposed to call exactly once within our asynchronous handler in order to notify the test framework that this specific test is done.

See also

Unfortunately, at the time of writing, many of the more complex JavaScript community modules are not yet migrated to Odoo 9.0, so there are not many examples of client side tests in the wild. Consult the `web` module's tests for some examples: `https://github.com/OCA/OCB/tree/9.0/addons/web/static/test`.

Debugging your client side code

For debugging server side code, this book contains a whole chapter, that is, *Chapter 7, Debugging and Automated Testing*. For the client side part, you'll get a kick start in this recipe.

Getting ready

This recipe doesn't really rely on specific code, but if you want to be able to reproduce exactly what's going on, grab the previous recipe's code.

How to do it...

What makes debugging client side script hard is that the web client heavily relies on jQuery's asynchronous events. Given that breakpoints halt execution, the chance is high that a bug caused by timing issues will not occur when debugging. We'll discuss some strategies for this later:

1. Turn on debug mode by selecting **About** in the top right user menu, and clicking **Activate developer mode**. For details, consult the *Chapter 1, Installing the Odoo Development Environment*, recipe *Activate developer tools*.

2. In a JavaScript function you're interested in, call the debugger:

   ```
   debugger;
   ```

3. If you have timing problems, log to the console in some JavaScript function:

   ```
   console.log("I'm in function X currently");
   ```

4. If you want to debug during template rendering, call the debugger from QWeb:

   ```
   <t t-debug="" />
   ```

5. You can also have QWeb log to the console by saying the following:

   ```
   <t t-log="myvalue" />
   ```

All of this relies on your browser offering appropriate functionality for debugging. While all the major browsers do that, we'll only look at Chromium here for demonstration purposes. To be able to use the debug tools, open them by clicking the top-right menu button and selecting **More tools | Developer tools**:

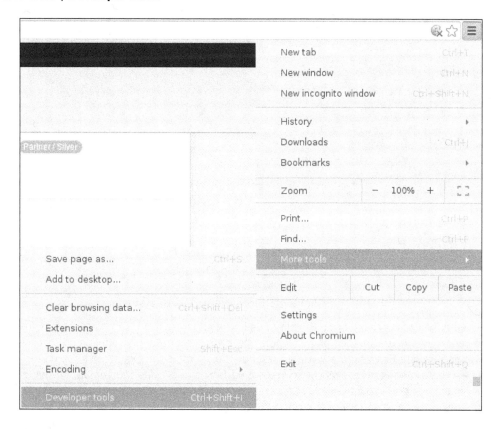

How it works...

When the debugger is opened, you should see something similar to the following screenshot:

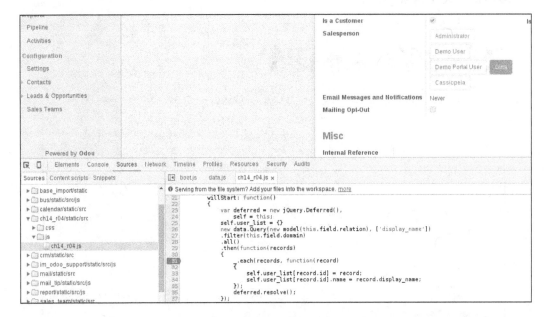

Here, you have access to a lot of different tools in the separate tabs. The currently active tab in the screenshot is the JavaScript debugger, where we set a breakpoint in line 31 by clicking on the line number. Every time our widget fetches the list of users, execution should stop at this line and the debugger allows you to inspect variables or change their value. Within the watch list to the right, you can also call functions to try out their effects without having to continuously save your script file and reload the page.

The `debugger` statements described above will behave the same as soon as you have the developer tools open: execution will stop and the browser will switch to the **Sources** tab, with the file in question opened and the line with the `debugger` statement highlighted.

The two logging possibilities from above will end up in the tab **Console**. This is the first tab you should inspect in case of problems anyways, because if some JavaScript code doesn't load at all because of syntax errors or similar fundamental problems, you'll see an error message there explaining what's going on.

There's more...

Use the **Elements** tab to inspect the DOM representation of the page the browser currently displays. This will prove helpful to make yourself familiar with the HTML code existing widgets produce, but also allows you to play with classes and CSS attributes in general. This is a great resource for testing layout changes.

The **Network** tab gives you an overview which requests the current page made and how long it took. This is helpful to debug slow page loads, as you'll usually see the culprit in one glance here, represented by a long bar. Then you can check on the server side why this call takes as long as it does. Also, this view helps you to determine if it makes sense to parallelize calls; this would look like several long bars, one after another. If you select a request, you can inspect the payload passed to the server and the result returned, which helps you to figure out the reason for unexpected behavior on the client side. You'll also see the status codes of requests made, for example 404, in case a resource can't be found, for example because you misspelled a file name.

For other browsers, you'll have to look up similar functionality in the documentation. Firefox for example has the very powerful firebug addon, which lets you perform most of the mentioned actions.

As stated above, debugging becomes complicated as soon as asynchronous operations are involved. Breakpoints are of limited use here because they interrupt code execution and the call stack won't contain the place where an event handler was attached, but mostly internal jQuery functions and the browser's implementation of the event system. The **Profiling** tab helps you here by showing call graphs, including timings. This can hint at event handlers being called in the wrong order. Another strategy is to spread out `console.log` statements throughout your handlers in order to plot a sort of call graph in the JavaScript console. Before diving into this, have a critical look at all your custom code in order to check if you forgot to return `super`'s result in case it is a deferred object. This is a very common cause of timing problems.

16
Server Deployment

In this chapter, we will learn about the following tasks:

- ▶ Installing Odoo for production use
- ▶ Adapting the configuration file for production
- ▶ Setting up Odoo as a system service
- ▶ Configuring a reverse proxy and SSL
- ▶ Using buildout for repeatable builds

Introduction

We have seen in *Chapter 1, Installing the Odoo Development Environment*, in the recipe *Easy installation from source*, and in *Chapter 2, Managing Odoo Server Instances*, in the recipe *Standardizing your instance directory layout*, how to set up a development environment. The requirements for a production environment are slightly different. This chapter covers the specificities of the deployment of Odoo.

Installing Odoo for production

Installing Odoo in the production phase is not very different from installing Odoo for development. While there are several possible approaches, this recipe proposes a set up that is close to the development installation explained in *Chapter 1, Installing the Odoo Development Environment*, in the recipe *Easy installation from source*, and in *Chapter 2, Managing Odoo Server Instances*, in the recipe *Standardize your instance directory layout*.

Getting ready

We expect that you have a development instance ready. In this recipe, we assume the following:

- The project of your instance is managed in the same way as suggested in *Chapter 2, Managing Odoo Server Instances*, in the *Standardize your instance directory layout* recipe. We will use `https://github.com/login/project.git`. This repository should contain the configuration file of the instance used during development, the specific addons of the instance, and any helper script that you may have created in the context of the project.

> **Caution:**
>
> If the configuration files of your project include security information such as passwords, you should not push the project on a public service such as GitHub. Use an internal Git repository or a private GitHub project.

- The deployment server is running Debian Jessie (but it should work with little change on derived distributions such as Ubuntu; see *Chapter 1, Installing the Odoo Development Environment*, for more on this).

- You have `root` access to the final server using `ssh` or `sudo`. If you don't, you will have to find a system administrator to assist you in the configuration.

- You know the final fully qualified domain name under which the server will be accessed.

How to do it...

To install Odoo for production, you need to carry out the following steps:

1. As root, install the dependencies and build dependencies:

```
# apt-get install git python2.7 postgresql nano python-virtualenv \
  gcc python2.7-dev libxml2-dev libxslt1-dev \
  libevent-dev libsasl2-dev libldap2-dev libpq-dev \
  libpng12-dev libjpeg-dev node-less node-clean-css \
  xfonts-75dpi xfonts-base
# wget http://nightly.odoo.com/extra/wkhtmltox-0.12.1.2_linux-jessie-amd64.deb
# dpkg -i wkhtmltox-0.12.1.2_linux-jessie-amd64.deb
```

2. As root, create a user called `odoo`:

```
# adduser odoo
```

3. Configure the PostgreSQL database:

```
# sudo -u postgres createuser odoo
# sudo -u postgres createdb -O odoo odoo_project
```

4. As odoo, clone the project repository:

```
# su odoo
$ mkdir ~/odoo-prod
$ cd ~/odoo-prod
$ git clone https://github.com/login/project.git project
$ mkdir -p project/src
```

5. As the odoo user, clone the Odoo source code:

```
$ cd project/src
$ git clone -b 9.0 --single-branch https://github.com/odoo/odoo.
git odoo
```

6. Create virtualenv and install the dependencies:

```
$ virtualenv ~/env-odoo-9.0
$ source ~/env-odoo-9.0/bin/activate
$ pip install -r odoo/requirements.txt
```

7. Clone all third-party addon repositories in the project/src subdirectory:

```
$ git clone -b 9.0 https://github.com/OCA/partner-contact.git
```

8. Create the ~/odoo-prod/project/bin directory:

```
$ mkdir ~/odoo-prod/project/bin
```

9. Create a script to easily start Odoo in the production environment in ~/odoo-prod/project/bin/start-odoo:

```
#! /bin/sh
PYTHON=~odoo/env-odoo-9.0/bin/python
ODOO=~odoo/odoo-prod/project/src/odoo/odoo.py
CONF=~odoo/odoo-prod/project/production.conf
${PYTHON} ${ODOO} -c ${CONF} "$*"
```

10. Make the script executable:

```
$ chmod +x ~/odoo-prod/project/bin/start-odoo
```

11. As root, uninstall gcc:

```
# apt-get remove gcc
```

How it works...

Most of the recipe is identical to what is described in *Chapter 1, Installing the Odoo Development Environment*, but there are a few key differences.

We are using a dedicated system user with login `odoo`. This enables us to control who has access to the account, for example, by configuring the `sudo` or `ssh` authorized keys. It also allows us to give this user as few permissions as possible, in case the instance is compromised.

The database user linked to this account does not have any privilege, not even database creation. We create the database externally, just once. In case the instance is compromised, an attacker won't be able to create additional databases on the server.

The Odoo script we are creating will be used in the recipe *Set up Odoo as a system service* later in this chapter. It uses the `production.conf` configuration file, which is explained in the next recipe, *Adapting the configuration file for production*.

We uninstall `gcc` at the end of the process so that if an attacker gains access, he will not be able to use this to recompile executables locally.

At the end of this recipe, your server is not ready yet. You will need to refer to the recipes *Adapting the configuration file for production*, *Set up Odoo as a system service*, and *Configure a reverse proxy and SSL*, which are described in this chapter.

There's more...

Here are a few more important points to consider when preparing the deployment of your instance.

Server dimensioning

What should you use for a server? Pretty much any physical server these days is more than enough to handle an average sized Odoo instance with about 10 simultaneous users. Since virtual machines typically have fewer resources provisioned, you will need to pay a little more attention to this if you are planning to run on a VM. Here are a few key figures to get you started. Obviously, they will need fine tuning to match your use of Odoo.

A small Odoo instance needs at least 1 GB of RAM. Don't be shy on this; the last thing you want to happen is your server swapping. 2 to 4 GB is a good starting point. Give your server, at the very least, two CPU/cores. If you are running the PostgreSQL server on the same host, provision at least four CPU/cores, and add 1 GB of RAM for the database. The additional CPU/cores will be used by the Odoo workers that are covered in the next recipe, *Adapting the configuration file for production*.

The source code of your instance will eat up 1 to 2 GB of hard disk if you are keeping the Git history, which we recommend in this recipe. The file store (`data_dir` in the configuration file) will grow as the instance is used, and the growth heavily depends on what you are doing in the instance. Start with 5 GB, which should give you plenty of time before getting full, and monitor the disk usage. If you are running the database on the same host, give plenty of disk space to the partition that will contain the database working files, starting at 50 GB.

You will also need space for the on-site backups, both of the database and the file store. A lot can depend on your backup plan; 200 GB is a good starting point.

PostgreSQL tuning

Discussing **PostgreSQL tuning** is beyond the scope of this book. You may want to check out the books *PostgreSQL 9 Admin Cookbook* or *PostgreSQL 9.0 High Performance*, both from Packt Publishing, for an in-depth coverage of these topics.

The default configuration of PostgreSQL is generally very conservative and meant to prevent the database server from hogging all the system resources. On production servers, you can safely increase some parameters in the `postgresql.conf` file to get better performance. Here are some settings you can use to get started:

```
max_connections = 100
shared_buffers = 256MB
effective_cache_size = 768MB
work_mem = 10MB
maintenance_work_mem = 64MB
checkpoint_segments = 16
wal_buffers = 8MB
checkpoint_completion_target = 0.9
```

You will need to restart PostgreSQL after modifying these settings.

The `pgtune` utility can help in finding a suitable configuration. You can install it by running the following:

```
sudo apt-get install pgtune
```

To get a suitable configuration, you can run the following:

```
$ pgtune -T OLTP -i /etc/postgresql/9.4/main/postgresql.conf \
-M 1073741824 -c 100
```

The options we use are as follows:

- ▸ `-T OLTP` to get a configuration for an on line translation processing database
- ▸ `-i` to get the original configuration file
- ▸ `-M` to specify the amount of memory for PostgreSQL (in kB); our example uses 1 GB
- ▸ `-c` to specify the maximum number of connections

If your instance is heavily loaded, you will benefit from separating the database server and the Odoo server onto two different hosts. Don't use two virtual machines running on the same physical server if you are getting down to this; use two physical servers with a high speed network connection between both. In that case, you will need to ensure that the `pg_hba.conf` file on the database server host allows password authenticated connections on the database from the Odoo server, and that the `postgresql.conf` file lets the PostgreSQL server listen in on the network interface connecting both servers.

Source code version

When cloning Odoo and the third-party dependencies, you may want to ensure that you are using the exact same revision as the one you had in developments. There are several ways to do this:

- You can manually mark down the version SHA1 of the local revision in a file, record this in the project repository, and make sure you are using the same revision on the production server
- You can use tags or branches on forks of these repositories in your GitHub account
- You can use `git submodule` to tie these revisions to the repository of your project
- You can use buildout to manage the various dependencies and freeze the revisions (see the following recipe *Use buildout for repeatable builds* for more information on this)

Why not use the Linux distribution packages provided by Odoo?

You can do that and you will get started much faster because a lot of things are handled for you by the packages. However, there are a few issues with using the packaged source; most importantly, you cannot easily patch the source code of Odoo, which is easier if you run from the source. Granted, this is not something you have to do every day, but being able to use the standard development tools to achieve this, rather than manually applying and tracking patches on production servers, is a precious help and a gain of time. You may also be using the Odoo Community Association branch of Odoo, (`https://github.com/OCA/OCB`) for which no packages are provided.

Backups

The recipe does not cover **backups**. At the very least, you should have the cron task on the server running a daily backup. A simple and basic solution is to edit the `crontab` file as root by running `crontab -e` and to add the following lines:

```
@daily su postgres -c pg_dumpall | gzip > /backups/postgresql-$(date
+%u).dump.gz
@daily tar czf /backups/odoo-data-$(date +%u).tgz /home/odoo/odoo-
prod/project/data
```

Don't forget to create the /backups directory. The backup files should not be stored on the same hard disk, and ideally, they would be mirrored on a server in a different physical location. Check these backups on a regular basis; having backups that you can't restore when you need them is useless.

The proposed solution is to keeps daily backups of the last 7 days, which means you will lose one day of work in case of a problem. There are more advanced solutions available for PostgreSQL that allow point-in-time recovery. You will find more information about this in the book *PostgreSQL 9 Admin Cookbook*, Packt Publishing. Similarly, there are many Linux tools, such as duplicity (http://duplicity.nongnu.org/), which you can use for file backups allowing easy management.

See also

For more information on the Odoo Community Association branch of Odoo, see the recipe *Easy installation from source* in *Chapter 1, Installing the Odoo Development Environment*.

Adapting the configuration file for production

In *Chapter 1, Installing the Odoo Development Environment* we have seen how to save the configuration of the instance in a file. We used the default values for lots of parameters, and if you've followed the *Standardize your instance directory layout* recipe in *Chapter 2, Managing Odoo Server Instances*, as well as the previous recipe for the production installation, you should now have that same configuration file in the production environment. This recipe shows how to derive a configuration file that is suitable for use in production.

Getting ready

We assume that you have installed Odoo on the production server with the previous recipe, *Install Odoo for production*. We assume that you will be running PostgreSQL on the same server as Odoo.

You may want to install the pwgen utility to generate random passwords.

We are describing the steps here as if you were running them on the production server, but they can also be executed on your development server, since the new configuration file is added to the Git repository of the project that we use to deploy on the production server.

How to do it...

To adapt the configuration file for production, you need to follow these steps:

1. Create a new configuration file for production based on the development file:

   ```
   $ cd ~/odoo-prod/project
   $ cp development.conf production.conf
   ```

2. Edit the production configuration file.

3. Change the addons path to match the production base directory:

   ```
   addons_path = /home/odoo/odoo-prod/project/src/odoo/addons,/home/
   odoo/odoo-prod/project/src/odoo/openerp/addons,/home/odoo/odoo-
   prod/project/src/partner-contact
   ```

4. Change the data directory:

   ```
   data_dir = /home/odoo/odoo-prod/project/data
   ```

5. Change the server log path to match the production base directory:

   ```
   logfile = /home/odoo/odoo-prod/project/logs/odoo.log
   ```

6. Configure log rotation:

   ```
   logrotate = True
   ```

7. Configure the logging handlers:

   ```
   log_level = warn
   log_handler = :WARNING,werkzeug:CRITICAL,openerp.service.
   server:INFO
   ```

8. Adapt the database connection parameters:

   ```
   db_host = False
   db_maxconn = 64
   db_name = odoo-project
   db_password = False
   db_port = False
   db_template = template1
   db_user = False
   ```

9. Configure the database filter, and disable database listing:

   ```
   dbfilter = odoo-project$
   list_db = False
   ```

10. Change the master password:

    ```
    admin_password = use a random password generated with e.g. pwgen
    ```

11. Configure Odoo to run with workers:

    ```
    workers = 4
    limit_memory_hard = 4294967296 # 4 GB
    limit_memory_soft = 671088640 # 640MB
    limit_request = 8192
    limit_time_cpu = 120
    limit_time_real = 300
    ```

12. Only listen on the local network interface:

    ```
    xmlrpc_interface = 127.0.0.1
    netrpc_interface = 127.0.0.1
    ```

13. Save the file, and add it to the Git repository:

    ```
    $ git add production.conf
    $ git commit -m "add production configuration file"
    ```

How it works...

Most of the parameters shown in this recipe are explained in the *Manage Odoo server instances* recipe in *Chapter 1, Installing the Odoo Development Environment*.

In steps 3, 4, and 5, we change the addons path and the log file. In case you are developing in an environment with the same layout as the production environment, this is required because Odoo expects absolute paths in the configuration file.

Step 6 enables log rotation. This will cause Odoo to configure the logging module to archive the server logs on a daily basis, and to keep the old logs for 30 days. This is useful on production servers to avoid logs eventually consuming all the available disk space.

Step 7 configures the logging level. The proposed setting is very conservative and will only log messages with at least the WARNING level, except for werkzeug (CRITICAL) and openerp. service.server (INFO). For more information on the log filtering, refer to *Chapter 7, Debugging and Automated Testing*, where you will find the recipe, *Producing server logs to help debug methods*. Feel free to tune this to your taste.

Step 8 configures the database settings. This will work if you are running the PostgreSQL database server locally and have set it up as explained in the previous recipe. If you're running PostgreSQL on a different server, you will need to replace the False values with the appropriate connection settings for your database instance.

Step 9 restricts the database available to the instance by configuring a database filter. We also disable the database listing, which is not strictly necessary given that the regular expression we set in `dbfilter` can only match one single database. It is still a good thing to do though, in order to avoid displaying the list of databases to anyone, and to avoid users connecting to the wrong database.

Step 10 sets a nontrivial master password for the instance. The master password is used for database management through the user interface, and a few community addons also use it for extra security before performing actions that can lead to data loss. You really need to set this to a nontrivial value. We propose using the `pwgen` utility to generate a random password, but any other method is also valid.

Step 11 configures Odoo to work with **workers**. In this mode, Odoo will create a number of worker processes (in this example, 4) to handle HTTP requests. This has several advantages over the default configuration in which the request handling is performed in separate threads, which are given as follows:

- Requests can be handled in parallel, making better use of multiple cores or CPUs on the server (Python threads are penalized by the existence of the Global Interpreter Locks (GIL) in the Python interpreter).

- It is possible to terminate one of the workers depending on resource consumption. The following table gives the various resource limits that can be configured:

Parameter	Suggested value	Description
`limit_memory_hard`	4294967296	This is the maximum amount of RAM a worker will be able to allocate. We recommend using 4 GB as some processes launched by Odoo can allocate some large amounts of RAM.
`limit_memory_soft`	671088640	If a worker ends up consuming more than this limit (640 MB in our setting), it will be terminated after it finishes processing the current request.
`limit_request`	8192	A worker will be terminated after having processed this many requests.
`limit_time_cpu`	120	This is the maximum amount of CPU time allowed to process a request.
`limit_time_real`	300	This is the maximum amount of wall clock time allowed to process a request.

Step 12 configures the internal Odoo web server to only listen on the local interface. This means the instance will not be reachable from other servers. This enables us to configure a **reverse proxy** on the same server to access the server and to force encrypted connections. Take a look at the *Configure a reverse proxy and SSL* recipe later in this chapter.

There's more...

When running with workers, you may encounter some issues specific to this mode:

▸ If you get strange errors when running with workers, with `lessc` or `wkhtmltopdf` not working as intended (for example, prematurely exiting with a `-11` or `-6` status), then you likely have `limit_memory_hard` set to a value that is too low. Try raising it a bit, as the default value is notoriously too low.

▸ If you get timeout errors when performing long operations (this includes CSV imports and exports and addon module installations), try increasing the `limit_time_cpu` and `limit_time_real` parameters, as there too the default value is quite low. If you have a reverse proxy, you may want to check its timeout limit too (although this will not prevent the transactions from completing).

▸ If your instance gets completely stuck when printing reports, try raising the number of workers. This can be a deadlock caused by `wkhtmltopdf` blocking up all the available workers while printing.

> In any case, always validate the setup before going to production, and remember to test printing reports when enabling workers.

Set up Odoo as a system service

For a production instance, it is very important that the Odoo server gets started when the computer reboots. On current Linux systems, there are different ways of achieving this, depending on the distribution and the server setup; either it is an init script, or a `systemd` configuration. This recipe shows how to do both.

Getting ready

We assume that you followed the first two recipes to install and configure your Odoo instance. Especially the deployed source of Odoo, which is at `/home/odoo/odoo-prod/project/src/odoo/`, and the configuration file of the instance, which is at `/home/odoo/odoo-prod/project/production.conf`. The scripts also makes use of the `start-odoo` script created in step 9 of the *Install Odoo for production* recipe.

You will first need to find out which initialization system is running on your system. For this, run the following:

```
$ dpkg -l systemd
```

If the last line of output starts with `ii systemd`, then `systemd` is available on your system. Otherwise, you are probably running `sysvinit` (on a system running an old Debian variant) or upstart (on an Ubuntu-based system).

How to do it...

Now that you know which version of the initialization system you are running, you can choose how to configure Odoo.

Configuring systemd to start Odoo

To configure **systemd** to start Odoo, you need to perform the following steps:

1. As root, create a file called `/lib/systemd/system/odoo.service`, with the following contents:

   ```
   [Unit]
   Description=Odoo 9.0
   After=postgresql.service


   [Service]
   Type=simple
   User=odoo
   Group=odoo
   ExecStart=/home/odoo/odoo-prod/project/bin/start-odoo


   [Install]
   WantedBy=multi-user.target
   ```

2. As root, register the service:

   ```
   # systemctl enable odoo.service
   ```

3. As root, start the service:

   ```
   # service odoo start
   ```

4. To stop the service, you can run the following:

   ```
   # service odoo stop
   ```

Configuring sysvinit or upstart to start Odoo

To configure `sysvinit` or `upstart` to start Odoo, you need to perform the following steps:

1. As root, copy the `init` file provided by Odoo to `/etc/init.d`:

   ```
   # cp src/odoo/debian/init /etc/init.d/odoo
   # chmod +x /etc/init.d/odoo
   ```

2. As root, edit that file to change the environment variables defined at the top of the script (we only list the ones which need changing as follows, with the appropriate values):

```
DAEMON=/home/odoo/odoo-prod/project/bin/start-odoo
```

3. In the same file, also modify the _start function as follows:

```
function _start() {
    start-stop-daemon --start --quiet --pidfile $PIDFILE
--chuid $USER:$USER --background --make-pidfile --exec $DAEMON
}
```

4. As root, register the daemon with sysvinit or upstart:

```
# update-rc.d odoo defaults
```

5. As root, start the service:

```
# /etc/init.d/odoo start
```

6. If you want to stop the service, you run the following:

```
# /etc/init.d/odoo stop
```

How it works...

The three configurations, systemd, sysvinit, and upstart, use some configuration files or scripts to know which programs must run when the server boots. The configurations provided in the recipe will need small adaptations to match the paths of your instance.

 Don't forget to reboot your server and check that Odoo is properly started!

There's more...

If you are using the buildout method described in the *Use buildout for repeatable builds* recipe, you will need to adapt the paths to use the start_odoo script created by the recipe.

Configure a reverse proxy and SSL

In order to avoid all the information between the users' browsers and the Odoo server, that is to be sent in clear over the network, it is necessary to use the HTTPS protocol that encrypts the exchanges. Odoo cannot do this natively, and it is necessary to configure a reverse proxy that will handle the encryption and decryption on behalf of the Odoo server. This recipe shows how to use nginx (http://nginx.net) for this.

Getting ready

You should know the public name of the server and configure your DNS accordingly. In this recipe, we will use `odoo.example.com` as the name of your server.

If you want your Odoo instance to be visible by all browsers, you will need to get an **SSL certificate** signed by a recognized **Certification Authority** (**CA**). Using a self-signed certificate can also be made to work, but modern browsers tend to refuse these.

To generate an SSL key, you can use the following process:

1. Install `openssl`:

   ```
   $ sudo apt-get install openssl
   ```

2. Generate the key for your server:

   ```
   $ mkdir ~/sslkey
   $ openssl genrsa -out ~/sslkey/server.key 2048
   ```

3. Generate a signing request:

   ```
   $ openssl req -new -key ~/sslkey/server.key -out ~/sslkey/server.csr
   ```

4. The preceding command will ask you a series of questions about your company and your Odoo server's URL. Don't get these wrong or your certificate will be unusable.

5. You will be able to send the file, `~/sslkey/server.csr`, to a Certification Authority (CA) of your choice. The CA will send you back a file called `server.crt`, which we will use in the recipe.

How to do it...

In order to access your instance using HTTPS via `nginx`, you need to follow these steps:

1. As root, install `nginx`:

   ```
   # apt-get install nginx
   ```

2. As root, create a configuration file in `/etc/nginx/sites-available/odoo-80`:

   ```
   server {
     listen [::]:80 ipv6only=off;
     server_name odoo.example.com;
     access_log /var/log/nginx/odoo80.access.log combined;
     error_log /var/log/nginx/odoo80.error.log;
   ```

```
      location / {
        rewrite ^/(.*) https://odoo.example.com:443/$1 permanent;
      }
    }
```

3. Create a configuration file in `/etc/nginx/sites-available/odoo-443`:

```
server {
    listen [::]:443 ipv6only=off;
    server_name odoo.example.com;
    ssl on;
    ssl_certificate /etc/nginx/ssl/server.crt;
    ssl_certificate_key /etc/nginx/ssl/server.key;
    access_log /var/log/nginx/odoo443.access.log combined;
    error_log /var/log/nginx/odoo443.error.log;
    client_max_body_size 128M;
    gzip on;
    proxy_read_timeout 600s;
    index index.html index.htm index.php;

    add_header Strict-Transport-Security "max-age=31536000";
    proxy_set_header Host $http_host;
    proxy_set_header X-Real-IP $remote_addr;
    proxy_set_header X-Forward-For $proxy_add_x_forwarded_for;
    proxy_set_header X-Forwarded-Proto https;
    proxy_set_header X-Forwarded-Host $http_host;

    location / {
      proxy_pass http://localhost:8069;
      proxy_read_timeout 6h;
      proxy_connect_timeout 5s;
      proxy_redirect http://$http_host/ https://$host:$server_port/;
      add_header X-Static no;
      proxy_buffer_size 64k;
      proxy_buffering off;
      proxy_buffers 4 64k;
      proxy_busy_buffers_size 64k;
```

```
        proxy_intercept_errors on;
    }


    location /longpolling/ {
        proxy_pass http://localhost:8072;
    }


    location ~ /[a-zA-Z0-9_-]*/static/ {
        proxy_pass http://localhost:8069;
        proxy_cache_valid 200 60m;
        proxy_buffering on;
        expires 864000;
    }
}
```

4. As root, link the configuration file in /etc/nginx/sites-enabled/:

   ```
   # ln -s /etc/nginx/sites-available/odoo80 /etc/nginx/sites-
   enabled/odoo80
   ```

   ```
   # ln -s /etc/nginx/sites-available/odoo443 /etc/nginx/sites-
   enabled/odoo443
   ```

5. As root, remove /etc/nginx/sites-enabled/default:

   ```
   # rm /etc/nginx/sites-enabled/default
   ```

6. As root, copy the ssl certificate and server key to the appropriate directories

   ```
   # mkdir -p /etc/nginx/ssl
   ```

   ```
   # chown www-data /etc/nginx/ssl
   ```

   ```
   # mv server.key server.crt /etc/nginx/ssl
   ```

   ```
   # chmod 710 /etc/nginx/ssl
   ```

   ```
   # chown root:www-data /etc/nginx/ssl/*
   ```

   ```
   # chmod 640 /etc/nginx/ssl/*
   ```

7. As Odoo, edit the production configuration file of the instance to enable proxy_mode:

   ```
   proxy_mode = True
   ```

8. As root, restart your odoo instance and nginx:

   ```
   # service odoo restart
   ```

   ```
   # service nginx restart
   ```

How it works...

We are using nginx as a reverse HTTP proxy. Incoming HTTP and HTTPS connections are handled by nginx, which delegates the processing of the requests to the Odoo server. The Odoo server is configured to only listen on the local loopback interface (127.0.0.1) on port 8069 for normal requests (xmlrpc_port) and port 8072 for the long polling requests (longpolling_port). You may need to adapt the port numbers to your configuration.

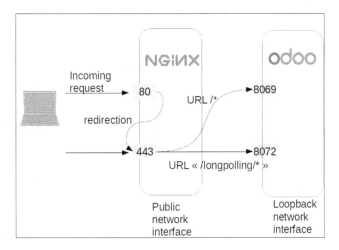

The recipe sets up two files. The first one is the configuration for incoming connections on port 80 using the HTTP protocol. We don't want these because they are in clear text, meaning that the passwords can be sniffed. Therefore, we set up nginx to redirect the URLs permanently to port 443 using the encrypted HTTPS protocol.

The second file is a bit more complex and configures the way nginx should handle connections using the HTTPS protocol:

- The first configuration block configures the SSL protocol, the encryption key, and certificate, as well as the log file's location.

- The second block sets some headers on the requests to handle the proper reverse proxying over HTTPS.

- The location / block defines the default processing of incoming requests; they will be proxied to the Odoo server listening on port 8069.

- The location /longpolling block handles queries made on URLs starting with /longpolling, which are then forwarded to Odoo on port 8072. These connections are used by the bus addon module to send notifications to the web client.

- The location ~ /[a-zA-Z0-9_-]*/static/ block uses a regular expression to match the URLs of the static files of Odoo modules. These files are rarely updated, and so we ask nginx to cache them in order to lighten the load on the Odoo server.

There's more...

This recipe focuses on the nginx configuration. You may be more familiar with other tools such as the Apache web server and `mod_proxy`. In this case, you can of course use these to achieve a similar setup.

See also

▸ For more information about the various nginx configuration options, see `http://nginx.org/en/docs/`.

▸ For a tutorial on the configuration of Apache2 as a reverse proxy and the use of a personal certification authority, take a look at `http://antiun.github.io/odoo-reverse-proxy-howto/`.

Use buildout for repeatable builds

So far, we have been manually setting up our instances. This cries for automation, and maybe you have already written a shell script to download the proper version of the addons your instance needs and streamlined the process. It turns out that there is a tool meant to help with doing this called **buildout**. Buildout is a Python-based build system for creating, assembling, and deploying applications from multiple parts, some of which may be non-Python-based. It lets you create a buildout configuration and reproduce the same software later.

This recipe shows how you can start using buildout to ensure you have the same setup in the development and production servers.

Getting ready

We assume that your instance only has a dependency on the server-tools project of the Odoo Community Association, and that your user-specific addon modules are living in the `local/addons` subdirectory of the project.

We also expect you to have installed the build dependencies of Odoo. Refer to steps 1 to 3 of the *Install Odoo for production* recipe in this chapter. This recipe is better used first on a development machine and later deployed on a production server.

How to do it...

In order to use buildout to build your project, you need to follow these steps:

1. On your development server, create a new work directory:

   ```
   $ mkdir ~/odoo-dev/project-buildout
   $ cd ~/odoo-dev/project-buildout
   ```

2. Create a file called `buildout.cfg`:

   ```
   [buildout]
   parts = odoo
   find-links = http://download.gna.org/pychart/

   [odoo]
   recipe = anybox.recipe.odoo:server
   OCA = https://github.com/OCA
   version = git https://github.com/odoo/odoo.git odoo 9.0 depth=1
   addons = git ${odoo:OCA}/server-tools.git parts/server-tools 9.0
     git ${odoo:OCA}/partner-contact.git parts/partner-contact 9.0
     local local/addons

   options.limit_memory_hard = 4294967296
   options.limit_memory_soft = 671088640
   options.limit_request = 8192
   options.limit_time_cpu = 120
   options.limit_time_real = 300
   options.xmlrpc_port = 8069
   options.longpolling_port = 8072
   options.workers = 0

   [versions]
   zc.buildout = 2.5.0
   anybox.buildout.odoo = 1.9.1
   setuptools = 19.7

   Babel = 1.3
   Jinja2 = 2.7.3
   Mako = 1.0.1
   MarkupSafe = 0.23
   Pillow = 2.7.0
   ```

```
Python-Chart = 1.39
PyYAML = 3.11
Werkzeug = 0.9.6
argparse = 1.2.1
decorator = 3.4.0
docutils = 0.12
feedparser = 5.1.3
gdata = 2.0.18
gevent = 1.0.2
greenlet = 0.4.7
jcconv = 0.2.3
lxml = 3.4.1
mock = 1.0.1
ofxparse = 0.14
passlib = 1.6.2
psutil = 2.2.0
psycogreen = 1.0
psycopg2 = 2.5.4
pyPdf = 1.13
pydot = 1.0.2
pyparsing = 2.0.3
pyserial = 2.7
python-dateutil = 2.4.0
python-ldap = 2.4.19
python-openid = 2.2.5
pytz = 2014.10
pyusb = 1.0.0b2
qrcode = 5.1
reportlab = 3.1.44
requests = 2.6.0
six = 1.9.0
suds-jurko = 0.6
vatnumber = 1.2
vobject = 0.6.6
wsgiref = 0.1.2
xlwt = 0.7.5
```

3. Create a configuration file for the production environment:

```
[buildout]
extends = buildout.cfg

[odoo]
options.limit_memory_hard = 4294967296
options.limit_memory_soft = 671088640
options.limit_request = 8192
options.limit_time_cpu = 120
options.limit_time_real = 300
options.workers = 4

options.data_dir = project/data

options.xmlrpc_interface = 127.0.0.1
options.netrpc_interface = 127.0.0.1
options.xmlrpc_port = 8069
options.longpolling_port = 8072

options.log_level = warn
options.log_handler = :WARNING,werkzeug:CRITICAL,openerp.service.
server:INFO

options.admin_password = generate with pwgen

options.listdb = False
options.db_host = False
options.db_port = False
options.db_user = False
options.db_name = odoo_project
options.dbfilter = ^odoo_project$
options.proxy_mode = True
```

4. Create a configuration file for the development environment:

```
[buildout]
extends = buildout.cfg

[odoo]
options.db_name = odoo_dev
options.dbfilter = ^odoo_dev$
options.log_level = info
```

5. Create a `virtualenv` without `setuptools`:

```
$ virtualenv sandbox --no-setuptools
```

6. Download the current version of the `bootstrap.py` file:

```
$ wget https://raw.github.com/buildout/buildout/master/bootstrap/
bootstrap.py
```

7. Run the `bootstrap.py` script:

```
$ sandbox/bin/python bootstrap.py
```

8. On your development machine, you can create a development environment by running the following:

```
$ bin/buildout -c dev.cfg
```

9. On the production server, you would create a production environment by running the following:

```
$ bin/buildout -c prod.cfg
```

10. To start the instance, run the following:

```
$ bin/start_odoo
```

11. Commit the files to Git:

```
$ git init
$ git add buildout.cfg prod.cfg dev.cfg bootstrap.py local/addons
$ git commit -m "initialize project with buildout"
```

How it works...

Buildout works by processing a configuration file, which is called `buildout.cfg` by default. This file uses a syntax close to `ConfigParser` (with a few extensions) to describe the desired target environment. There is one mandatory section, `[buildout]`, which contains a `parts` entry listing the sections to process. Most sections have a `recipe` entry that gives the name of a buildout recipe to use to build the section. There are lots of recipes available (take a look at `http://www.buildout.org/en/latest/docs/recipelist.html` for a partial listing), and different recipes can be combined in a single configuration file. Each recipe supports its own configuration settings. Recipes are Python modules, usually made available from PyPI.

Buildout configuration files are extensible and support parameterization:

▸ A configuration file can *extend* another one; configuration settings are added or overwritten by the extending file.

▸ Configuration settings can refer to the value of other settings using the `${section:name}` syntax.

▸ In step 1, we prepare our base `buildout.cfg` configuration file. We define a section called `[odoo]` and set the `anybox.recipe.odoo` parameter as the buildout recipe in charge for this section. Here are the settings we use:

  ❑ `version`: This defines the Odoo version we want. Here, we are using the latest version from the 9.0 branch on GitHub. The depth options limit the Git clone depth to speed up the installation.

  ❑ `OCA`: This is a custom setting used to simplify the URLs of the OCA addons we are listing in the following settings, using the `${odoo:OCA}` variable.

  ❑ `addons`: This lists the addons directories to install, one by one. The syntax is `protocol URL destination revision options`. The Git protocol will use Git to clone a repository. The local protocol will use a local directory (and revision must not be provided in this case). Other available protocols are `hg` (for mercurial repositories), `svn` (subversion), `bzr` (bazaar). The revision can be a tag, a branch, or a commit identifier.

The `[versions]` section is a standardized buildout section used to specify the versions of the Python dependencies that will be installed in the environment. It is important to fix the version of `zc.buildout`, `anybox.buildout.odoo`, and `setuptools` in this section to ensure the repeatability of the build, which is what we do in the first two lines of the section. The `anybox.buildout.odoo` recipe is able to find the names of the dependencies from the Odoo server version, but not the versions. To generate this list, we copied the `requirements.txt` file for the Odoo codebase and replaced the `==` operator with `=`.

The `prod.cfg` and `dev.cfg` files extend the base configuration defined in `buildout.cfg`. In the `[odoo]` section, they both define settings with names starting with `options.` (Mind the dot): buildout will use these when generating a configuration file for the instance with the options set as specified in the configuration file. If you've read the recipe *Adapting the configuration file for production* in this chapter, the `prod.cfg` file should be familiar.

In order to ensure that the buildout environment is insulated from the system Python, we use a **virtualenv** (called `sandbox` in this recipe) configured to not have `setuptools` available. We use this virtualenv to run the `bootstrap.py` script that we downloaded from the buildout source code repository. The role of `bootstrap.py` is to prepare things for buildout to work, including installing buildout itself. A script, `bin/buildout`, is created in the directory of the build to run buildout.

You can then manage your buildout configuration in a version management system such as Git. It is recommended that you store the `bootstrap.py` file together with the buildout configuration file; this file evolves with buildout, and since we are freezing the version of buildout in the configuration file, we need to keep the `bootstrap.py` file that we know will work with this version.

To run buildout, just execute the `bin/buildout` script with the `-c` option to specify a configuration file. This will do several things:

- ► Odoo gets installed in the `parts/` subdirectory
- ► The specified addons are installed in the specified subdirectory (we recommend that you use `parts/` for this too)
- ► The dependencies of Odoo and any additional dependencies are installed in the `eggs/` subdirectory
- ► A configuration file is created in `etc/odoo.cfg` with the appropriate value for `addons_path` and all the options specified in the buildout configurations
- ► A helper script `bin/start_odoo` is created; it uses the generated configuration file and the installed Python dependencies

There's more...

If one addon module that you need requires an external Python dependency, you can add it to the `[odoo]` section using the `eggs` setting. For instance, to add `unicodecsv` to the buildout, use the following:

```
[odoo]
eggs += unicodecsv

[versions]
unicodecsv = 0.14.1
```

Temporary merges

During development, it can be useful to merge pending pull requests in the various projects used by the project. The buildout recipe supports this through the merges option. Suppose your project uses OCA/partner-contact and OCA/product-attribute, and you need to merge the PR 237 and 249 on partner-contact and the PR 132 on product attribute, then you can write the following in your buildout configuration file:

```
[odoo]
OCA = https://github.com/OCA
version = git https://github.com/odoo/odoo.git odoo 9.0 depth=1
addons = git ${odoo:OCA}/partner-contact.git parts/partner-contact 9.0
    git ${odoo:OCA}/product-attribute.git parts/product-attribute
9.0
merges = git origin parts/partner-contact pull/237/head
    git origin parts/partner-contact pull/249/head
    git origin parts/product-attribute pull/132/head
```

The syntax for the merge option using the git protocol is `<remote> <local repository> <refspec>`. We use here the reference for pull requests provided by GitHub.

A word of caution

This feature is very useful during development but should be avoided for deployment in production. The merged branches can evolve and be rebased or overwritten without notice. It is better that your deployment depends on non-merged PR so as to use a personal fork of the project on which you will do the merges yourself to ensure that you get repeatable builds. Also, note that the buildout `freeze-to` option, which is explained next, does not work with `merges`.

Freezing a buildout

To ease deployment, it is possible to use some advanced commands. The `freeze-to` option can be used to generate a buildout configuration file that freezes the revisions of Odoo and all the addons:

```
$ bin/buildout -c prod.cfg -o odoo:freeze-to=frozen-prod.cfg
```

You can then run buildout with the `frozen-prod.cfg` file to get the exact same versions of the files.

You can also extract the source code to a separate directory, with the `extract-downloads-to` option:

```
$ bin/buildout -c frozen-prod.cfg \
-o odoo:extract-downloads-to=../production
```

The directory production now contains a `release.cfg` file, and a `parts/` directory with the source code (but not the git history). If the target server is running the same version of Linux as the server you are working on, you can deploy the production environment without compiling any dependency by performing the following steps:

1. Copy the required file to the `production/` directory:

   ```
   $ cp -r develop-eggs eggs buildout.cfg prod.cfg bootstrap.py \
   ../production
   ```

2. Make an archive of that directory:

   ```
   $ cd ..
   $ tar cjf production-1.0.tar.bz2
   ```

3. Copy that archive on the production server using a suitable procedure (USB key or `rsync`, for instance).

4. On the production server, unpack the archive and install the version with the following:

   ```
   $ tar xf production-1.0.tar.bz2
   $ cd production
   $ virtualenv sandbox --no-setuptools
   $ sandbox/bin/python bootstrap.py
   $ bin/buildout -c release.cfg
   ```

See also

▸ The full documentation for the buildout recipe is available at `http://docs.anybox.fr/anybox.recipe.odoo/current/index.html`.

Index

Symbols

@api.one decorator 98, 99

A

abstract models
  using, for reusable model features 89-91
access control lists 127
actions
  ir.actions.act_window.view 185
  parameters, passing 190-193
  specific view, opening 184, 185
addon module
  changes, applying 42, 43
  creating 48, 49
  data files 54
  file structure, organizing 52-55
  installing 48, 49
  installing, from GitHub 40, 41
  list, updating 31-33
  manifest, finishing 49-52
  Python code 54
  versus addon 29
  web assets 54
addons path
  configuring 30, 31
addon updates 229-231
API code
  old API code, porting to new API 143-151
API decorators
  defining 96-98
attrs attribute
  used, for dynamic form elements 207
automated actions
  using, on event conditions 288-291
  using, on time conditions 283-287

B

backups 351
base_suspend_security
  URL 127
bootstrap
  URL 318
buildout
  about 362
  freezing 369, 370
  temporary mergess 369
  URL 367, 370
  using, for repeatable builds 362-368
built-in workflows
  inspecting 291-294
business logic
  in model, extending 114-117
buttons
  adding, to forms 189, 190

C

calendar views 212, 213
category
  URL 51
Certification Authority (CA)
  about 358
  personal 362
client-side code
  debugging 340-343
  tests, writing for 336-339
client-side QWeb templates
  using 331-333
command line interface 157
community repository
  URL 330

model
adding 55-57
business logic, extending 114-117
computed fields, adding 82-84
constraint validations, adding 80, 81
data fields, adding 66-70
features adding, inheritance used 87-89
features copying to another model, delegation
   interface used 91-93
fields, limit accessing 241, 242
hierarchy, adding 78, 79
methods, defining 96-98
monetary field, adding 73
order, defining 64-66
related fields stored, exposing 85
relational fields, adding 74-77
representation, defining 64-66
security access, adding 238-241

module
creating, scaffold used 61, 62

module tests
writing, Python unit tests used 168-171
writing, YAML used 164-167

monetary field
adding, to model 73

N

namespaces
using 219-221
nginx
configuration options, URL 362
URL 357
noupdate
about 317
using 224-226

O

Odoo
backups 350, 351
Git, configuration 7
installing, for production 345-348
installing, from source 2-5
instance, starting 7, 8
PostgreSQL configuration 6, 7
PostgreSQL tuning 349, 350

server, dimensioning 348, 349
setting up, as system service 355
source code, downloading 7
source code version 350
starting, systemd configuring for 356
starting, sysvinit or upstart configuring for
   356, 357
updating, from source 25, 26
URL 323
virtual environments (virtualenv) 5, 6
Odoo Community Association (OCA)
about 8, 29, 173
maintainer quality tools, using 173-178
Odoo developer tools
activating 22-24
Odoo environments
managing, start command used 9, 10
Odoo maintainers
URL 5
Odoo server databases
managing 10, 11
Odoo shell
used, for interactively calling methods 157,
   158
Odoo superuser 127
onchange methods
about 104
calling, on server side 141, 142
defining 138, 139
operators 195

P

parameters
passed to handlers, consuming 302-304
passing, to actions 190-193
passing, to forms 190-193
path
accesibility, from network 295-297
openerp.http.request 299
openerp.http.route 297
return values 297, 298
pdb
URL 164
Pivot views 213-215
poedit
URL 264

werkzeug
  URL 295
widgets
  adding, to form view 186
window action
  adding 180-183
wizard
  about 91, 133
  and code reuse 136
  writing, to guide user 133-136
Wkhtmltopdf
  about 5
  URL 5
workflow definitions
  URL 294
write()
  extending 117-120

X

XML files
  used, for loading data 221-224
XMLRPC 309

Y

YAML
  files, used for loading data 228, 229
  used, for writing module tests 164-167

www.ingramcontent.com/pod-product-compliance
Lightning Source LLC
LaVergne TN
LVHW081330050326
832903LV00024B/1097